Entrepreneurship Today

Swati Bhatt

Entrepreneurship Today

The Resurgence of Small, Technology-Driven Businesses in a Dynamic New Economy

palgrave
macmillan

Swati Bhatt
Department of Economics
Princeton University
Princeton, NJ, USA

ISBN 978-3-031-11497-7 ISBN 978-3-031-11495-3 (eBook)
https://doi.org/10.1007/978-3-031-11495-3

Cover illustration: Marina Lohrbach_shutterstock.com

This Palgrave Macmillan imprint is published by the registered company Springer Nature Switzerland AG
The registered company address is: Gewerbestrasse 11, 6330 Cham, Switzerland

For Anjali and Ishaan
Whose strategies for figuring it out might well have made a startup

Preface

Owning one's livelihood is a dream for many people. The chance to figure it out and envision one's creation in the wider world confers acknowledgment. There is a place in this world for everyone and knowledge of this certainty provides grounding amidst uncertainty and ambiguity.

About a decade ago, my foray into strength training at the local gym connected me with Keith Harper, the trainer for some of the varsity sports teams at Princeton University. Keith's dream was to engage more deeply with the community that had been part of his life since he moved here from Trinidad as a teenager, and start his own personal training business and gym. With a sunny disposition and self-taught technical skills, he plunged into modifying a fitness app and creat a version that worked for his particular vision. Putting together his savings with some financial assistance from his girlfriend Caitlyn's family (now wife) he searched the neighborhood of Mercer County for an appropriate space. It was not a smooth search, as most landlords were reluctant to lease space to a dark-skinned young man with dreadlocks who traced his ancestry to Trinidad. Keith's engagement with the local community, resourcefulness, practical insights, eternal optimism and initiative prevailed—he "figured it out" and has been, for the past seven years, the successful owner of a hybrid gym in Princeton, combining online routines with in-person training.

Keith's story made me cognizant of the exigencies of startups and their founders. The path from idea to implementation of the fitness application, was slow and labyrinthine, requiring both creativity and patience and I wondered how this particular story would generalize across time and across different parts of the country. This led me to investigate the world of startups, both young and mature, across two decades spliced by the terrorist acts of September 2001, the Great Recession and now COVID-19. Creativity and ideas at the young startup stage have endured steadfastly across the entire time period, and in fact, acquired momentum during the decade of 2010–2020. However, low survival rates of mature startups stand as testimony to the complex and unpredictable nature of the entrepreneurial world. Robust early-stage startup activity complemented with community-based support as the enterprise matures could ensure durability of the business. Nevertheless, the entrepreneurial culture reflected in young startup trends portends optimism and hope.

As with startups so also with research and writing, it is a team effort. This book has benefited enormously from the dedicated research assistance of Melissa Woo, a brilliant and promising junior at Princeton University.

Interactions with students, both in class and outside, have prompted much of my research over the years. Their incisive questions and out-of-the box thinking deepened my understanding. Thank you Khadijah Anwar, Aidan Chodorow, David Chang, Nelson Dimpter, Amichai Felt, Grace Hong, Max Jacobsen, Pooja Parmar, Amelia Paternoster, Kathryn Postiglione, Aiden Quayle, Louisa Sarofim, Zachary Shevin, and Yasmine Zein.

The economics department at Princeton University has been my intellectual home for the past 30 years and I am grateful for the open spirit of inquiry it has consistently nurtured. My colleagues, Leah Boustan and Ilyana Kuziemko provided both encouragement and counsel, for which I am deeply appreciative. Many thanks to Christina Lipsky, Laura Sciarrotta, Laura Hedden, and Kristin Rogers who have always had my back.

Writing a book places tremendous demands on one's family. My daughter, Anjali and my husband, Ravin, have been stalwart supporters. My son, Ishaan, as an adult with autism, has learnt to "figure it out" on an ongoing basis—as a sous-chef in a popular restaurant it is as if he was in the startup world all the time.

Princeton, USA Swati Bhatt

Contents

List of Figures

PART I

Patterns in the Data: 1994–2021

CHAPTER 1

Introduction

It started before the pandemic. Virality, impatience with delay, the order-online-for-delivery-or-takeout model, the direct-to-consumer model—these phenomena emerged when we became connected on a massive scale. There was an era when time moved slowly—information traveled at a sluggish pace, and events occurred in a long, drawn-out sequence. News of President's Lincoln's assassination in 1865 was available to readers of the Times of London 13 days after the fact. Today it would happen in seconds. The conception of the internet, based on the notion of openness in its architecture, occurred in the early 1970s with the idea of a web of connections enabling information sharing between research institutions and scientists in universities around the world.

Global connectivity and the speed of information exchange accelerated with introduction of the World Wide Web by Tim Berners Lee in 1989 while working at CERN, and its software was put in the public domain in April 1993. Mobile communication technology and cloud storage and computing, widely available since 2007 when the iPhone was introduced, expanded the network of connected persons, granting them the ability to communicate anywhere and anytime. Instantaneous connectivity ensured that the speed of information exchange would escalate, that information would diffuse within moments across the global network [1, 2].

Information-sharing inaugurated new ideas and inspired a new vision for emerging business enterprises. As computer use and access to the web

S. Bhatt, *Entrepreneurship Today*,
https://doi.org/10.1007/978-3-031-11495-3_1

grew, businesses broke new ground in the late 1990s. Over-enthusiasm among investors led to the dot-com bubble. The Nasdaq Composite Index rose 400% between 1995 and March 2000, then crashed and gave up all the gains by October 2002. Some newly created enterprises, such as Amazon, Qualcomm, and Akamai Technologies (a backbone of internet infrastructure and the world's largest distributed computing platform) have survived and dominate their respective markets today.

This book investigates the U.S. entrepreneurial scene over these captivating years for startup activity and innovation, beginning in 1994, just before the dot-com boom, to 2020. These years were punctuated by the events of September 11, 2001, the Great Recession of December 2007 through June 2009 and the pandemic [3]. Analyzing new business establishments over this time period, 1994–2020, I submit six propositions.

First, there was a resurgence of entrepreneurship from 1994 through the present. In fact, there was a striking resurgence of the startup landscape from 2010 to 2020, which I define as the years of the mobility revolution. The early glamor years of 1994–2007 comprise the desktop revolution. The mobility revolution dominated the desktop revolution. It was not merely a recovery of entrepreneurship but rather a revitalization in which new business formations traced a steep ascent during 2010–2020, surpassing that of the earlier period.

Second, new businesses were launched predominantly in the small-firm segment—businesses less than 1 year in existence with fewer than 100 employees—over the 1994–2020 period. However, there was a dearth of young businesses with more than 400 employees. Those that survived the first year stayed small in terms of employment. The renaissance of entrepreneurial activity took place primarily at the community level with small businesses.

Third, the Mississippi River is a significant geographical marker. Since state laws and regulations play an important role in new business formation, I define the country by states rather than counties or metropolitan areas. States west of the Mississippi exhibit stronger entrepreneurial vitality than states east of it. Eleven of the highest-ranking states in startup performance are in the western area, with the Pacific and Mountain region states dominating—Nevada, Utah, Washington, Idaho, and California. The exceptions are Massachusetts in New England, Virginia and Florida in the South, and Wisconsin in the East North Central region. Of the fifteen weakest performers, nine states are east of the Mississippi.

Fourth, population of states and population density do not correlate with entrepreneurial activity. While 56% of the U.S. population in 2022 resides east of the Mississippi, states with greater population such as New York and Pennsylvania are not among the highest-ranking in startup formation. Some states with medium populations such as Missouri and Massachusetts account for much new business activity. The agglomeration of highly skilled individuals in densely populated locations does not necessarily predict entrepreneurship. Population density is also not predictive of a vibrant business culture. Nine of the ten most densely populated states do not rank highly in business dynamism—all ten are east of the Mississippi. California and Texas, the two most populous states, together account for a fifth of the American population (20.76%). Both are west of the Mississippi, but only California is among the top-ranking states in entrepreneurial activity.

Population growth rates, on the other hand, strongly correlate with business formation: six of the fastest-growing states exhibit a growing new business community, including Idaho, Nevada, Utah, Texas, South Carolina, and Washington. With the exception of South Carolina, these states are all west of the Mississippi. Digging deeper, the growth in these states is largely driven by Latinos, who account for a larger share of entrepreneurs in the mobility revolution compared with any other racial or ethnic group, including Asians, Blacks, Native Americans, and Whites.

Fifth, the professional and business sector, which includes technical services such as research and development, is the driver of not only the national economy but also of the economies of the leading states in the mobility revolution. Some states' economic activity was super charged by this sector during the past decade, such as Missouri, Massachusetts, and California. In Washington, Nevada, and Utah, this sector was second in importance, while in Idaho and Washington, it was third and fourth in terms of contribution to the states' economy, respectively.

And sixth, nascent establishments were inadequately rooted in the economy and exited between 1 and 4 years after inception during the years leading up to the Great Recession, dwindling progressively after 2010. New businesses peter out not because of inadequate funding, as venture capital has been prolific during these years, but due to scarce mentoring and nurturing in the early months.

Preservation of this entrepreneurial enthusiasm is the critical issue. To ensure endurance of these new businesses beyond the early years timely counsel and networking can be pivotal. Founders may be passionate about their idea but have little experience with execution. Recognizing the problem is a starting point. Awareness of, and sensitivity to, a community's needs and fears can provide the electrifying idea. When juxtaposed with a nurturing community, it can create a culture of risk-taking. Awareness of problems and mutual trust among peers are the prerequisites for entrepreneurship.

Contrary to the popular belief that founders have to be inventors, they are more likely to be engines of implementation, having perceived a problem in their environment. The industries and sectors in which startups flourish are complementary to those that incorporate breakthrough inventions. New glamorous technologies seduce potential founders into believing that the essence of developing a new business must involve the incorporation of the latest patent or discovery. On the contrary, an effort to incorporate a giant leap in technology is likely to increase the fragility of new enterprises.

The focus on growth at all costs suggests a misunderstanding of the concept of scaling, which is the response of economic organizations to changes in size. Young businesses are evolving systems and the outcome of simply growing subscribers or customers is not well understood. Increasing the scale of organizations often relies on linear thinking. Such thinking would imply, for example, if Missouri had 17,890 young startups and a state population of 3.7 million in 2019, then a state with double the population, say Pennsylvania with 7.7 million will have double the number of young startups, or 35,780 young establishments. In fact, in 2019, Pennsylvania had 21,574 startups which is 20% more than Missouri.

Human organizations, like many social and biological systems, are complex adaptive systems which means that the whole is different from the simple sum of its elements. Firms self-organize by adapting and growing in response to changes in the environment, an outcome called emergent behavior.[1]

[1] Applying the concept of scaling to networks of connections would also display emergent behavior. Social networks evolve and adapt to the changing environment and the outcome of adding more nodes, more connections does not commensurately improve the outcome. Society could be over-connected.

What Is a Startup?

A few clarifying definitions will elucidate these propositions. What is a startup, and what do we mean by the term entrepreneurship? Is a new barbershop considered a startup? A new delicatessen? Does an organization need to have patents to be considered a startup? Using the expressions new business ventures and startups interchangeably, let us be clear about a few terms.

The term startup conjures a new business with rapidly escalating employees and sales, but also rapidly rising costs. There are scant profits. In reality, a startup *starts* as a small business with an idea and a few employees. The exact moment of job creation varies by the idea, the market, and the environment. I take the stance that at the very early stage, a startup is a small business. As it matures, it adds workers in a process that could be swift or long drawn. One cannot dismiss a small and young business from qualifying for startup status simply due to its gradual and cautious job creation. Only in a backward look at the trajectory of the business can one identify a firm as a startup which escalated its payroll within the first few years.

A startup could be based on an **invention,** which is a completely new solution to a new problem, one that was not previously obvious. For example, the smartphone, which combined computing with mobility, was an invention. **Innovation** is a new solution to an old problem. The addition of traffic lights mounted with sensors to detect the extent of waiting traffic ingeniously solved the twin problems of congestion and car-idling time. Startups that launched mobile payments and banking are another example. **Improvement** is a more efficient way of addressing an old problem. It could be manifested as technology that saves time or work hours, such as home automation and wearable technology like fitness bands equipped with sensors to monitor health. Smartphones have become sensors, collecting and sharing data from our vehicles through applications such as Waze or Google Maps. Sensors establish links between fleet vehicles and head offices to allow optimal utilization by sharing status, location, and the requirements of vehicles. In agriculture, the implementation of sensors in the field allows farmers to obtain details about soil condition, such as moisture, acidity, nutrient levels, and temperature. Farmers can control irrigation, making water use more efficient.

Reorganization of an enterprise is another manifestation of a startup. The enterprise, or startup, is an organization of individuals, usually with one or two people as the founders or leaders. From a practical perspective, reorganization is best understood by clarifying what it is not. It is not a job redefinition, which is the same task in another job. Reorganization involves a shake-up of the business by creating new connections between employees, adding or eliminating members and jumpstarting the functionality of the enterprise. That same delicatessen is reorganized upon the addition of a Korean cook, who adds kimchi to the standard mustard-laden turkey-on-rye sandwich.

Reorganization doesn't sound as dramatic as innovation, yet together with invention and improvement these facets constitute the basis of most new businesses. Unpacking the idea of startups, with a renewed emphasis on reorganization, is important because any change spurs an incremental, imperceptible change in risk-taking attitudes of the individuals related to the initial network. The very idea of change permeates the thinking of the entire community and all the capabilities required of a thriving, dynamic economy. It promotes an appreciation of risk rather than fear due to its very simplicity and ordinariness.

To be clear, all reorganization is not related to new ventures. Incumbent firms may reconfigure their operations such that it is not a simple makeover or window dressing but a genuine reorganization. One of the stodgiest businesses, banking, is now offering online capability via Zelle, the digital interbank network. Funds can be transferred, and checks deposited without a physical trip to the bank. Medical records from multiple providers are collated and can be accessed via health care apps provided by various employers. MyPennMedicine, an application provided by the Hospital of the University of Pennsylvania, provides a coherent body of records of all past services, test results, and visits, and a direct messaging feature that connects you with the doctor. No more phone calls and long waits in doctors' offices to obtain answers to questions.

A portable skill set is the defining characteristic of a startup. The idea that workers would stay in the same jobs for a lifetime has passed with the digital revolution initiated by the emergence of the World Wide Web, but even more definitively after the advent of the mobile digital revolution in the past decade with the smartphone and cloud computing. Amazon's cloud, the Amazon Web Server, was introduced in 2006, and the iPhone, combining computers with mobile communication, in 2007.

The time has come for skill portability to be manifested on a large scale so as to be more than a mere bump in the data. Old jobs can be redefined or reorganized using technology and transformed into a portable skill set. This has been termed the *app economy*. The past two decades have attested to a restructuring of the U.S. economy in a shift toward increasing online activity—remote work and business organizations built around online platforms of activities which connect suppliers directly to buyers.

What we are witnessing today, often referred to as "the Great Resignation", is in fact a reorganization using technology to create portable skill sets. The increase in the number of self- employed individuals has challenged the common perception of business. In October 2021, the U.S. Census Bureau published a report separating data on employer businesses from data on businesses without paid employees, called non-employer businesses. These are businesses that have no paid employees and that are subject to no federal corporate income tax. They comprise self-employed individuals operating sole proprietorships, cover nearly every sector of the U.S. economy, and are especially prominent in some industries.

Researchers and policymakers have talked about startups as a vehicle to promote (a) innovation and (b) job creation and paid little attention to the third aspect of startups, which is (c) engaging with the community and personal satisfaction. It was observed in past research that startups led to job creation. In 2010, the Kaufman Foundation said, "[W]ithout startups, there would be no net job growth in the U.S. economy. This fact is true on average, but also is true for all but seven years for which the U.S had data going back to 1977". However, the report also makes an important clarifying point: "these are counts of jobs within the firm itself, not its impact on other firms". This is a crucial acknowledgement[2] [4].

I believe this syllogism is misleading: First, one defines firms that have been in business for less than 1 year as startups. Second, one observes in past data that startups tend to create jobs. As a consequence, the conclusion is that if there are no net jobs created, there are no startups. The startup deficit is equivalent to a jobs deficit. The mistaken

[2] The Kaufmann analysis is based on the Business Dynamics Statistics dataset from the Bureau of Labor Statistics, which documents the age of an establishment. This data was available for the first time in 2008 and became incorporated in research as in the paper by Haltiwanger et al. [5].

logic becomes particularly pernicious when job creation is the objective in later years—the syllogism is applied to selectively promote job-creating establishments.

When it was determined that there was a startup deficit, policymakers sought to promote new business development with the idea that new jobs would be created if they selected sectors and regions accordingly. The community-building aspect of new businesses was ignored, and worse, fledgling enterprises were not provided the incubation that would enable healthy growth to maturity, after which there would be job creation.

In Lawrenceville, New Jersey, The Gingered Peach is a quaint bake-shop started in 2011 with family and friends as assistants. It has since become hugely successful as evidenced by long lines every morning for their croissants, blueberry muffins, cinnamon French toast rolls, and other breakfast pastries. However, they have not scaled up by adding more locations nor have they expanded the size of their kitchens. What they have accomplished is inducing similar firms to enter the local community. Wildflowers, a gluten-free bakery, and also a mom-and-pop business, has opened down the road, not to mention the entry of a Starbucks franchise. This franchise creates jobs, but it would show up in the data as jobs added by the mature and older firm, Starbucks Incorporated. Whereas, at least in the early days, The Gingered Peach would show up in the data as creating no jobs, since all workers were family members, and the jobs created by Wildflower would not be attributed to The Gingered Peach. The growth in startups in Lawrenceville would be zero since no new jobs were created. In a personal interview with the manager in January 2022, it was learned that the startup has now matured into a small business with multiple employees and nation-wide shipping. In my opinion, there were two new startups in the town in 2011, adding to its downtown vitality. The impact on the community and the bonds created among the hungry locals waiting in line on a cold, Saturday morning is ignored by the focus on job creation. The very bonds created have led to local carpenters finding new assignments, electricians connecting with a small home builder, not to mention my own interaction with a landscape designer whom I ended up hiring.

To summarize, this book considers entrepreneurial activity as work defined by invention, innovation, improvement, and reorganization of work/tasks into portable skill sets. Characterizing startups as non-employer establishments that have been in existence for less than a

year with fewer than 100 employees, I find a steady upward trend in startup activity over the years 1994–2020, as depicted in Fig. 1.1.

I posit three forces driving entrepreneurship over the past two decades. The first is digital connectivity. The second is a pervasive sense of mistrust in institutions, which leads to the third, more recent phenomenon, a deeper desire to engage in the community.

The business wisdom in this book is that a risk-taking culture is created by the bonds of mutual trust in a tightly knit community, where resourcefulness, practical intelligence and initiative are encouraged, even applauded. It does not mean transparency because private information can be the lifeblood of startups. But it does mean a social ethos that the rules of the game are accepted by all and that the process must be inclusive of all constituents. The corollary is that, in a trust-based environment, building community networks is an investment in the future, a display of hope. The marvel of this nation is its optimism, its forward- looking attitude and a belief in advancing rather than mulling over both the great and the shameful past. That same business wisdom correspondingly implies that an entrepreneurial resurgence takes place precisely because of optimism.

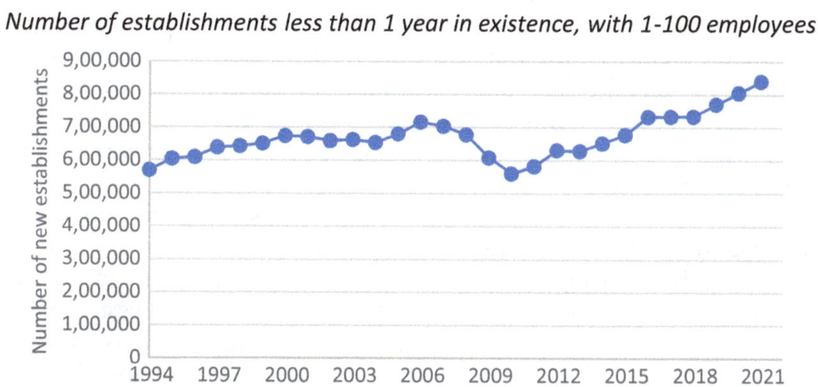

Fig. 1.1 Total number of startups: 1994–2020 (*Source* Business Employment Dynamics Data by Age and Size, BLS)

Connectivity

First, digital communication technology has made connectivity—constant, ubiquitous, and continuous—the new norm. Communication and information transfer between individuals is unimpeded. Interactions between individuals, despite being separated by space and time, take place on an anywhere–anytime basis. Consequently, economic activity, which depends upon social interactions, is frictionless. While I buy my laptop from Apple, the locally-based GeekSquad, or alternatively HelloTech, services the device. Rather than patiently waiting for some customer service agent based on another continent to service my device I have immediate access to a local business that has eliminated search costs and other such frictions. This is the *direct-to-consumer*, *same -day delivery* model, with minimal retail space and low inventories.

This rapid diffusion of, and instantaneous access to, information led to two changes: an increase in content and an increase in time-sensitivity. The ability to communicate anywhere, anytime has supported an increase in content in the form of images, short-form videos, and text. Sharing experiences, gossiping about people and transmitting rumors are all bonding mechanisms, instilling a sense of belonging to some larger group. The gossip triad, consisting of people who send this informal communication, people who receive it and the target, is based upon trust, trust that the recipient will not rebuke or report the sender. Along with details about the target, the rules and guidelines of a society's culture are also transmitted, where culture is "defined as an information-based system that organizes social interactions and helps people to fill basic social and biological needs" [6].

The content tsunami is best illustrated by TikTok. This short-form video platform has captivated the younger demographic in terms of hours spent on it. Introducing an interactive feature between users and content creators, called streamers, has led to the development of livestreaming. Twitch, the largest livestreaming platform, hosts the two most popular interactive games of 2021, Fortnite and League of Legends. In fact, League of Legends is played by around 8 million people every day. In 2020, 15% of U.S. adults between the ages of 18 and 34 watched livestream videos several times a day. Virtual learning in the form of short videos on YouTube and the Khan Academy website offer educational content. Online videos provide step-by-step solutions to problems, which many people find more instructive than reading text. The video captures the mind more readily by drawing upon multiple sensory stimuli [7].

The anywhere–anytime conception of the world has bestowed a sense of urgency, an acute sensitivity to the passage of time. Time sensitivity is perceived as a higher value for each hour, a sense of impatience with lengthy conversations, and a move toward communicating with short text messages. As the speed of information transmission increases, the number of actions undertaken within a given time period expands. The higher activity level is perceived as an increase in the speed of time, making each hour more valuable. By cramming more action into a day, the "cost" of diverting an hour to chat with your grandmother is measured by the activity forfeited. If the chat is less entertaining than the activity, you feel cheated. Communicating in "byte"-sized text messages is one manifestation of this phenomenon.

Multiple online choices for consumption of content encourage individuals to cram more activities, more information into their waking hours. Rather than make choices between activities by accurately assessing the time needed to consume any one activity, there is a tendency to squeeze multiple activities into any given time period—multitasking. The corresponding information overload or content tsunami has led to an exorbitant demand for attention. Constrained by a fixed supply of mental capacity, or cognitive bandwidth, the result is an attention deficit. The manifestation of this deficit, and the content tsunami, is choice fatigue diagnosed by a decrease in basic comprehension. The attention deficit clouds judgment and decision-making and reduces mental acuity by increasing the personal costs of information processing[3] [8].

Choice fatigue or decision fatigue can become a hurdle for would-be entrepreneurs when there are multiple decisions to be made in the early stages of a business. It could mean the entrepreneur reverts to simplified rules of thumb or the availability heuristic. It might be easier for a local electrician to order standardized tools from, say Amazon, than check out a local supplier who is a mere 10 miles away. Paradoxically, that supplier might be more informed about local conditions, such as the age of the electricity grid, and have a network of local contacts and knowledge that can be valuable as the business grows. The belief that the decision

[3] This attention deficit is not to be confused with the neurodevelopmental condition attention-deficit/hyperactivity disorder (ADHD), a mental health issue designated as DSM-5 by the U.S. Centers for Disease Control and Prevention.

to choose between the two has to be made instantly, that there is an urgency to this process, can lead to decision paralysis. Overwhelmed by both multiple choices and an urgency in making the decision can leave the fledgling founder in a state of confused paralysis.

Time sensitivity, manifested as impatience and immediacy, is frequently expressed as the convenience factor in individual decision-making.[4] Much like maximizing one's well-being, minimizing the time required for activities has become a powerful driving force in determining lifestyles. It creates a demand for new services and products, and may generate preference reversals in a non-rational manner. Preferences have changed in the sense that eating at one's place of work or home is no longer considered a necessity, but a luxury. People are willing to shell out large delivery fees or pay in intangible ways such as forgoing waiter service at the table. This higher willingness to pay suggests an increase in demand for this discretionary service.

Similarly, delivery of both perishable and non-perishable food has become a part of daily living for many individuals who feel time-constrained, whether or not they are truly pressed for time. Notably, food consumption via the order-online-for-takeout-or-delivery model predated the pandemic. Services were offered via a website or mobile app. DoorDash, the online order and food delivery app, was introduced in 2013, and Instacart, the grocery delivery and pickup service, in 2012. As evidence of this growing trend, the leisure and hospitality sector had the largest job gains, in the last quarter of 2021, relative to the same quarter in 2020 [9].

Cynicism and Mistrust of Government Institutions and State Authority

Second, there has been an erosion of trust in institutions. According to Fig. 1.2, the past two decades have witnessed a secular decline in public trust in government [10]. Armed with data and computing power, individuals have developed a new social consciousness about the power of

[4] A higher shadow price of time is another way of describing this phenomenon. The shadow price is a technical term for hidden price or implicit price. As this price increases, people respond by cutting their estimates of how long each activity will take. They do not cut activities, but rather think that the same activities can be done in less time. Hence the feeling of impatience.

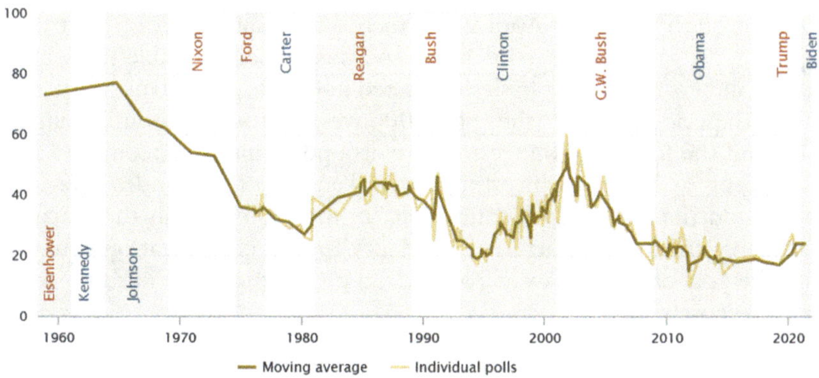

Fig. 1.2 Public trust in government near historic lows (*Source* Public Trust in Government: 1958–2021, Pew Research Center)

startups, of owning one's livelihood, to overcome inequality, both of opportunity and of outcome.

Are cryptocurrencies a symbol of this mistrust, an alternative to the shared belief in currencies backed by the sovereign power of the state? Benjamin Ho writes in his 2021 book *Why Trust Matters: An Economist's Guide to the Ties that Bind Us:*

> In fact, a better way to think about money is that money was a way to keep track of trust. In hunter-gatherer societies, a lot of economic life was governed by gift exchange. I share my hunt as a gift, in the hope that you will share your hunt next time. As societies grew, it became more and more difficult to keep track of who owes whom a favor. People began using markers to keep track of favors. The earliest markers became the earliest form of writing. Other markers developed into money. [11]

Most of the activity on the Bitcoin blockchain is not based on economically significant activities but is a "byproduct of the Bitcoin protocol design as well as the preference of many participants for anonymity", according to Makarov and Schoar et al. [12]. Furthermore, mining capacity itself is highly concentrated, with the top 10% of miners controlling 90% of the world's capacity to generate Bitcoins, and therefore dominating ownership. There is also a geographic concentration of miners, with 60% to 80% of mining capacity located in China between

2015 through 2020. In April 2021 there was a shutdown of electricity supply in Xinjiang province in China, and this made it possible to identify a set of miners that were physically located in China. But far more remarkable is the evidence that "the top 1000 investors control about 3 million BTC and the top 10,000 investor own around 5 million bitcoins".

It seems as if private investors have taken over the mantle of central banks, and the European Central Bank in the euro area, in the issuance and management of money. This tendency toward centralization conflicts with the goal of moving away from federal governance. The need for trust hasn't been eliminated.

The New World of 2020–2022

A powerful force binding communities today is the **shared experience** of sheltered isolation during the pandemic. This shared experience has formed a connection, a bond of trust. Having faced a once-in-a lifetime crisis of epic proportions, people may be more tolerant of risk and more willing to share it. Attitudes toward risk change when individuals face such an unimagined shock. They become emboldened by having passed through the crisis and survived. That it was possible to live a reasonable life under such formidable circumstances can be empowering. Individuals now have the confidence to implement ideas that have been germinating for months and launch their own businesses. Since June 2020, new business creation has risen to levels not recorded since the dot-com revolution.

These are also the years of the **Great Resignation**, when according to a Prudential survey, more than 25% of workers left a job. The pandemic energized individuals, creating a zest for living, but with a new lifestyle, new jobs, or new tasks. After more than a year of isolation, many workers are reconsidering their lifestyle choices, perhaps valuing more flexibility and agency in their work patterns. The reasons for career switching are better work-life balance (27%), better compensation (26%), and the desire to try a new career/job (26%), according to the survey. More than 30% of millennials plan to work for a different employer once the pandemic has retreated, compared with 24% of Gen Xers and 10% of boomers. More than three-quarters of those surveyed said they think employers should expand remote work options post-pandemic, while nearly half said they would switch jobs if their current employer didn't offer flexible or remote work options [13].

New business ideas would have shriveled in the absence of financing. It has been argued that the resurgence of new businesses might have been held back by disparities in access to capital. Certain communities are disproportionately impacted by access to finance. "Black-owned startups start smaller and stay smaller over the entire first eight years of their existence", write Fairlie and Desai [14].

Government or public sector financial assistance might have been the key to unlocking many new businesses, particularly among underrepresented communities. Vice President Kamala Harris makes this point in a 2021 *Forbes* magazine article:

> Traditional banks and venture capital firms have not always seen the vision of women entrepreneurs and those of color. Community lenders, on the other hand, were founded to see that vision. Community lenders understand the value in providing access to capital in communities of color and low-income communities—and because they do, they add value to those communities and our country. [15]

However, the public sector help might have simply been the tipping point. As John Haltiwanger writes: "The surge in applications for likely employer businesses is arguably not because of, but despite, the PPP [public-private partnership] program". He continues:

> After all, PPP money went only to old businesses, thereby giving them a competitive advantage with respect to anybody who wanted to start a new business after February 2020. Government help was also frequently slow to arrive, which implies that the real driver of new business formation was not the government but just the underlying wealth and hopefulness of individual Americans. [16]

That last statement drives home the third thesis of this book, which is the desire for community engagement.

The business wisdom in this book is that a risk-taking culture is based on mutual trust which emerges in a tightly networked community. It does not require complete transparency because private information can be the lifeblood of startups. But it does mean a social ethos, an expectation that contracts will be honored, and confidence in the economic playbook, that the rules of the game are accepted by all. Institutions and preferences will change, but the process must be inclusive of all constituents [17, 18]. The corollary is that trust implies hope. Businesses are formed, not in spite of, but because of, adversity.

Entrepreneurship and Community

Entrepreneurial activity tends to signal optimism in the world in general and in the economy in particular. A surge in microbusinesses can, however, be followed by a demise further down the road. Therefore the more seeds planted, the higher the probability that some will germinate. Policymakers would do well to add these microbusiness owners to their radar screens, not merely due to their ability to create jobs but also because of their impact on the community.

Community relationships cultivate trust through long-standing family and social ties and can obviate the need for explicit contracting arrangements. These agreements can avert the problem of insufficient information or asymmetries of information. Cooperation in a community often relies on reciprocity and moral obligations, compared to impersonal enforcement procedures. As Sam Bowles writes in his book,

> "over the past two decades, behavioral experiments have provided hard evidence that ethical and other regarding motives are common in virtually all human populations". And that "policies advocated as necessary to the functioning of a market economy may also promote self-interest and undermine the means by which a society sustains a robust civic culture of cooperative and generous citizens." Furthermore, "while some economists imagined that in a distant past Homo economicus invented markets, it could have been the other way around: the proliferation of amoral self-interest might be one of the consequences of living in the kind of society that economists idealized". [19]

The disruptive effect of technology has unsettled many Americans, prompting a reevaluation of the balance between institutions, both government and large business organizations, and their own community. Community can be defined along the lines of religion or neighborhood or some larger interest. "Once we understand that the community matters, then it becomes clear why it is not enough for a country to experience strong economic growth – the professional economist's favorite measure of economic performance", writes Raghu Rajan [20]. The community is the third pillar. "The human need for relationships and the social needs of the neighborhood may well provide many of the jobs of tomorrow",

Rajan writes. Communities provide a sense of belonging and identity through the narratives portrayed and the shared values established. Attitudes toward risk are one of those shared values.

The Plan

The data examined cover the period 1994–2020, with young startups defined as businesses with fewer than 100 employees and less than 1 year in existence. Mature startups are businesses with 1 to 4 years in operation and fewer than 400 employees. Part I of the book groups the data on an establishment size by state by population grid. The following patterns emerge.[5]

1. There was a startup resurgence over the period 1994–2020. Young startups, under one year in existence, have fewer than 100 employees with few new ventures with over 500 employees.
2. Splitting this period by the years of the Great Recession, the 1994–2007 period is defined as the **desktop digital revolution (DR I)** and the post-2010 period as the **mobility digital revolution (DR II)**. The startup trend in DR II exceeds that in DR I.[6] Chapter 2 explains this story.
3. Scrutinizing the data at the state level, states east of the Mississippi are ineffective as startup incubators while most of the activity lies west of the Mississippi, with the exception of Massachusetts, Wisconsin, and Georgia, as discussed in Chapter 3.
4. Population and population density across states are uncorrelated with entrepreneurial activity in that state. Chapter 4 studies startups per capita, normalizing by working age population. The composition of top-ranking states is unchanged, but the rankings are rearranged.
5. These businesses are in technology-driven markets, requiring higher skills. It is the application of technology to traditional production methods that is propelling this resurgence.

[5] This analysis is based on data from the Business Employment Dynamics database of the Bureau of Labor Statistics, the U.S. Census Bureau, and the Kaufmann Foundation covering the period 1994–2020 [21].

[6] The trend in the number of startups is the level of entrepreneurial activity after accounting for noise and recurring seasonal factors.

6. New establishments face a high infant mortality rate. Chapter 5 examines the data for new businesses in the 1–4-year range with fewer than 500 employees, called the mature startups, and finds that new establishment trends are stronger for young startups compared with mature startups over the years 1994–2020. This suggests that starting businesses is not the problem. Rather, sustaining their development and growth with support services is the principal policy issue.

   Part II of the book takes a more abstract view of entrepreneurship, starting with a summary of the results in Chapter 6 followed by a discussion of the technology landscape, and the difference between invention and implementation.
7. Chapter 7 addresses the importance of incubation and mentorship, the absence of which spells the demise of fledgling businesses. The bane of startups is the focus on rapid scaling perpetrated by investors, whose motive may be rapid exit after accumulating the return to their initial investment. What is needed perhaps, is "ridiculously intrusive monitoring" to sustain the young seedlings of business, as David Tobenkin put it in a 2021 *Wired* magazine article [22].
8. "Even seasoned entrepreneurs face long odds that do not necessarily improve with time. Roughly one-third of new businesses fail within two years, half within five years, and two-thirds within 10 years, according to a U.S. Small Business Administration analysis of new business survival rates from 1994–2018. … Minority entrepreneurs face additional challenges; on average, they have less household wealth and less access to mainstream grants, loans, and equity investors, and they often serve less affluent communities than white-owned businesses" [22].
9. Chapter 8 explores experience, age, education, gender, and race in the context of young businesses. This chapter unpacks the paradox presented by the simultaneous presence of a declining labor force participation rate among prime working age adults, a decrease in productivity growth rates in the past decade and a startup revolution.
10. Chapter 9 pivots to the current post-pandemic outlook, and Chapter 10 concludes by highlighting the principal points in the book and some policy suggestions.

For a quick overview of the main results, the reader might proceed directly to the summary in Chapter 6 and the discussion of entrepreneurship in subsequent chapters, skipping the literature survey below and the empirical details in Chapters 2–5.

The Backdrop: A Short Survey of Related Current Research

Entrepreneurship research has been dominated by a labor market perspective in much of the academic literature. The consistent decline in the number of jobs created by new businesses over the past 25 years is the central research issue. For instance, Fig. 1.3 examines the number of jobs created in the context of young businesses, less than a year old, based on data from the Bureau of Labor Statistics. This decline in jobs created by startups is then interpreted as a startup deficit. It is paradoxical to conceive of a technology-driven startup resurgence that is labor intensive. The point of a science and engineering-based new business frontier is reducing the requirement of a large workforce. A startup with two workers skilled in writing computer code can create a business that has large revenues and equally large numbers of suppliers and distributors, who are all part of the independent contractor network.

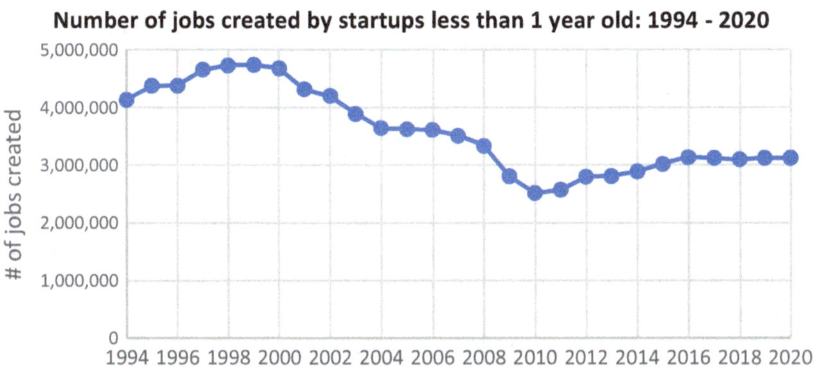

Fig. 1.3 Number of jobs created by startup businesses that were less than one year old in the U.S. from 1994–2020 (*Source* Bureau of Labor Statistics, compiled by Statista)

A decade ago, Hurst and Pugsley [23] found that "many young and small business owners in the U.S. economy state they do not have aspirations for high growth, but rather often started businesses for non-pecuniary reasons like time flexibility or personal goals". They show that most small businesses have between 1 and 19 employees, making up roughly 20% of the workforce [23]. These are confined to 40 narrowly defined industries with a standardized product or service. These businesses remain small and are rarely innovative. Furthermore, policymakers interested in innovation "may want to consider more targeted policies as opposed to creating policies that target the universe of small business" [23].

From this angle, there has been a **startup deficit** since before the Great Recession as measured by the number of jobs created by young businesses [22]. In research where startups are defined by years in existence and the period examined is 1980–2014, Alon et al. wrote in 2018, "Over the last three decades, the U.S. business sector has experienced a collapse in the rate of new startups, alongside an enormous reallocation of economic activity from entrants and young firms to older incumbents". In terms of the macroeconomic impact, they write, "Our results suggest that the startup deficit and subsequent aging of the U.S. business sector have had a considerable impact on aggregate productivity... [reducing] aggregate productivity by roughly 0.10 percentage point a year from 1980–2014" [24].

Further, the authors find a **decline in business dynamism** over the same period as reallocation of workers across the productivity spectrum was sluggish. Young firms are more responsive to productivity differentials, and if there are fewer startups, there is less job reallocation. The "decline in responsiveness is especially large in the high-tech sector", which suggests a "significant drag on aggregate productivity" [24]. The theory is that if a certain sector produced more output per worker, it should as a matter of course attract more workers, since they would be paid more. When this reallocation does not occur, the economy is said to be sluggish and lacking in business dynamism.

Business endurance beyond the first few years is the riskiest aspect of startups but plays a crucial role in job growth. Decker et al. [25] find that most young firms either exit within 10 years or remain small. But few firms exhibit very high growth in terms of job creation. This suggests that

> the rate of business startups and the pace of employment dynamism in the U.S. economy has fallen over recent decades and this downward trend accelerated after 2000. A critical factor in accounting for the decline in business dynamics [the processes of entry, exit, expansion, and contraction] is a lower rate of business startups and the related decreasing role of dynamic young businesses in the economy"[7]. [25]

In addition to job growth, I believe the focus on declining productivity in the U.S. economy since 1990 has researchers looking for plausible causes. The antecedent factors that fit the data are those associated with a decline in job growth, namely, new establishments or startups. Hence, the focus on the startup deficit. If young establishments do not produce jobs, the data will show a decline in startups [26].

In a 2021 paper examining employer businesses over the period 1979–2007, Karahan, Pugsley, and Sahin observe that the sluggish supply of labor since the 1970s explains the long-run decline in the U.S. startup rate. The definition of startup is "the share of new employers as a fraction of all employers", which approaches startups from a new employer perspective rather than a new establishment viewpoint. New establishments may still be founder-run and may not have hired new employees, as measured by payroll. The founders of these new establishments could be joint owners and therefore will not show up in the U.S. Census Bureau's Longitudinal Business Database.[8] The authors argue that startups by definition need new employees, and if the labor supply is decreasing, there must accordingly be adjustments at the entry margin, which means fewer startups. "The slowdown in the U.S labor supply growth can explain up to 60 percent of the declining startup rate and up to 70 percent of startups' decline in employment share. Ultimately, growing labor supply requires growing labor demand, which can only arise through entry of new firms. … This feature makes the startup rate highly responsive to change in labor supply growth", Karahan et al. write [27].

These papers focus on one category of entrepreneurs, "transformational" or scale-up entrepreneurs that contribute heavily to job creation.

[7] Data from the Business Dynamics Statistics and the Longitudinal Business Database, maintained by the U.S. Census Bureau, are used in the papers referenced above as well as in this book.

[8] Karahan et al.'s measure of startups is crucially dependent upon the definition: "the share of new employers as a fraction of all employers."

On the other hand, "subsistence" entrepreneurs provide employment for the entrepreneur and a few others, most likely family members, and do not grow. Therefore, "when people discuss the importance of entrepreneurs in job creation and productivity growth, they are envisioning transformational entrepreneurs, not subsistence entrepreneurs", according to Antoinette Schoar [28]. Both categories of entrepreneurs imply risk-bearing, an assessment of medium to long-term market conditions to gauge the risk-reward tradeoff, and therefore should properly be evaluated as part of the same business segment. Policies that purport to encourage innovation would do well to address attitudes toward risk, which are more likely to be affected by community networks than by financial incentives.

Most research on startups has defined them as firms (which include all establishments owned by that organization) that add to job growth. As discussed above, it is misleading to dismiss a particular subset of startups as being unimportant simply because they don't add to job growth. The culture of risk taking is felt across the entire spectrum of new enterprises, and even if the motive of some startups is to stay small, they may influence others to enter the fray and scale up. Therefore, it would be enlightening to consider the entire world of new businesses, not simply those that add to employment.

Emphasis on the correlation between jobs and startups obscures a deeper focus on the effects of young firms on the environment and other nascent enterprises and founders. The Kaufmann Foundation is the exception. Its unique and more comprehensive statistic, the Rate of New Entrepreneurs, "captures all new business owners, including those who own incorporated or unincorporated businesses, and those who are employers or non-employers", according to Travis Howe and Sameeksha Desai. It measures the percent of population that starts a new business, a trend that has not declined over 1994–2020, and, in fact, has shown a meaningful upturn in 2020 [29].

In practice, publicly available data categorize startups in conjunction with employment, a format followed in this book. Viewing recent data from the perspective of establishment size conjointly with employment growth, a newer picture emerges. According to a news release from the U.S. Bureau of Labor Statistics, Business Employment Dynamics Summary, "In the third quarter of 2020, firms with 1– 49 employees had a net employment increase of 1.4 million. Firms with 50 – 249 employees had a net employment gain of 529,000. Firms with 250 or more employees had a net employment increase of 2.0 million" [30].

This suggests that there was strong job growth at very small businesses with 1–49 employees and very large businesses with more than 250 employees. Also, small businesses lost fewer employees during the sharp downturn in the second quarter of 2020 compared with the over-250 employee businesses: 4.6 million jobs lost compared with 7.7 million. Using data from the Business Formation Statistics, Dinlersoz et al. [31] confirm this escalation in new business formation [31].

A 2021 paper by Catherine Fazio et al., expanding on the idea that entrepreneurship is a "key foundation of economic dynamism" in terms of job creation and economic resilience, examines how entrepreneurship varies by state and by geographies within states [32]. In particular, drawing on state level new business registration records from 2019 and 2020 for Georgia, Kentucky, New York, Tennessee, Texas, Vermont, Washington, and Florida, the authors find "a more than 20% increase in new business registrations in 2020 compared to 2019. Additionally, locations including a higher proportion of wealthy, Black residents are associated with higher 'startup formation rates'".[9] They also find that the CARES Act of 2020 and the Supplemental Act of December 2020 are associated with higher startup formation rates. While they recognize that the joint occurrence of the pandemic and the social justice movements of 2020 might have stimulated entrepreneurship, the authors attribute startup resurgence to federal stimulus, arguing that "potential Black entrepreneurs face less access to bank finance".

In the past few years, larger numbers of Americans have started online microbusinesses. "Online microbusinesses are defined as businesses with a discrete domain name and an active website. About 90% of these online businesses employ fewer than 10 employees", according to Matthew Smith et al. [33] Moreover, these entrepreneurial trends are widespread as "[t]he number of unincorporated, self-employed Americans reached 9.44 million in October 2021—one of the highest numbers since the 2008 financial crisis" [33]. Lower entry barriers for starting a microbusiness include "widely available broadband, greater digital fluency, and a more mature e-commerce marketplace that simplifies website creation, marketing, and online sales". A July 2021 survey by GoDaddy found that

[9] The startup formation rate is defined as the difference in ventures between 2020 and 2019 divided by the sum of ventures in both years.

55% of the 4,000 individuals surveyed were single owners, such as retirees, stay-at-home moms, and students. Many of these individuals would be classified by national and state level data as non-employed. These micro businesses launched rapidly as 63% of those started in 2020 needed less than $5,000 in capital [34].

The new role model is the self-made rich, the true American Dream. Smith and his co-authors show that most U.S. households in the top 0.1% of income distribution in 2014 received their income from human capital and skills rather than land or inherited financial capital. The primary source of this income is recorded as tax-favored private business profit or pass-through business income.[10] "Most top earners are pass-through business owners", they write. "In 2014, over 69% of the top 1% and over 84% of the top 0.1% earn some pass-through income. Typical firms owned by the top 1–0.1% are single-establishment firms in professional services or health services". Moreover, "[t]op entrepreneurial income is large relative to all other income components. For example, among million-dollar earners, 44% of fiscal income ... is pass-through entrepreneurial income". These are self-made millionaires since "across income definitions and top income groups, more than three out of four of top earners in the parent-linked sample did not have top 1% parents" [33].

If, in 2014, the primary source of income at the very top of the income distribution ladder was self-made business income, then surely that must define the career path for job seekers. This is reinforced by the fact that most of this entrepreneurial income can be attributed to human capital—there is an "84% decline in profits" upon an owner's death, according to Jeremy Hartman and Joseph Parilla [34]. The defining role model is formed by noting that, "a typical firm owned by the top 0.1% is a regional business with $20 million in sales and 100 employees, such as an auto dealer, beverage distributor, or large law firm", the researchers find [34].

Since the start of the pandemic, online businesses grew fastest among groups that were most impacted by the economic distress. Hartman and Parilla write, "Black owners account for 26% of all new microbusinesses, up from 15% before the pandemic. Similarly, women-owned businesses surged to 57% of new microbusiness starts, up from 48%". Consequently,

[10] Smith et al. write: "Most top business income comes from private 'pass-through' businesses that are not taxed at the entity level; instead, income passes through to the owners who pay taxes on their share of the firm's income" [33].

they write, the recent swell of microbusinesses warrants greater attention from policymakers to understand how these nascent owners can be supported. Owners need mentoring help with online business skills, digital marketing, capital, and networking. Ultimately, a shift in mindset is as important as policy change. Many local economic growth policies focus on target industries or chase well-documented metrics such as job creation. But microbusiness owners do not fall neatly into traditional economic development strategies. They are following a passion—not an industry—and need access to skills training, capital, and affordable broadband rather than a job fair [34].

Bibliography

1 *The Times*, Assassination of President Lincoln. https://en.wikisource.org/wiki/The_Times/1865/News/Assassination_of_President_Lincoln.
2 Cerf, Vincent. 2013. The Open Internet and the Web. *CERN*. https://home.cern/news/opinion/computing/open-internet-and-web.
3 National Bureau of Economic Research. 2021. US Business Cycle Expansions and Contractions. https://www.nber.org/research/data/us-business-cycle-expansions-and-contractions.
4 Kaufmann Foundation. 2010. The Importance of Startups in Job Creation and Destruction. https://www.kauffman.org/wp-content/uploads/2019/12/firm_formation_importance_of_startups.pdf.
5 Haltiwanger, John, Ron Jarmin and Javier Miranda. 2008. Business Formation and Dynamics by Business Age: Results from the New Business Dynamics Statistics. https://www.census.gov/content/dam/Census/library/publications/2008/adrm/CES/BDS_Business_Formation_CAED_May2008.pdf.
6 Baumeister, Roy et al. 2004. Gossip as Cultural Learning. *Review of General Psychology* 8(2). https://journals.sagepub.com/doi/pdf/10.1037/1089-2680.8.2.111.
7 Statista. 2021. https://www.statista.com/statistics/297071/us-social-media-live-streaming-video-usage-age-group/#statisticContainer.
8 Bhatt. 2019. *The Attention Deficit*. Palgrave Macmillan.
9 Bureu of Labor Statistics, Leisure and Hospitality. 2021. https://www.bls.gov/iag/tgs/iag70.htm.
10 Pew Research Center. 2021. https://www.pewresearch.org/politics/2021/05/17/public-trust-in-government-1958-2021/.
11 Ho, Benjamin. 2021. *Why Trust Matters: An Economist's Guide to the Ties that Bind Us*. Columbia University Press.

12 Makarov, Igor and Antoinette Schoar. 2021. Blockchain Analysis of the Bitcoin Market. *NBER Working Paper 29396*. https://www.nber.org/system/files/working_papers/w29396/w29396.pdf.
13 Prudential's Pulse of the American Worker Survey conducted by Morning Consult in March 2021: AWS_Is-This-Working_Fact Sheet_FINAL.pdf. https://news.prudential.com/presskits/pulse-american-worker-survey-is-this-working.htm.
14 Fairlie, Robert W. and Sameeksha Desai. 2021. State Report on Early-Stage Entrepreneurship in the United States: 2020. https://ssrn.com/abstract=3827254.
15 Harris, Kamala. 2021. Kamalanomics: Vice President Kamala Harris Outlines Her Vision of Inclusive Entrepreneurship. https://www.forbes.com/sites/kamalaharris/2021/06/01/kamala-harris-kamalanomics-vice-president-inclusive-capitalism-entrepreneurship.
16 Haltiwanger, John. 2021. Entrepreneurship during the Covid-19 Pandemic: Evidence from the Business Formation Statistics. *NBER Working Paper 28912*. http://www.nber.org/papers/w28912.
17 Rose, D. C. 2011. *The Moral Foundations of Economic Behavior*, New York: Oxford University Press.
18 For a full discussion of markets see Herzog, Lisa. 2021. Markets. *The Stanford Encyclopedia of Philosophy* (Fall 2021 Edition), Edward N. Zalta (ed.) https://plato.stanford.edu/archives/fall2021/entries/markets.
19 Bowles, Sam. 2016. *The Moral Economy: Why Good Incentives Are no Substitute for Good Citizens*. Yale University Press.
20 Rajan, Raghuram. 2019. *The Third Pillar: How Markets and the State Leave the Community Behind*. Penguin Press.
21 Kaufmann Foudation, 2022. https://www.kauffman.org/entrepreneurship/.
22 Tobenkin, David. 2021. More Black and Hispanic Entrepreneurs Are Open for Business. *Wired Magazine*, December 20. https://www.wired.com/story/more-black-hispanic-entrepreneurs-open-business/.
23 Hurst, E. and B. Pugsley. 2011. What Do Small Businesses Do? *Brookings Papers on Economic Activity* 43(2): 73–142.
24 Alon, Titus, David Berger, Robert Dent, Benjamin Pugsley. 2018. Older and Slower: The Startup Deficit's Lasting Effects on Aggregate Productivity Growth. *Journal of Monetary Economics*, October.
25 Decker, Ryan, John Haltiwanger, Ron Jarmin and Javier Miranda. 2014. The Role of Entrepreneurship in US Job Creation and Economic Dynamism. *Journal of Economic Perspectives* 28(3): 3–24.
26 Decker, Ryan, John C. Haltiwanger, Ron S. Jarmin and Javier Miranda. January 2018. Changing Business Dynamism and Productivity: Shocks vs. Responsiveness. *NBER Working Paper No. 24236*.

27 Karahan, Fatih, Benjamin Pugsley and Aysegul Sahin. 2021. Demographic Origins of the Startup Deficit. *Federal Reserve Bank of New York Staff Reports, no 888*. https://www.newyorkfed.org/medialibrary/media/research/staff_reports/sr888.pdf.
28 Schoar, A. 2010. The Divide Between Subsistence and Transformational Entrepreneurship. *Innovation Policy and the Economy* 10: 57–81.
29 Howe, Travis and Sameeksha Desai. April 2021. Entrepreneurship in Economic Crises: A look at Four Recession Periods between 1978 and 2018 in the United States. *Kaufmann Foundation Working Paper.*
30 Bureau of Labor Statistics. 2021. https://www.bls.gov/news.release/cewbd.nr0.htm.
31 Dinlersoz, E., Dunne, T., Haltiwanger, J. and V. Penciakova. 2021. Business Formation: A Tale of Two Recessions. *Federal Reserve Bank of Atlanta Working Paper 21-01.*
32 Fazio, C., J. Guzman, Y. Liu and S. Stern. 2021. How Is Covid Changing the Geography of Entrepreneurship? Evidence from the Startup Cartography Project. *NBER Working Paper 28787*. http://www.nber.org/papers/w28787.
33 Smith, Matthew, Danny Yagan, Owen Zidar and Eric Zwick. 2019. Capitalists in the Twenty-First Century. *The Quarterly Journal of Economics* 134(4): 1675–1745. Also at https://doi.org/10.1093/qje/qjz020.
34 Hartman, Jeremy and Joseph Parilla. 2022. Microbusinesses Flourished During the Pandemic. Now We Must Tap into Their Potential. https://www.brookings.edu/blog/the-avenue/2022/01/04/microbusinesses-flourished-during-the-pandemic-now-we-must-tap-into-their-full-potential.

CHAPTER 2

Business Dynamism Over 1994–2020

The term startup conjures many varieties of new businesses. In general, there are multiple milestones or stages that locate the business in its lifespan. First, there is the idea stage, or equivalently, the seed stage, where a problem is discovered. Second, a possible solution is imagined and enshrined in the value proposition. Third, the solution is tested among an initial group of users, going through multiple iterations before getting to stage four, where customer acquisition is accelerated. The fifth stage is the expansion stage where new markets are explored.

Young Versus Mature Startups

Integrating the second solution stage and the third testing stages, I label this early stage as **young startups**. At this stage, it is quite likely that profits are non-existent or negative. The fourth stage, involving sustainable scaling, is labeled **mature startups**. There may be positive profits at this milestone. The idea stage, which precedes both can be as short as a few months to a few years and is typically not documented in the data. Expansion into new markets at the fifth stage is another stage and has ambiguous length in terms of years. Hence, the data examined will encompass two broad stages: startups and mature startups; the first and fifth stages are not examined. Economists and policymakers have been despairing over the lack of business dynamism until recently

S. Bhatt, *Entrepreneurship Today*,
https://doi.org/10.1007/978-3-031-11495-3_2

and attributed that to a startup deficit. That debate, briefly discussed in Chapter 1, might be settled by clarifying definitions and by examining the data.

For the purposes of this book, startups are defined as establishments less than 1 year in existence, with less than 100 employees, and mature startups as those with 1–4 years and less than 500 employees. An establishment, as defined by the Bureau of Labor Statistics, is the basic unit of production of goods or services, usually at a single location.[1] A firm is a legal construct, usually embodies several establishments and is identified by the employer tax identification number (EIN) at the Internal Revenue Service of the Treasury Department. **In essence, according to the Bureau of Labor Statistics, a startup is a business opening that reports positive employment for the first time in the current year or equivalently, a firm that employed its first worker in the current year.**

The age of an establishment is the time span between the first instance an establishment reports positive employment and the reference period, which is the survey period. Note that this is a self-reported measure where survey-takers choose among the following different age categories: less than 1 year, 1–4 years, 5–9 years, 10 years and older, and all ages [1].

Theoretically, one could define small business in terms of revenue cutoffs or employee cutoffs or age cutoffs. For instance, a startup could be one with less than $50,000 in sales or less than 50 employees or less than 5 years in existence. Since we are interested in new venture activity, using revenue as the measure of size may be misleading. For instance, the minimum revenue that would sustain businesses in an industry with high overhead costs, such as the trucking industry will be larger than that required to tide over a business with low fixed costs, such as the fast-food industry. The U.S. Small Business Administration defines size by the amount of money a business makes as well as employment. In the fast food industry, there were over 37,000 establishments with less than 5 employees in 2017 but they accounted for only 4% of the sales in this industry. If we are interested in firms that were responsible for more than 50% of the industry's revenue, then perhaps the cutoff should be moved up to firms with fewer than 250 employees as these accounted for 52% of the $253billion in revenue in 2017. In truck transportation the firms that

[1] The analysis uses data drawn from the Labor Department's Business Employment Dynamics at the Bureau of Labor Statistics (BLS) as well as the Commerce Department's U.S. Census Bureau and the Bureau of Economic Analysis.

accounted for 41% of the industry revenue had more than $100 million in sales in 2017. In this case, a small trucking business would be defined by an establishment with less than $5 million in revenue [2].

The emergent nature of entrepreneurship directs us to define startups not in terms of revenue earned, since many startups begin to report positive earnings only after a year or two in operation. However, employee count need not march in tandem with sales. It could be possible for a young business to have a fairly large employee count. Consequently, we define a startup in terms of age and employee count.

Under this definition startups only include employer businesses, which comprise those business with paid employees.[2] In 2019, for example, there were 7.959 million employer establishments with paid employees, but 26.485 million non-employer establishments with no paid employees. There are non-employee businesses such as sole proprietorships, which are not included in the measure. Given that this form of business organization also represents new business establishments, my analysis provides a conservative estimate of startups. This undercounting leads to a discounting and neglect of women and minority entrepreneurs. In 2019, for example, of all the businesses without paid employees, 41% were owned by women, with $300b in receipts, and 32.7% of these non-employer businesses were owned by minorities, with $306b in receipts. Sole proprietorships constituted the largest sub-heading in 2019, with 22.9 million establishments and sales of $816 million. Among the various sectors, professional, scientific, and technical topped the list with 3.726 establishments and revenues of $178 million [4].

Effectively, for every employer establishment there were three non-employer establishments, with just under half of them owned by women and one-third owned by minorities. Most non-employers are self-employed individuals operating unincorporated businesses (sole proprietorships). According to the Non-Employer Statistics website, part of the U.S. Census, "The majority of all business establishments in the United States are non-employers, yet these firms average less than 4 percent of all sales and receipts nationally. Due to their small economic impact and small workforce, these firms are excluded from most other Census Bureau

[2] The U.S. Census proposes the same definition in its Business Dynamics Statistics dataset [3].

business statistics (the primary exception being the Survey of Business Owners)”.[3]

This exclusion can be misleading due to its narrow focus, as discussed in Chapter 1. If a business has no employees today and contributes little to national sales revenue does it not have any community significance or collective repercussion? The behavioral spillovers resulting from each new enterprise in a community can coalesce into a powerful contagion, much like individuals walking at their own pace across the newly built London Millennium Pedestrian bridge in 2000, causing the entire structure to sway sideways with amplitudes up to 7 cm., leading many engineers to panic. The tendency of a crowd to fall into step is a consequence of the instability. Bridge motion causes walkers to adjust their pace, the forces from random right and left footsteps do not negate, and the feedback leads to oscillation [5].

Synchronized swaying can be the outcome of many socio-economic phenomena. It is not conscious copying in the sense of “fear-of-missing out” or the availability heuristic. This “wobble and synchrony” arises from independent individual actions taken simultaneously. So also, independent germination of new firms could lead to a synchronized collective confidence which may inspire grander changes. As we ponder the trajectory of startups below, it would be appropriate to reflect on the non-employer businesses that are going under the radar in these diagrams.

Proceeding with this understanding, the trajectory of startups, business openings that reported positive employment by March of the year, is shown in Fig. 2.1 below.

Startup ventures trended upward from 1994 and peaked in 2007 before plunging over the years 2008–2009. The upward trend resumes in 2010 and continues to the present. A clear pattern is discernable with 2007 as a watershed year. After peaking in 2007, the number of startups trended down through the 2008–2009 financial crisis, but then remarkably, pivoted in a relentless upward trajectory from 2010 to the present.

In the recent history of digital communication technology, the year 2007 was a turning point. The past 26 years are dotted with milestones that have influenced the trail of the economy, starting with 1994, when we had commercialization of the web via the web browser on the desktop

[3] See the Non-Employer Statistics (NES) website at [4].

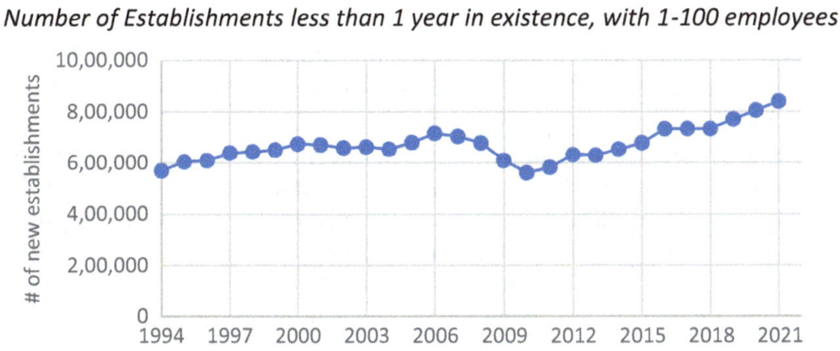

Fig. 2.1 Total number of startups: 1994–2020 (*Source* Business Employment Dynamics Data by Age and Size, BLS)

computer. Then, on January 9, 2007, Apple CEO Steve Jobs, dressed in his customary jeans and black turtleneck, introduced the iPhone at the MacWorld convention in San Francisco with the introduction,

> This is a day that I have been looking forward to for two and a half years. Every once in a while, a revolutionary product comes along that changes everything. Apple has been very fortunate. It's been able to introduce a few of these into the world.
>
> 1984 – we introduced the Macintosh. It didn't just change Apple. It changed the whole computer industry.
>
> In 2001, we introduced the first iPod. And it didn't just change the way we all listen to music; it changed the entire music industry.
>
> Well, today we're introducing three revolutionary products of this class. The first one is a widescreen iPod with touch controls. The second is a revolutionary mobile phone. And the third is a breakthrough Internet communications device. So, three things: a widescreen iPod with touch controls; a revolutionary mobile phone; and a breakthrough Internet communications device.
>
> An iPod, a phone . . are you getting it? These are not three separate devices, this is one device, and we are calling it iPhone. Today, Apple is going to reinvent the phone, and here it is.

He teased that Apple was about to "*reinvent the phone*" and "*make a leapfrog product that is way smarter than any mobile device has ever been and super-easy to use*". Today, it is clear that Apple did just that, with some inventions along the way such as the mouse for the Mac, the click wheel for the iPod and multi-touch for the iPhone. Steve Jobs ends with a Wayne Gretsky quote, "*I skate to where the puck is going to be, not where it has been*" [6].

The introduction of the world-wide-web in 1994 heralded the first digital revolution, the desktop revolution. These were the years of the browser wars where digital activity was focused on the personal computer. Label these years period I, the years of the desktop digital revolution. Subsequently, period II, the years 2010–2020, reflected the mobile digital revolution ignited by the game-changing technology of mobile communication embedded in the smartphone. As Jobs said, the introduction of the iPhone in March 2007 heralded this new revolution. A closer examination of the underlying changes in business activity over the 26-year period is thus made possible by a deeper dive into the desktop revolution covering the years 1994–2007 and the mobility revolution, over the years 2010–2020, following the invention of a game-changing technology, the smartphone.

This pattern is best illustrated by considering 2007 as the base year and normalizing startup activity in all other years relative to this base year, 2007. Consequently, startup activity in all other years is to be interpreted as a fraction of new business created in 2007. Such a normalization enables comparisons across states which differ in population and other structural features. In a sense, we are measuring a given state's startup activity relative to its own performance in a previous year.

To illustrate this interpretation, consider the case of California, one of the leading states in entrepreneurial activity. Startups in this state were 18.7% higher in 2019 compared to the base year, 2007, as seen in Fig. 2.2. A state that we will discuss in detail in Chapter 3, Missouri, in a *carpe diem* manner, exhibited a dramatic rise in venture funded activity of 48% from 2007 to 2020. New York and Florida, on the other hand did not have a robust recovery after the Great Recession, with a decline in activity of negative 3.3% and meagre growth of 4.6% in 2020 compared to 2007, respectively.

Figure 2.3 shows national startup activity as a fraction of the base year, 2007 or equivalently, indexed by 2007. Observe that the *average* startup activity per year for young firms, under 1 year in existence, over the period 1994–2020 was an anemic, but statistically positive rate of 0.36%. Like the heights of growing children, the average increase in height over the teenage years obscures the differential growth in the early teen versus the

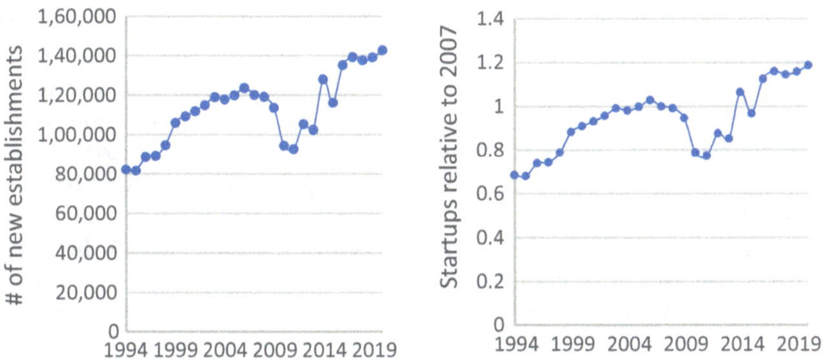

Fig. 2.2 California startups: 1994–2020 (*Source* Business Employment Dynamics Data by Age and Size, BLS)

late teens. Similarly, rather than considering the average rate of growth in startups across all the years, the trend rate of growth of startups is 0.006, measured by the slope of a line drawn through the 27-year data. (Fig. 2.2) In other words, new establishments increased at the rate of 0.6% per year over the period 1994–2020.

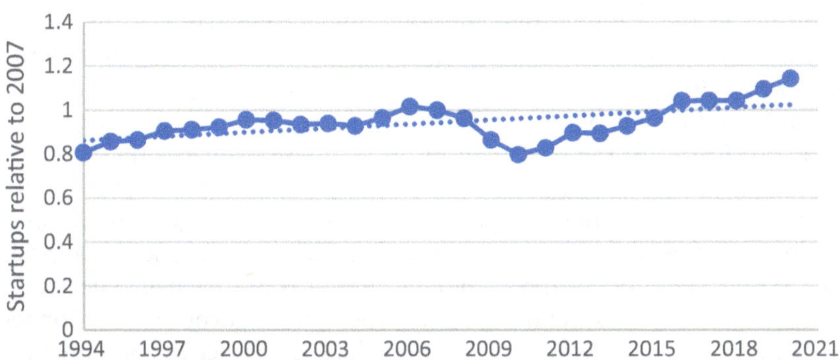

Fig. 2.3 Startups, *indexed by 2007*[4]: 1994–2020 (*Source* Business Employment Dynamics Data by Age and Size, BLS)

[4] *Indexing refers to dividing the data series by a base year in order to make comparisons.*

This weak picture is driven by the impact of the unusual events of 2008–2009, during which there were more startup failures and exits than entrants. The Great Recession ravaged the economy in the form of lost jobs and long periods of unemployment. The preceding years were characterized by an enormous rise in housing prices, record levels of household debt supported by toxic mortgages and systematic breaches in accountability.

Starting around 1994–1995, there was an expansion in U.S. housing construction that accelerated in the early 2000s. Average home prices more than doubled between 1998 and 2006 and roughly 40% of private sector job creation was in the housing market. In 2007, losses on mortgage-related financial assets began to cause stress in global financial markets, hitting several large financial firms. The turbulence in financial markets worsened in 2008, when the Federal Reserve provided liquidity and support through a range of programs. In March 2008, the investment bank Bear Stearns was acquired by JPMorgan Chase, with the assistance of the Federal Reserve. In September 2008, Lehman Brothers filed for bankruptcy protection, and the following day AIG, a large insurance and financial services company, received support from the Federal Reserve. The ensuing economic contraction worsened, ultimately becoming deep and protracted, with U.S. GDP falling by 4.3% which was the worst downturn since World War II. This was the Great Recession, which, according to the National Bureau of Economic Research, was the period between December 2007 through June 2009, which I summarize as the years 2008–2009 [7, 8].

But the ensuing economic collapse had far-reaching effects. More than the actual lost jobs, the challenge for most households was the dramatic increase in uncertainty. The inability to plan around a household budget led to many socio-economic problems such as increased stress, poorer health outcomes, delays in marriage, and changes in household composition. With state budgets impacted, education was distorted as reflected in lower graduation rates, school closings, and teacher turnover. The longer the period of unemployment for an individual, the larger the potential for scarring on future employment prospects. This factor could alter choices, attitudes, and perceptions toward risk taking.

When people lose their homes in foreclosures, as happened in many parts of the country, they don't emerge unscathed from this experience. It affects their world view—one's home is integral to one's sense of well-being. Emerging from this experience, rattled and shaken, people

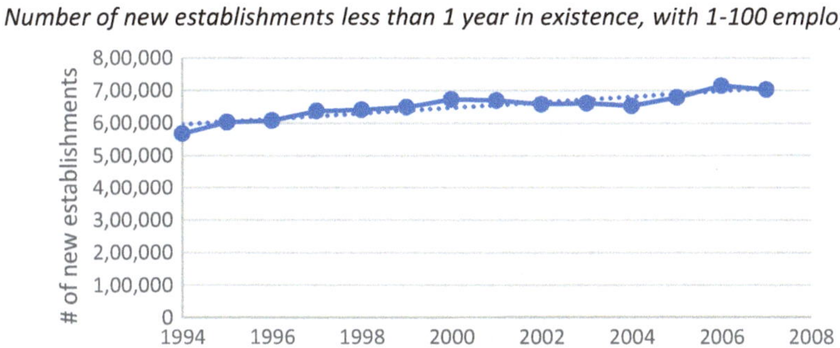

Fig. 2.4 Total number of startups: 1994–2007 (*Source* Business Employment Dynamics Data by Age and Size, BLS)

reorganized their lives and their thinking. Consequently, rather than looking at the 26-year stretch as one structurally coherent time period, it would improve our understanding of the dynamics if we split the time period into two and drop the years of the Great Recession years of 2008 and 2009.

Tracing the data through the two time periods, the picture changes remarkably. For the earlier time frame, period I, which is 1994 through 2007, the trend rate of growth is **1.12%.** (Figs. 2.4 and 2.5) And then, in the later time frame, period II which is 2010 through 2020, there is an impressive rate of increase in new establishments of **3.31%** per year. (Figs. 2.6 and 2.7) **This is the result that drives the thesis of entrepreneurial renaissance.** The slow and nearly imperceptible improvement in startups during the desktop digital revolution is vastly overtaken by the grand escalation to over 3% during the mobility digital revolution.

Scale of Startups

The analysis was expanded to larger startups, those with more employees and yet under one year in existence. Establishments with 100–499 employees that were less than 1 year old were **disappearing** at the rate of 64 establishments per year after peaking in 1998. Perhaps the excitement generated by the introduction of widespread personal computing along with access to the web of information led to an onslaught of new

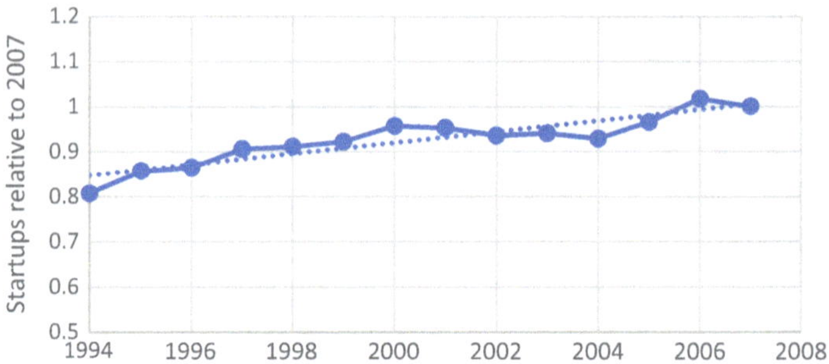

Fig. 2.5 Startups, *indexed by 2007*: 1994–2007 (*Source* Business Employment Dynamics Data by Age and Size, BLS)

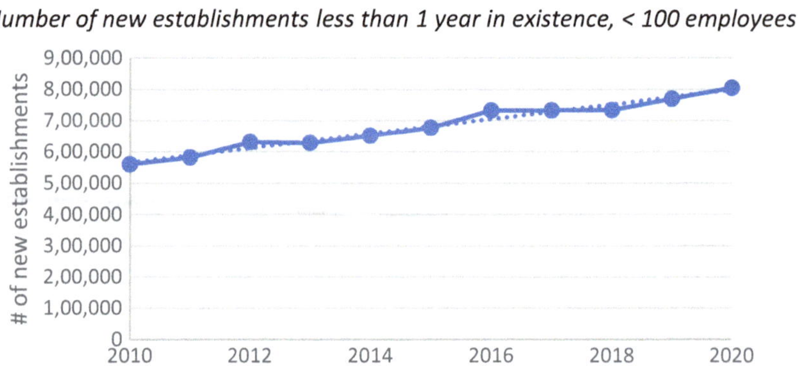

Fig. 2.6 Total number of startups: 2010–2020 (*Source* Business Employment Dynamics Data by Age and Size, BLS)

enterprises loaded with employees, but with limited focus as to the exact objective. Ironically, Google was yet to come—it began operations as a small firm in September 1998. Amazon started as a website that sold only books in July 1995. In those early days, book publishers required retailers to order at least 10 books at a time. Amazon was so cash strapped that the firm ordered the one book they needed along with nine copies of a little-known book on lichen, which was mostly out of stock. Amazon didn't scale until after the initial public offering in May 1997 at $18 per

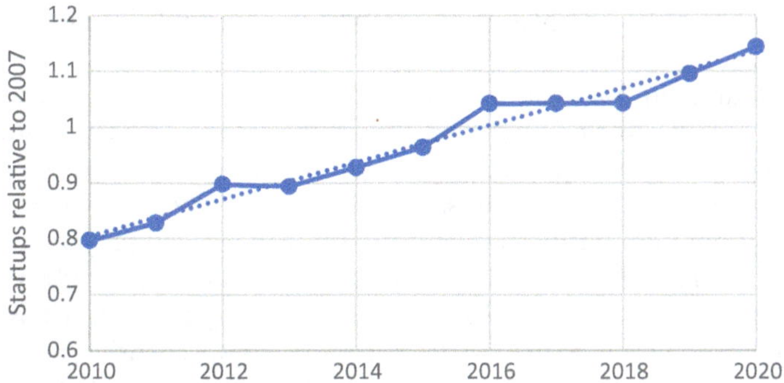

Fig. 2.7 Startups, *indexed by 2007*: 2010–2020 (*Source* Business Employment Dynamics Data by Age and Size, BLS)

share when it started to expand beyond books. Jack Ma launched Alibaba in China in December 1998 [9].

Further confirming our hypothesis that the entrepreneurial resurgence is driven by small firms, with less than 100 employees, there were no job gains in medium to larger establishments, as defined by payroll count, a result that is consistent with past work on the startup deficit. These results reinforce the idea propounded in this book that young startups are small, with less than 100 employees, and less than a year into life.

The result that entrepreneurial activity was sustained and strengthened over these 26 years, is checked for robustness by investigating different data sets, which provides an alternative view of the picture. Casting a wider net using survey data, the Kaufmann Foundation results converge with the results presented above. In addition, tax records, based on non-survey-based data are less liable to errors and biases from self-reported information so they provide a robustness check.

Kaufmann Foundation Data

Defining the rate of new entrepreneurs as the percent of the adult, non-business owner population that starts a new business, the Kaufmann Foundation reinforces these patterns, as shown in Fig. 2.8. There is a distinct peak around 2009, with an uneven trajectory over the subsequent years, before the startling rise in 2020. As depicted, entrepreneurship is a rare skill but the sharp upturn in 2020 is suggestive of new vigor in business activity [10, 11].

The Kaufmann Foundation Indicator encompasses a broad measure of entrepreneurship, including all new business owners, regardless of business size or origin. "As such, it includes businesses of all types... It captures all new business owners, including those who own incorporated or unincorporated businesses, and those who are employers or non-employers". This index is calculated using microdata from the Current Population Survey, a monthly survey conducted by the U.S. Census and the Bureau of Labor Statistics. It is a more comprehensive measure of entrepreneurs than the startup measure we examine. The focus for this book is young businesses, under 1 year in existence, while the Kaufmann index does not separate business by age. Because the Rate of New Entrepreneurs covers firms of all sizes, there is likely to be some averaging across this wider business landscape, such that sharp increases in one direction are dampened by equally sharp decreases in the other, resulting in a more muted overall measure, compared to that shown in Figs. 2.5 and 2.7.

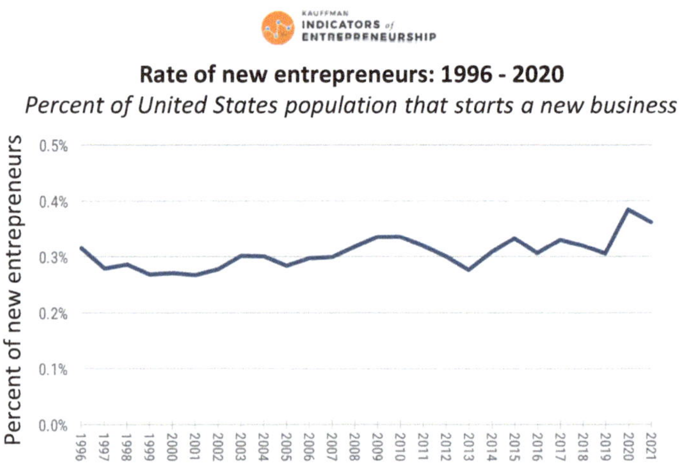

Fig. 2.8 Rate of new entrepreneurs, Kauffman Foundation: 1996–2020 (*Source* Kaufmann Indicators of Entrepreneurship)

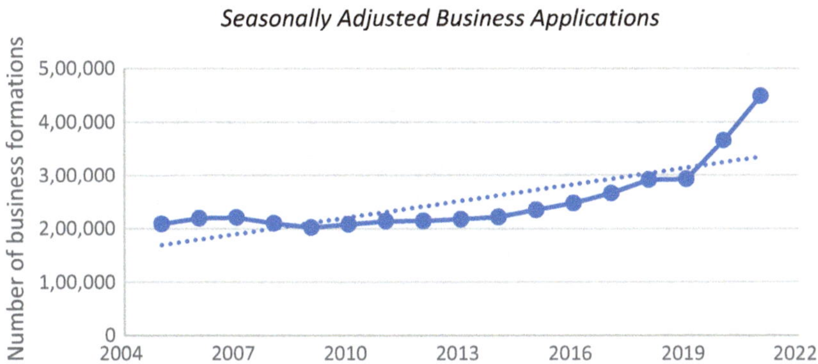

Fig. 2.9 New business formations: 2004–2022 (*Source* Business Formation Statistics, U.S. Census Bureau)

Results Based on Tax and Administrative Data

Using tax and administrative records, data from the recently created Business Formation Statistics (BFS) at the Census Bureau points to a rise in early stage new business formations as shown in Fig. 2.9 [12]. This figure depicts a statistically significant rise in projected new business formations since approximately 2004. Pointedly, this picture demonstrates no **decline in startup trend.**

The BFS describes business applications (BA) for tax IDs, which is the Employer Identification Number (EIN) through filings of form SS-4 with the Internal Revenue Service of the Treasury Department. Business applications with planned wages (WBA) indicate a wages-paid date and are a subset of total applications and provide information on actual business formation, in contrast to projected business formation [13]. Actual business formation, as shown in Fig. 2.10, shows a positive trend during years 2013–2021, when data were available.

The Mobility Versus the Desktop Digital Revolution

The rate at which new businesses enter in the years 1994–2007, the desktop revolution years, is 1.12% per year while the rate during the mobility revolution years of 2010–2020 is 3.31% per year. What explains

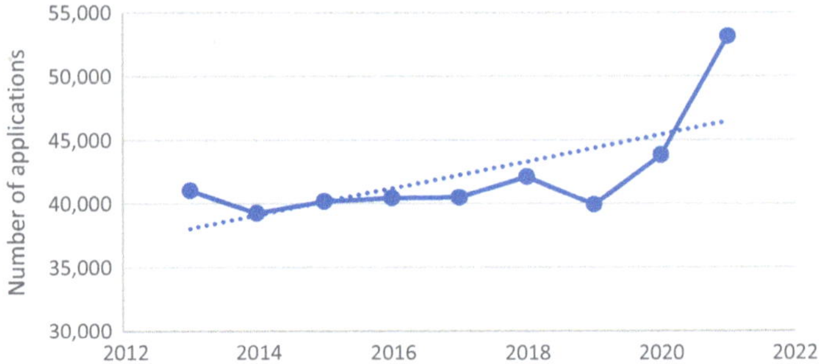

Fig. 2.10 Business applications with planned wages: 2013–2021 (Business Formation Statistics, U.S. Census Bureau, FRED)

this sharp upturn? One headline event was the announcement of a new technology in January 2007, the iPhone, suggesting that many of the new businesses are following the often-cited model of the *app economy.* There is, however, another aspect that bears consideration. It takes time. The incorporation of new inventions into trade and commerce is a slow, uneven process with multiple setbacks and barriers to smooth adoption. These hurdles to implementation can be mitigated by a mentoring system where founders are assisted with the art of business creation and the architecture of its implementation. I return to this topic in Chapter 6. Here the topic of delay is an integral part of the mechanics of exchange—production processes and demand perceptions, the buying and selling—is examined.

Paul David elaborates upon this delay hypothesis by drawing an analogy to past inventions. Electricity, the driver of the second industrial revolution (steam power, in 1870, powered the first industrial revolution) did not exhibit the productivity enhancement until the "expansionary macroeconomic climate of the 1920s". This delay was due to the sluggish pace of factory electrification which meant replacing the old model of mechanization due to steam and water with new, electrified factories—this rested upon physical depreciation and slow obsolescence of urban locations. "Likewise, the contributions to the improvement in economic welfare in the form of faster trip speeds and shorter passenger waiting times afforded by electric streetcars, and later by subways, all remained largely uncaptured by the conventional indexes of real product and productivity" [14].

Daron Acemoglu points out this phenomenon, calling it the reinstatement effect, in another context: the impact of automation. Technology, he argues, allows capital to replace labor in some tasks, which he calls the *task displacement effect*. There is, at first, the productivity effect coming from increased efficiency of labor (higher value added) in non-automated tasks as well as businesses substituting cheaper capital for labor. As a consequence, the economy becomes richer and people are able to buy more. This creates new tasks, *the reinstatement effect*, as firms reinstate workers into *new tasks* for satisfying this new demand [15]. The problem that the U.S. economy has faced over 1987–2017, based on Acemoglu's research, is the mismatch—the skills needed for the new tasks are not aligned with those available. People who have lost jobs due to automation or the application of technology to production, do not have the newer skills demanded for newer types of products and services.

During the past decade skill levels have caught up and the technology has become user-friendly. Tasks are being outsourced to businesses that specialize in one skill set, such as web design. Such specialization generates a reshuffling of tasks, which is different from task displacement or task creation. Reshuffling of tasks not only redeploys existing workers in new ways but ropes in suppliers and customers as partners in an efficient matching process. Reallocating new as well as altered tasks brings a sense of ownership and job significance to the workforce, motivating individuals and enhancing productivity.

On the demand side, the onslaught of information has created a content tsunami. Unlike an economic commodity, it is not subject to disposal once it has been released. It can result in overload, like an electrical circuit that has been jammed with excess demand for electricity. A circuit consists of wiring, a breaker and the devices it powers, and with an overload, the breaker trips, shutting off the power supply to that circuit. Cognitive bandwidth circuits are comprised of mental wiring and demand for mental capacity but do not come with circuit breakers or fuses. The information overload leads to a deficit of attention whose outcome is cognitive apathy and diminished acuity [16]. Decision-making is compromised as is awareness of the economic environment, making it harder to evaluate market trends.

The Big Quit, or what is commonly called the *Great Resignation*, is, in a manner, testimony to the delay hypothesis [17]. Thompson writes, "'Quits', as the Bureau of Labor Statistics calls them, are rising in almost every industry.... But this level of quitting is really an expression of optimism that says, We can do better". The balance of power between employers and employees has shifted in the pandemic and recentered individuals' identities from work to some undefined, possibly wider worldview [18]. Surging numbers of new establishments and jobs over the past two years could be because of (i) an increase in time available to ponder about new ventures (ii) a forced change in identity as workers shifted to remote work and a family-friendly work environment and (iii) a new flexibility in work hours under remote work. Note that all three factors contribute to the recent big quit. Longer term trends of job gains and losses, in the context of escalating entrepreneurial activity, over the period 1994–2020 are explored in Chapter 9.

This chapter has made a strong case for a reawakening of new business creation, most prominently in the years following the Great Recession. It is worth noting that these results are robust, buttressed by multiple major surveys conducted periodically (by week, month, quarter and year) by the U.S. Census Bureau and the Bureau of Labor Statistics.[5] Nevertheless, it remains important to recognize that all data are imprecise and have some element of noise, and that the ensuing results are to be accepted with appropriate caveats.

We turn now to explore the trend in new establishments at the state level: how have individual states fared in entrepreneurial activity over the period, 1994–2020. Can we explain why the Southern Region, represented by the rising star of Georgia, exhibits strong business activity? Chapter 3 explains precise state-by-state patterns.

Data Map

Data relevant for this book are from the U.S. Departments of Labor and Commerce. Following is a data map sketching the principal links between data files; it is not comprehensive. The appendix provides details.

[5] The US Census Bureau sources data from the Longitudinal Employer-Household Dynamics dataset (LEHD) which is fueled by inputs from (i) administrative records on employment which is based on unemployment insurance benefits (UI) (ii) social security data (SS) (iii) federal tax records (IRS) (iv) the Quarterly Census of Employment and Wages – QCEW (v) American Community Survey (ACS) and (vi) Business Dynamics Statistics (BDS).

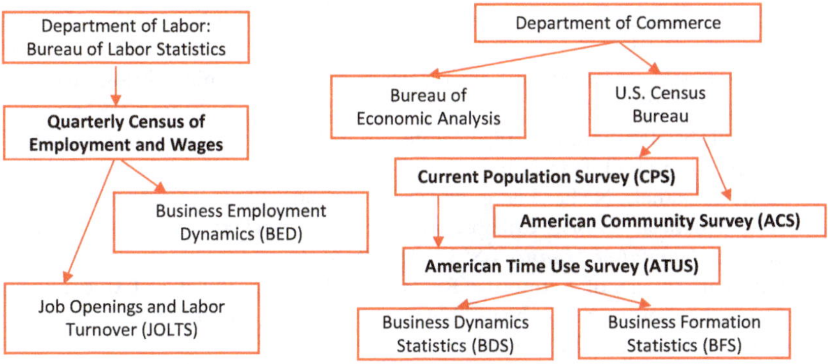

Fig. 2.11 Data Map (*Source* Author's creation)

All data in this and following chapters are accessed from the following websites.

- https://www.bls.gov/bdm/
- https://www.bls.gov/bdm/business-employment-dynamics-data-by-age-and-size.htm
- https://www.bls.gov/news.release/cewbd.tn.htm]
- https://www.bls.gov/bdm/entrepreneurship/bdm_chart1.htm
- https://indicators.kauffman.org/series/earlystage.

Bibliography

1 For details on definitions see the Business Employment Dynamics section of the Bureau of Labor Statistics at https://www.bls.gov/bdm/business-employment-dynamics-data-by-age-and-size.htm.

2 Hait, Andrew. 2021. The Majority of U.S. Businesses Have Fewer Than Five Employees. *U.S. Census Bureau*. https://www.census.gov/library/stories/2021/01/what-is-a-small-business.html.

3 U.S. Census. Definition of Startup. 2022. https://www.census.gov/library/stories/2022/02/united-states-startups-create-jobs-at-higher-rates-older-large-firms-employ-most-workers.html.

4 Non-Employer Statistics. 2022. https://data.census.gov/cedsci/table?q=NONEMP2018.NS1800NONEMP&tid=NONEMP2018.NS1800NONEMP&hidePreview=true.

5 Ouellette, Jennifer. 2018. New Study Sheds More Light on What Caused the Millennium Bridge to Wobble. https://arstechnica.com/science/2018/10/new-study-sheds-more-light-on-what-caused-millennium-bridge-to-wobble/.
6 Steve Jobs Presentation of iPhone in 2007. Steve Jobs iPhone 2007 Presentation (Full Transcript).
7 Covitz, Daniel, Nellie Liang and Gustavo Suarez. 2013. The Evolution of a Financial Crisis: Collapse of the Asset-Backed Commercial Paper Market. *Journal of Finance* 68(3): 815–848.
8 National Bureau of Economic Research. 2021. US Business Cycle Expansions and Contractions. https://www.nber.org/research/data/us-business-cycle-expansions-and-contractions.
9 Wang, Helen. 2015. Why Amazon Should Fear Alibaba. Forbes, July 8.
10 Kaufman Indicators of Entrepreneurship, 2022. https://indicators.kauffman.org/wp-content/uploads/sites/2/2022/03/2021-Early-State-Entrepreneurship-National-Report.pdf.
11 Kaufman Indicators of Entrepreneurship, 2021. https://indicators.kauffman.org/wp-content/uploads/sites/2/2021/05/2020-New-Employer-Business-Indicators-in-the-United-States_April2021.pdf.
12 The Business Formation Statistics (BFS) were first released on February 14, 2018. The BFS, produced by the U.S. Census, provides high frequency and timely measurements of early stage new business formations. Prior to BFS, the earliest indication of startups was the Census Bureau's Business Dynamics Statistics, which offers annual information on business entry with a two-year lag, or quarterly establishment openings which is based on employee count. BFS can offer monthly and even weekly insights. For details, see https://fred.stlouisfed.org/series/BABATOTALSAUS.
13 High-propensity business applications (HBA) are those that have a high probability of showing an actual payroll. This probability is based on characteristics, revealed on the applications, that are associated with a high rate of business formation such as payroll actualization. This would include any information that indicates employee hiring or a date for the first wages-paid. It also includes applications in certain sectors, such as accommodation and food services, portions of construction and manufacturing, retail, professional services, education and health care. Note that WBA is a subset of HBA. See the following site for details, https://www.census.gov/econ/bfs/pdf/bfs_current.pdf.
14 David, P. A. 1990. The Dynamo and the Computer: An Historical Perspective on the Modern Productivity Paradox. *The American Economic Review* 80(2): 355–361. http://www.jstor.org/stable/2006600.

15 Acemoglu, Daron and Pascual Restrepo. 2019. Automation and New Tasks: How Technology Displaces and Reinstates Labor. *Journal of Economic Perspectives* 33(2): 3–30. https://doi.org/10.1257/jep.33.2.3.
16 Bhatt, Swati, 2019. *The Attention Deficit*. Palgrave Macmillan.
17 Bloomberg. 2022. https://www.bloomberg.com/news/articles/2021-05-10/quit-your-job-how-to-resign-after-covid-pandemic.
18 The phenomenon of increasing numbers of workers quitting their current jobs in search of other alternatives was labelled the "Great Resignation" by Anthony Klotz in a Bloomberg interview on May 5, 2021. However, the title Big Quit labels the trend without inserting a momentous, significant or weighty adjective like "great" which alludes to a turning point. Did these quitters actually find "great" alternatives, other work that made them better off? We have yet to obtain data confirming that a corner has been turned.
19 Thompson, Derek. 2021. The Great Resignation. *The Atlantic*, October 15. https://www.theatlantic.com/ideas/archive/2021/10/great-resignation-accelerating/620382/.

CHAPTER 3

Entrepreneurial Activity at the State Level

Ubiquitous connectivity and instant access to information could homogenize populations in terms of ideas, values, and preferences. Social influence can become more powerful in highly embedded societies, leading to a convergence of tastes. The marketing world has shown us the power of persuasion in modifying or even changing our underlying desires. In the business world, there is reason to believe, therefore, that greater connectivity would increase opportunities to interact with individuals across the continent and that this would induce similarities in business ideas and strategies. This is most certainly not the case in the U.S.

Multiple patterns emerge across two decades and fifty-one states. Geography and historical immigration patterns have marked out different regions, divisions, and states. The four regions correspond to geographical boundaries such as the **West,** separated by the Rocky Mountains; the **Midwest,** which is north of the Missouri river but the western half is west of the Mississippi river; the **South**, whose eastern half is east of the Mississippi and the **Northeast**. Taking the rivers and mountains as boundaries, there are nine divisions: Pacific and Mountain, in the West; West and East North Central in the Midwest, separated by the Mississippi; West and East South Central, again separated by the Mississippi, and the South Atlantic, all in the South; and the Northeast comprising the Middle Atlantic and New England divisions. In the analysis that follows, the Mississippi river is an important compass since states east and west

S. Bhatt, *Entrepreneurship Today*,
https://doi.org/10.1007/978-3-031-11495-3_3

of the Mississippi have divergent paths in their entrepreneurial history. I examine the entrepreneurial landscape first by time, then by geography and finally by time entwined with geography.

Individuals prefer to interact on a common platform as is the case when the value of a messaging platform increases as more individuals join the user base. These are network effects, pervasive in the digital world, and most commonly encountered in social media platforms, such as Twitter, TikTok, YouTube (owned by Alphabet), and Instagram (owned by Facebook). By virtue of *wanting to be where everyone is*, the logic of connectivity rests upon these network effects. Digital communication technology could not have created the anywhere–anytime ubiquity of connections without shared platforms upon which they congregate.

Undoubtedly, the behemoths of the online world, such as Alphabet, Microsoft, Apple, Facebook, and Amazon are global entities arising from scale effects, or complementarities, both at the consumption level and at the production level.

Just as with people, so also with data–there are complementarities when a single platform contains copious amounts of data since patterns can be detected and a story can be told. When there are common features across groups of people, products and services can be customized according to their story. In order to store and process this volume of data, firms necessarily have to incur large fixed costs in developing and maintaining a cloud server. When Amazon recommends other products similar to the one being purchased, this cloud of data is the source of the advice.

However, at the more local and granular level, there need not be giant sized complementarities. These are the markets that enable individuals to obtain a livelihood and pursue a dream. The way we reorganized and coordinated during the pandemic, as when front-line workers and knowledge workers came together, as well as the hybrid work phenomenon of today, is pointing to a resourcefulness that has buttressed entrepreneurial activity over the past two decades. This creative energy varies across states, but some consistent patterns emerge, and it is to this subject that we now turn.

A quick look at the differences across the continent informs us that there is an increase in early-stage new business applications with planned wages in all but one division of the U.S. Figure 3.1, which is based on tax and administrative records from Business Formation Statistics (BFS) at the Census Bureau, illustrates the different paths in number of business applications over the years 2013–2021 for the 4 divisions in the

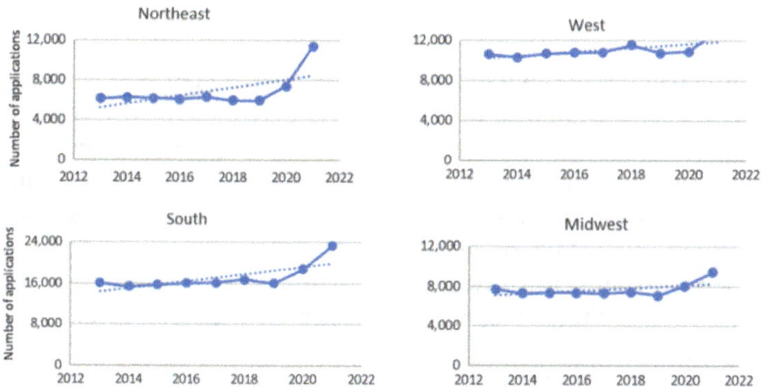

Fig. 3.1 Business applications with planned wages, by region: 2013–2021 (*Source* Business Formation Statistics, U.S. Census Bureau)

U.S. In particular, the Northeast, the West and South, all show positive activity during the years 2013–2021 (data availability was restricted to these years). The sustained increase in the number of business formations is quite remarkable, particularly since this growth is across a large swath of states. The Midwest, however, has an insignificant trend over the 2013–2021 period, perhaps the slowdown in activity in 2019 played a role in this sluggish response.

The more recent perspective illustrated in Fig. 3.1 is illuminating in that it reinforces the point made in Chapter 2. The thesis drawn there was that period I activity (1994–2007), when the trend rate of growth is **1.12%,** was inferior to period II activity (2010–2020) which shows an impressive rate of increase in new establishments of **3.31%** per year (Figs. 2.5 and 2.7). Recall that the overall trend rate of growth of startups was 0.6% per year. The slow growth in new business activity during the desktop digital revolution is vastly offset by the grand escalation to over 3% during the mobility digital revolution, an outcome that drives this book's thesis of entrepreneurial revitalization.

What are the patterns across different states and how do they compare by the entrepreneurial metric? To understand the complex interplay of multiple factors, we classify the data by time, then by geography and finally by population.

Time

Two-and-a half decades is a long time in the digital economy. In fact, if we dated the general awareness of the digital universe to the invention of the transistor at ATT's Bell Laboratories in December 1947, then less time has elapsed between then and the introduction of the personal computer in 1975, compared to our 26-year period.[1] Microsoft was founded in Albuquerque, New Mexico (1975) by Bill Gates and Paul Allen, childhood friends from Seattle, Washington. Apple was incorporated in 1977 by Steve Jobs and Steve Wozniak, to market the then best-selling personal computer, Apple II.

The years 1994–2020 saw the emergence of not only the World Wide Web in 1993, but also Amazon in 1995, Netflix in 1997, Google in 1998, Facebook in 2004, Shopify in 2004, Spotify in 2006 and many more landmark startups that have since become behemoths.

Netflix started out as an upstart DVD rental business in 1997 founded by Reed Hastings and Marc Randolph. But it did not remain merely as a convenient way to rent movies online, it morphed into watching movies online. Hastings and Randolph had a keen understanding of the market, that a user-friendly entertainment delivery model was needed. They edged out the few dominant cable companies, with a catalogue of over 5000 titles by 2000, just three years after inception. Along the way, Netflix introduced the subscription model in 1999 which focused on the consumer rather than the content—the goal was to enable content viewing for consumers and not to maximize viewership for a particular piece of content, or movie. The following year, in 2000, Netflix abandoned late fees [1].

Seven years later, in 2007, Netflix pivoted to streaming with Watch Now, at a time when viewers were unfamiliar with the technology. Does this sound like Apple and the introduction of the iPad in 2010, when no consumer demand existed since no such product existed? For Netflix, the aggregation of content onto its servers and then streaming it to users, was going to revolutionize the entire entertainment industry.

Streaming technology was known as video-on-demand or interactive television, well before Netflix popularized it. In June 1993, the band

[1] The transistor was publicly unveiled at the West Side Auditorium in Manhattan in the summer of 1951, at which point Bell Laboratories was compelled to share and license the transistor device [2].

Severe Tire Damage was performing at Xerox Parc, as proof of the research conducted on live Internet broadcasting by scientists and engineers. The scientists were working on Mbone or multi-cast backbone, a network built on the Internet for carrying multicast traffic.[2] Speeches by President Clinton have been carried live on Mbone. In November 1995, Mick Jagger of the Rolling Stones opened the first major livestreamed concert with the words, "I wanna say a special welcome to everyone that's, uh, climbed into the Internet tonight, and, uh, has got into the M-bone. And I hope it doesn't all collapse" [4].

The New York Times wrote in 1995, "[u]nlike conventional broadcasting, the Mbone can allow viewers and listeners to be broadcasters themselves. The Mbone is the Internet's multicast backbone, which functions as a network based on the Internet's framework" [5]. The Times also echoed Mick Jagger's concern about the Mbone jamming the Internet since audio and video signals are bandwidth hungry. In those early days, Mbone was restricted to scientific and research organizations.

But then, in 1995, the startup RealNetworks developed the first media player capable of live streaming, and later that year livestreamed a baseball game between the New York Yankees and the Seattle Mariners.

In 1996, HongKong Telecom (PCCW) Chairman Richard Li, son of billionaire Li Ka-shing, created a video-on-demand television service, iTV, using Internet technology, and held a launch ceremony for it in March 1998, a mere 3 weeks before Netflix mailed its first DVD [6]. But HongKong Telecom didn't just have to sell the service, it had to build the infrastructure and negotiate deals with the movie studios that held copyrights over the content. Onboarding consumers was its Achilles' heel: the service was discontinued in 2000, after HongKong Telecom was acquired by PCCW [7].

Spotify was developed in Sweden by Daniel Ek and Martin Lorentzon in 2006. The Supreme Court had put a halt to the peer-to-peer file sharing model of Sean Parker and Napster in the A&M Records, Inc v Napster, Inc case in October 2000, due to copyright infringement.

[2] Several sessions of the March 1992 meeting of the Internet Engineering Task Force, IETF, in San Diego were audiocast (live audio) using multicast packet transmission from the IETF site over the Internet to audiences at 20 sites on three continents. This was interactive in that participants could talk with one another, unlike radio broadcasts. There are three key elements to this livestream: hardware and software to generate and receive audio packets, "IP multicast rerouting to replicate packets efficiently for distribution to a large number of recipients and uncongested networks with sufficient bandwidth" [3].

Meanwhile Apple's iTunes was charging for downloading each individual piece of music or track. Ek and Lorentzon's innovation was in merging these two ideas: legitimize the functionality of peer-to-peer sharing via streaming, much like downloading without ownership. It was like renting music. The product was available for initial users, influential music bloggers in Sweden, by 2007. By restricting user invitations in the early stages, Spotify did not scale superfast, but concentrated on product development. By 2008, when the product was introduced in Sweden, the global music industry was in a tailspin with revenues plunging from $25.2 billion in 1999 to $16.9 billion in 2008 and then further to $14.8 billion in 2011 [8].

These are the stories of the startups launched during the time period under consideration in this book. There is also a story about startups at a more granular level. What were the ripple effects from the emergence of these Internet giants? Each driver for an Amazon delivery truck is a buyer of a variety of products and services. And demand for these services, in turn, could propel the germination of a new businesses, such as food and hospitality services and professional and business services.

The national trend in startup activity over the period 1994–2020 is shown in Fig. 3.2 (seen earlier in Chapter 2 as Figs. 2.1 and 2.2). Over the two and half decades, 1994–2020, startup activity was 0.6% per year, meaning that new businesses were created each year, across the U.S., at the rate of 0.6%. This paltry number suggests a startup weakness rather than robust activity. But pause to consider that these years were punctuated by a momentous economic upheaval, disrupting all plans and casting a deep shadow of uncertainty, as discussed in Chapter 2.

Consequently, we view the economic environment in two distinct epochs. The era before the Great Recession which comprises the years 1994–2007 and the era after the Great Recession, which would be the years 2010–2020. As in Chapter 2, label the first epoch as period I, the desktop digital revolution, and the second as period II, the mobility digital revolution. Recall, from Chapter 2, that the latter time period not only follows the Great Recession but also the introduction of the smartphone in 2007, a technology which unleashed the application-based economy.

In period I, the startup trend was **1.12%** growth per year, while the trend increased to **3.31%** during the later period, 2010–2020. In the post-2010 period, the average startup trend was significantly larger, suggesting that the digital mobility revolution, DR II was stronger in

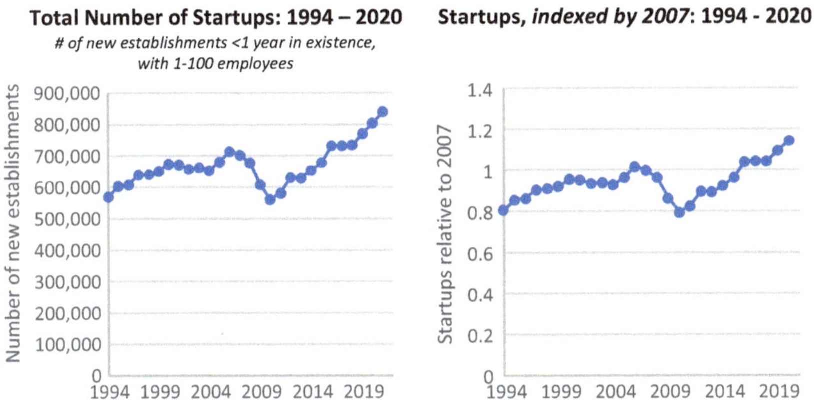

Fig. 3.2 Reproduction of Figs. 2.1 and 2.3 (*Source* Business Formation Statistics, U.S. Census Bureau)

terms of new business formation. For example, the data show that startup activity in 2010 was 80% of the peak level in 2007. But by 2016 it had recovered to 104% or more than the peak, steadily increasing to 114% of the 2007 peak by 2020. In 2000, startup activity was 95% of the 2007 level. See Figs. 3.3 and 3.4.

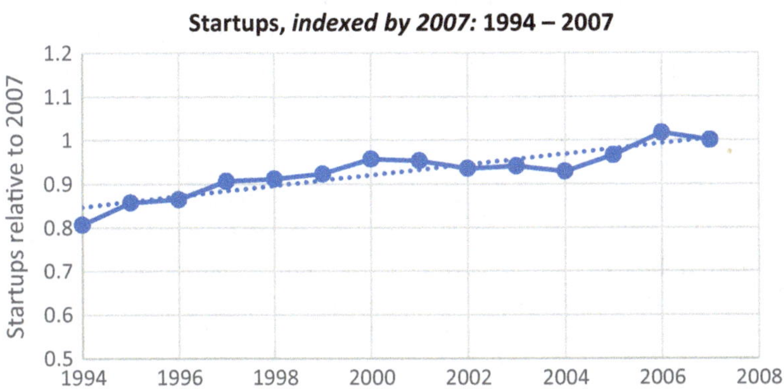

Fig. 3.3 Reproduction of Fig. 2.5 (*Source* Business Employment Dynamics Data by Age and Size, BLS)

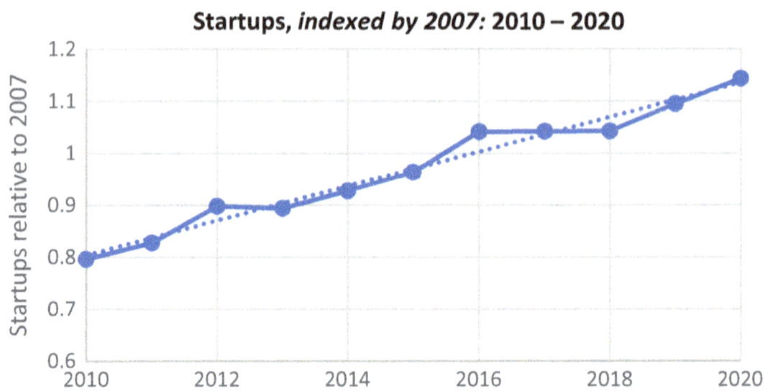

Fig. 3.4 Reproduction of Fig. 2.7 (*Source* Business Employment Dynamics Data by Age and Size, BLS)

Geography

Turning to the distribution of startup activity across the nation consider the map of the U.S. in Fig. 3.5, which shows startup activity over the time period 1994–2020. The lighter shaded states, in green, had higher startup activity and the darker states, in red, had lower business activity. It is quite apparent that a large fraction of new business activity took place in states west of the Mississippi river. Quite simply, the eastern portion of the country was lagging through the time period under consideration. However, make a note of the upcoming states, Georgia, North and South Carolina. These states stand apart from the others in the eastern half of the country, as we shall see in later illustrations.

Since movement between states is unencumbered, proximity might make a difference in the sense that entrepreneurial activity in a given state would have spillover effects on neighboring states. To take a non-U.S. example, Kenya and Tanzania are neighboring states, sharing a long east–west border. But Kenya has attracted foreign investments ranging from seed rounds to later stage venture capital during the past year of over $480 million through 45 deals, while Tanzania has attracted a paltry sum of $2.8 million through 5 deals [9].

These are two distinct sovereign nations with their own institutions and political structure. But they share a unique history of British colonialism. However, their political leadership had differing ideologies: Kenya had a more free market orientation under President Kenyatta, while Tanzania,

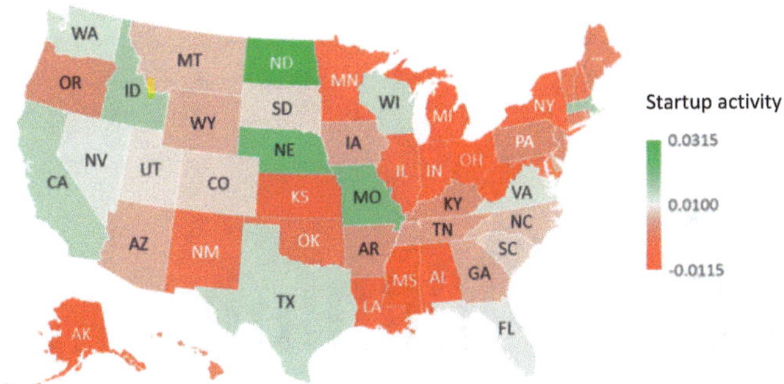

Fig. 3.5 Map of U.S. showing rate of startup activity by state: 1994–2020 (*Source* Business Employment Dynamics Data by Age and Size, BLS)

under Ujamaa was more socialist. Consequently, foreign investment followed the more liberal northern nation.

Similarly, back in the U.S. behind this broad generalization the details reveal some heterogeneity. The ranking of states with positive trends or positive startup activity is depicted in Fig. 3.6 while Fig. 3.7 exhibits this for states with negative trends. The fifteen states with the highest rate of startups across the entire period, 1994–2020, are: North Dakota, Nebraska, Missouri, Idaho, Massachusetts, California, Texas, Wisconsin, Washington, Virginia, Nevada, Florida, Utah, South Dakota, and South Carolina. Oil and gas exploration are the most important constituents of North Dakota's economy, but not in the neighboring state of Nebraska, where finance and insurance match manufacturing as the important sectors. Similarly, in Missouri, manufacturing is edged out by the professional and business services sector. The industry composition is discussed in more detail in Chapter 4.

Of these top performers 10 of the 15 represent states west of the Mississippi, while Massachusetts (the only state from New England), Wisconsin (from the East North Central Region), and Virginia, Florida, and South Carolina (from the South) hail from the east. Note that Pacific and Mountain regions are well represented by what I call the NUWMIC states, which as we shall see dominate the top ranks across multiple categories. The NUWMIC states are Nevada, Utah, Washington, Montana, Idaho, and California. Of these, all rank among the top 15, except Montana, trailing at number 17.

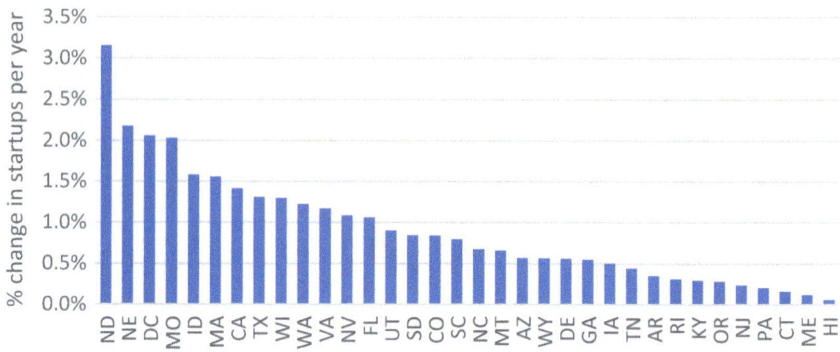

Fig. 3.6 States with positive startup trend: 1994–2020 (*Source* Business Employment Dynamics Data by Age and Size, BLS)

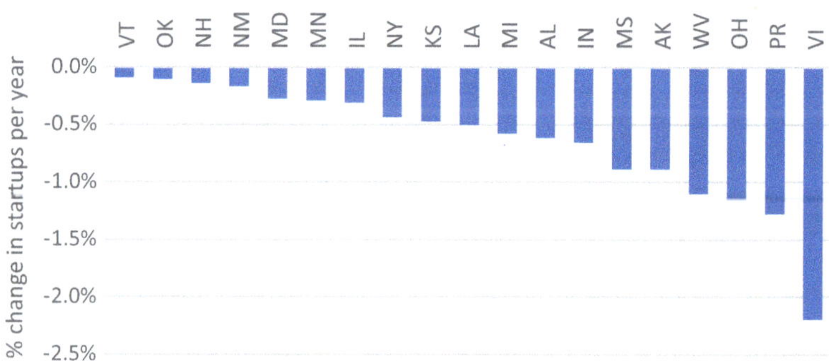

Fig. 3.7 States with negative startup trend: 1994–2020 (*Source* Business Employment Dynamics Data by Age and Size, BLS)

The fifteen weakest performing states include Ohio, West Virginia, Arkansas, Mississippi, Indiana, Alabama, Michigan, Louisiana, Kansas, New York, Illinois, Minnesota, Maryland, New Mexico, and New Hampshire. The cluster of states consisting of New Mexico, Louisiana, and Kansas are neighbors to Texas, one of the top-ranking states, but there is a sharp distinction in business activity across these proximate states. Together with Minnesota and Alaska, these five states are the only representatives of areas west of the Mississippi.

Of note is that neither Florida, New York nor Pennsylvania, the largest eastern states by population, rank in the top 10 during the overall period.[3] Paradoxically, Florida ranks at the top during the early years of 1994–2007, but then languishes during the second decade of this century. One can reasonably conclude that population has little effect on new business formation and that agglomeration of highly skilled individuals does not necessarily predict high entrepreneurship. California, one of the most populous states, ranks high in business formation, but so does Massachusetts and Missouri, which are sixteenth and eighteenth in population rank.

Population density is also not predictive since only Massachusetts can be counted among the 10 most densely populated states. In fact, nine of the top 10 most densely populated states are all east of the Mississippi and do not present as entrepreneurial. Agglomeration effects or benefits emanating from clustering of businesses do not appear to be important. From the perspective of fraction of the U.S. population, over half of the population resides east of the Mississippi (56%), but only 3 of the top 10 states listed above represent this region—Massachusetts, Wisconsin, and Virginia, which together account for a mere 6.38% of the American population. California and Texas together account for nearly a fifth of the American population (20.76%) [10].

However, population growth rates do correlate with new venture activity. Over the period 2010–2019, California's population was growing at the rate of 0.13% per year while Texas was growing by 1.24%. Of the states depicted in Fig. 3.6, Idaho, Nevada, Utah, Texas, Washington and Florida were amongst the states with over 1% population growth rates. Idaho's population, for example, was exploding at the rate of 1.96% Nevada surpassed the retirement state of Arizona with 1.66% compared to 1.6% respectively, and Utah follows at 1.58% In short, all the NUWMIC states grew by over 1% during the years 1010–2019, except Montana and California, which had population growth rates of 0.75% and 0.13% respectively.

[3] Hawaii and DC are not considered in these classifications, although they rank among the top 15. Hawaii's economy is idiosyncratically dependent upon tourism, making business activity seasonal. Washington D.C. being the nation's capital is similarly idiosyncratically dependent upon politics.

Time and Geography

Did these high performing states sustain their ranking across the two time periods? Was the desktop revolution as strong as the mobility revolution in the states listed above? Which states have shown entrepreneurship flourish during the desktop revolution years of 1994–2007?

The top 15 states in the desktop revolution in period I were: Florida, California, Idaho, Nevada, Utah, Arizona, New Jersey, Virginia, North Carolina, Montana, Washington, Wyoming, Georgia, Arkansas, and North Dakota, all with a startup trend of over 1% per year (Fig. 3.8). This means that new businesses were being added to the states' economies at the rate of over 1% per year. Florida, California, Idaho, Nevada, and Utah were adding young startups at the rate of over 2.5%. Note that these were establishments that were less than one year old with fewer than 100 employees.

The weakest states, the lowest 15, during the desktop era were (in increasing order, with Ohio being the weakest): Michigan, New Mexico, Massachusetts, Kentucky, Oklahoma, Illinois, Wisconsin, Kansas, Vermont, Alabama, Indiana, New York, West Virginia, Alaska, and Ohio (Fig. 3.9). These were states that were weak in new business formation, with young businesses exiting the economy at the rate of just under 1% per year. While Michigan had a smaller exit rate of 0.17% per year, Ohio saw the largest cessation of young establishments at the rate of 2%

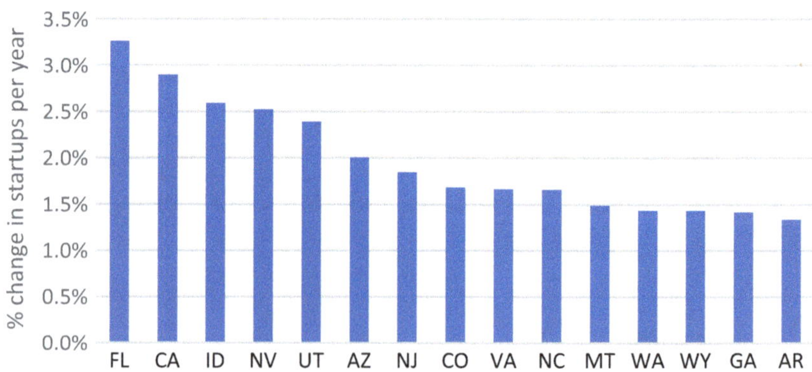

Fig. 3.8 Top 15 states with positive startup trend: 1994–2007 (*Source* Business Employment Dynamics Data by Age and Size, BLS)

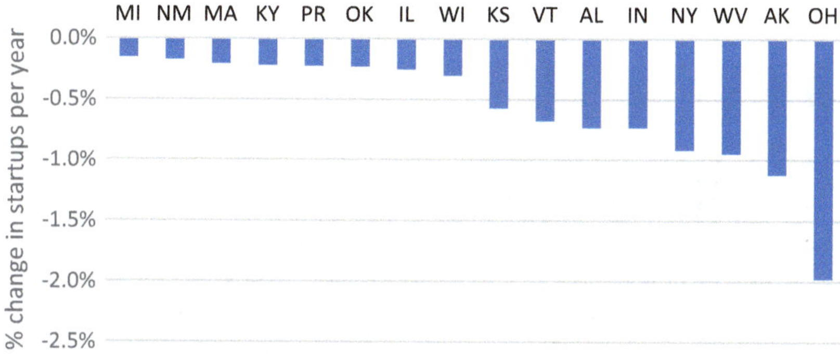

Fig. 3.9 Bottom 15 states with negative startup trend: 1994–2007 (*Source* Business Employment Dynamics Data by Age and Size, BLS)

per year. All these states were weak in incorporating new technologies unleashed by the introduction of the WWW in 1993.

Several hypotheses can be proffered as explanations of these rankings. The first is population, an idea mentioned earlier. California, Texas, Florida, NewYork, Pennsylvania, Illinois, Ohio, Georgia, North Carolina and Michigan are all large states in terms of population, but only four—California, Florida, North Carolina and Georgia—rank among the top 15 states in startup trend during the desktop revolution, 1994–2007. And only California and Georgia sustain their rank among the top 15 states during the mobility revolution, 2010–2020. This correspondence between population and startup activity does not extend for other states.

The second is state funded research and development. The presence of large state universities might be thought to play a role in germinating and launching startups. While this may be true for top ranking states California, Wisconsin and North Carolina, it is not the general case. In 2020, the largest employer in the state of New York was the State University of New York System, the University of New Mexico in that state, while simultaneously in Wisconsin the University of Wisconsin at Madison had the most employees as did the University of California system, the University of North Carolina system. Partners Health in Massachusetts was the largest employer in that state [11].

Third, one might hypothesize that the presence of a large global behemoth in the labor market might be a factor in slowing down the emergence of startups. From that perspective, it is consequential that the

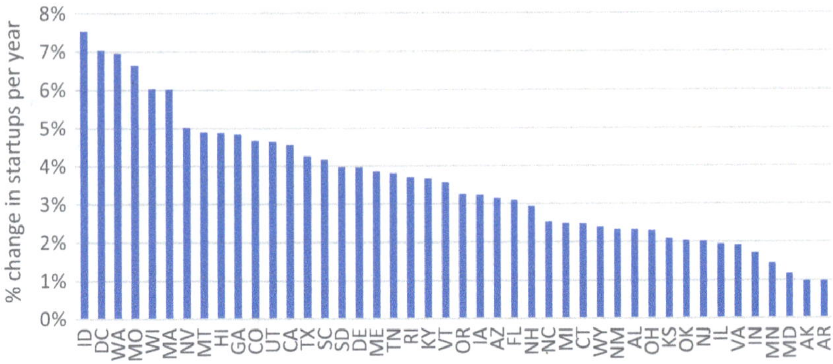

Fig. 3.10 States with positive startup trend: 2010–2020 (*Source* Business Employment Dynamics Data by Age and Size, BLS)

entire Southern Census Region in the U.S. is dominated by Walmart as an employer, from Texas in the West to Delaware in the East and Arkansas and Kentucky bordering the north. Walmart is also the largest employer in Montana and Wyoming. The presence of Georgia and the Carolinas in the top rankings of entrepreneurial activity, despite the dominance of Walmart in their labor markets, disproves this hypothesis.

Turning to the era of the mobility revolution in period II, 2010–2020, the top 15 states were: Idaho, Washington, Missouri, Wisconsin, Massachusetts, Nevada, Montana, Georgia, Utah, California, Texas, South Carolina, South Dakota, Colorado, and Delaware[4] (Fig. 3.10). The first 10 states were introducing new businesses at the rate of over 5% per year—and 7% in the case of Idaho, Washington and Missouri. Note the presence of all NUWMIC states, the cluster of states around the Pacific Northwest, as well as the rising star of the South, South Carolina. Only 5 states, Massachusetts, Georgia, South Carolina, Wisconsin, and Delaware are representative of regions east of the Mississippi.

Health care related facilities, hospitals, employed the largest number of people in Idaho (St Luke's Health System), Utah (Intermountain Healthcare), and Massachusetts (Partners Healthcare). Missouri has Walmart as its largest employer. Recall that the entire Southern Region has Walmart

[4] Hawaii and the District of Columbia ranked high but are not included due to their idiosyncratic nature. The nation's capital saw a blistering growth rate of 7% during the period 2010–2020. See the discussion later in the chapter.

as its largest employer, yet that does not appear to impede new ventures in states such as Georgia, North and South Carolina, and Missouri. To summarize, there appears to be no consistent kind of market or industry configuration that would predict the presence of entrepreneurs.

The resurgence in new business formations after the Great Recession was so powerful that most states showed positive new business activity. Few states had less than 1% growth in startups—North Dakota, Pennsylvania, Mississippi, Louisiana, West Virginia, Nebraska, and New York were among these weaker states. Curiously, North Dakota, and to a lesser extent Nebraska, was dominated by oil and gas exploration after 2015 when Congress lifted the ban on oil exports (Fig. 3.11).

New York and Pennsylvania were once again laggards with startup growth rates of less than 1%.

Whether it was their inadequate support structure, archaic regulation or lack of skills that prevented large states in the eastern half of the U.S. to embrace new technologies is not clear. Due to their large population and high density, one would expect that entrepreneurial networks would form rapidly, deploy new knowledge and spread *know-how or* first-hand details of business development. But this was not happening. Population growth rates, however, do correlate with startup activity, as mentioned above, and New York, Pennsylvania, and Ohio had sluggish population growth rates over the past decade of 0.4%, 0.2%, and 0.2% respectively. Compare that to the population growth rate of the contiguous U.S. which was 1%

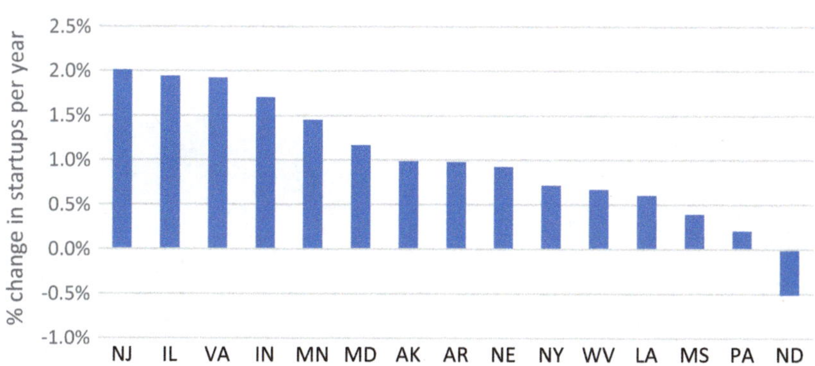

Fig. 3.11 Bottom 15 states with weakest startup trend: 2010–2020 (*Source* Business Employment Dynamics Data by Age and Size, BLS)

per year during 2019–2020 and it is clear that these large states, which together comprise 14% of the entire U.S. population, are slowing down in business dynamism.

Consolidating these observations, the following five points provide a comprehensive summary.

The Mississippi River

Rivers and mountains provide logical geographical markers, and the U.S. Census Bureau has made this simple by providing the following boundaries for the continental U.S. There are 4 regions and 9 divisions. Region 1, the Northeast, comprises Division 1 and 2: New England and the Middle Atlantic. Region 2 is the Midwest: East and West North Central (#3 and #4). Region 3, the South, is composed the South Atlantic (#5), East and West South Central (#6 and #7). Region 4 is the West, with the Mountain division (#8) and the Pacific (#9). The West and Midwest are west of the Mississippi, while the South, excluding the West South Central division, and Northeast are east of the river (Fig. 3.12).

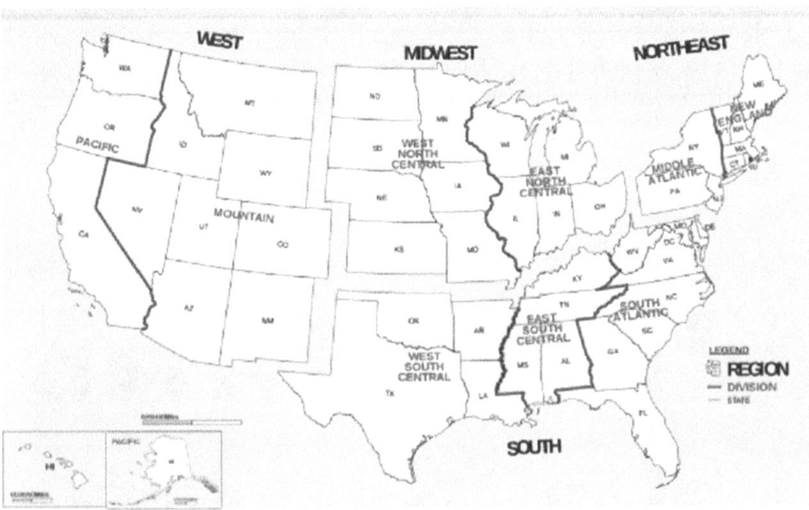

Fig. 3.12 Census regions and divisions of the United States (*Source* U.S. Census)

The Eastern side of the Mississippi consists of 26 states and 58% of the nation's total population in 2021. While visually, the river does not cut the continent half, it does break the nation into roughly equal halves in terms of population and number of states [12]. Therefore, the first observation to be made is that the Mississippi claims an important role in this discussion.

Recall that the rate of startup activity for the U.S. over the period 1994–2020 was **0.62%**. But the state level picture is asymmetric in the sense that while about half of the states in the nation are east of the Mississippi, only 8 of them have had an active entrepreneurial landscape during the past two and a half decades.

Over the entire period, 1994–2020, 11 of the top 15 states are west of the Mississippi (Fig. 3.6). The exceptions are Massachusetts, Wisconsin, Virginia, and Florida. On the other hand, 10 of the 15 bottom ranking states are east of the Mississippi river, with New Mexico, Minnesota, Kansas, Louisiana, Arkansas, being the 5 bottom-ranked states west of the Mississippi (Fig. 3.12).

Proximity might play a role in the clustering of states that performed well during period I. For example, the shared borders of California, Nevada, Utah, Idaho, and Montana, might play an important role in transmitting entrepreneurial sentiment. On the other hand, Kansas and Illinois are particularly noteworthy, as both are bordered by high-ranked states, Missouri, Nebraska, and Wisconsin, and yet show relatively mediocre entrepreneurial activity.

The unremarkable standing of Kansas is noteworthy, considering that it is surrounded by high performing states such as Missouri, Nebraska, and Texas. Why did Kansas not pick up on some of the entrepreneurial activity in these neighboring states, or capitalize on its location as the geographic center of the contiguous United States [10]. Wichita, the largest city in Kansas, is home to the aircraft industry, as Beechcraft, Cessna, Bombardier Jet, Airbus, and Spirit Aerosystems have design and manufacturing facilities in Wichita. A century ago, it was the destination of the cattle drive from Texas, but lost that role upon the development of the railroads. In the early 1900s oil was discovered, allowing oil wealth to promote entrepreneurship in the aircraft industry, becoming host to the first airplane factory in the U.S. Today, it is home to companies like Coleman, White Castle (the first hamburger chain in the U.S.) Pizza Hut, and Koch Industries.

In fact, as we will see in later chapters, Missouri remains exceptionally high ranking along other dimensions as well. Quite possibly, its location at the center of the United States might play a role.

During the desktop revolution, which is defined as period I, 10 of the top 15 states were **west of the Mississippi.** The highest-ranking states all exhibited startup growth rates ranging from over 3% for Florida and California to just under 2% for North Carolina and Virginia. Half of the states east of the Mississippi river saw stagnant (less than 0.1%) or negative startup trends with the exception of the South Atlantic states, New Jersey, Pennsylvania, Connecticut, Rhode Island, and Maine. The importance of Georgia and South Carolina cannot be overstated as both states remain in the higher ranks during the subsequent mobility revolution (Fig. 3.8).

During the mobility revolution, 11 of the 15 strongest performers were **west of the Mississippi**: Idaho, Washington, Nevada, Montana, Utah, and California are from the Pacific and Mountain census regions; Missouri and South Dakota from the West North Central Division; and Texas from the West South Central. The areas east of the Mississippi are represented by Wisconsin and Massachusetts from the East North Central and New England regions, with Georgia and South Carolina representing the South Atlantic region. All had startup growth rates exceeding 4% with Idaho at 7.5% and South Carolina at 4.2%. With over 40 states showing more than 2% growth in startups per year during the past decade (2010–2020), there was a robust response to the app economy that exploded during the second decade of the twenty-first century (Fig. 3.10).

The following cluster of states persist from the earlier period: Idaho, Utah, Montana, and Nevada from the Mountain Division and Washington and California from the Pacific Division. Recall that these states were given the acronym NUWMIC earlier in the chapter. There are three other states among the top 15 that are similarly consistent across many categories: Missouri from the West North Central Division; Wisconsin from the East North Central Division; and Massachusetts from the New England Division.

The Southern Region and the Rising Star of Georgia

Second, Georgia and South Carolina from the South Atlantic Division ranked among the top 15 during the mobility revolution, while seven of the eight states in this Division were among the top 15 states during the desktop revolution.[5] Georgia retains its top ranking during the entire time period. Georgia, **the rising star**, climbed from thirteenth spot in the earlier period to the eighth spot in the later period.

The NUWMICs

Third, for a state to rank among the top 15 in period I, the desktop revolution, and persist in this ranking during the mobility revolution, suggests enormous entrepreneurial spirit. There were two categories of states that comprise this unique feature. The cluster of states in the Mountain and Pacific division, the **NUWMICs**, were present among the top-ranking states across both the desktop and the digital revolution: Nevada, Utah, Washington, Montana, Idaho, and California. Proximity, in the sense of shared borders, might facilitate the easy movement of people across states thereby encouraging information exchange and the development of strong trust-based relationships.

Also important is the exposure to East Asia which would most likely build cultural ties that lead to increased trade ties, leveraging Asian intellectual capital into startups in the Western U.S.

These states, together with Georgia, were the only states that ranked in the top 15 in both periods.

Resilience

Fourth, the Great Recession was a period of tremendous upheaval and uncertainty, as we discussed in Chapter 2. Note that that California, Nevada, and Utah fell in rank upon progressing from period I to period II, while Idaho, Washington, and Montana rose. Nevertheless, the resilience of the NUWMIC states and Georgia is remarkable. The newcomer in the post-recession period, upholding the importance of the South, was South Carolina.

There were six states that dropped from the rankings in the post-recession years. Virginia, North Carolina, and Florida were possibly losing

[5] This result appears to differ from the suggestion of positive performance of the Southern Division during 2013–2021, based on the Business Formation Statistics data, as depicted in Fig. 3.1. However, it must be noted that the latter diagram presents an average across all the southern states, none of which rank in the top 10 in the overall rankings.

business activity to fast-growing South Carolina and Georgia within the South Atlantic Division. The other three, Arizona, Wyoming, and Arkansas may similarly have lost ground to the upcoming giant next door, Texas.

Wisconsin, Massachusetts, and Missouri made the most **dramatic turnaround** in activity in years following the Great Recession.

Weak Northeast Region

Fifth, the unseen fact in this geographical layout is the missing states. The Midwest and the Northeast of the U.S. remained ossified in the past, with the impressive exceptions being Missouri, Wisconsin, and Massachusetts which I single out here deliberately as we shall see this triumvirate reappear in other guises later. South Carolina makes an appearance in the post-2010 period, cementing the South Atlantic as the vanguard of the new digital transformation, as does South Dakota and Texas.

The low-ranking 10 states during the mobility revolution were Maryland, Arkansas, Arizona, Nebraska, New York, West Virginia, Louisiana, Mississippi, PR, Pennsylvania, and North Dakota (Fig. 3.11). Importantly, these states had startup activity less than 1% per year. The Northeast Census Region dominates this segment with 4 out of the 10 states coming from this region: New York, Pennsylvania, Maryland, and West Virginia. Recall that New York and Vermont were among the laggards in period I, **suggesting that much of the entrepreneurial activity during the past two decades has not been in the Northeast Region or the Midwest,** with the exception of South Dakota, Wisconsin, Missouri, and Massachusetts.

District of Columbia and Hawaii

Washington D.C. is a unique city in that it ranks high in startup activity over both periods, and across multiple years, but is not a state. Moreover, it is the nation's capital and as such supports an unusual economic environment. The city is one of the fastest growing metropolitan areas in the country with an annual population growth rate of over 2% since 2008. It was losing people in the first decade of the twenty-first century, particularly during 2002–2003 when it lost 1% of its population, quite likely a reaction to the bombings of September 11, 2001 [13].

The nation's capital has also been a crucible for startup ventures during the entire 26 years examined, 1994–2020. It has ranked among the top 10% of states in terms of entrepreneurial activity during those years. This activity was sustained during both the desktop revolution, where it ranked among the top 10, quickly rising to the second rank during the digital revolution. Normalizing for working age population, ages 18–64, the District retained its second rank in the country.

Hawaii ranks among the top 15 during the mobility revolution after one of the largest turnarounds in activity after the Great Recession. What is unique about this state? It is a rising technology nexus with three incubators, five accelerators, six investment funds, and six startup organizations. Blue Startups was ranked in the top 20 U.S. accelerators by TechCrunch. Starting from a tourist paradise with white sand beaches and perfect weather, with a minimal number of starutps, Governor David Ige called for $30 million to be spent on supporting innovative enterprises over the next six years, in his state of the state address before the legislature on January 25, 2016. "Sugar is gone" he proclaimed and needs to be replaced with a "new economic engine" which would deploy broadband for innovation across a vast range of industries such as agriculture, clean energy, healthcare, fashion and media and design. The state might be on the cusp of startup activity, which may be low in levels but ranks high in the rate of change [14].

State Level Illustrations

Individual states have far more interesting stories compared to the overall, perhaps bland picture. Consider the pattern for individual states. Figure 3.13 shows the picture for the top 15 states over the entire 26-year period, 1994–2020: North Dakota, Nebraska, Missouri, Idaho, Massachusetts, California, Texas, Wisconsin, Washington, Florida, Virginia, and Nevada. Figure 3.14 adds the rising stars: Utah, South Carolina, Montana, and Georgia.

Massachusetts, Missouri, and Wisconsin stand out as having rather tepid startup activity during period I but with a dramatic upsurge after 2010. Idaho and California's startup activity rose gradually to peak in 2007 but fell during the Great Recession and didn't recover before 2019.

All states have sharply rising activity after 2010, with the exception of Washington and Virginia. Washington is unusual in showing a dramatic upsurge in 2020 after a relatively quiescent 25-year stretch. North Dakota

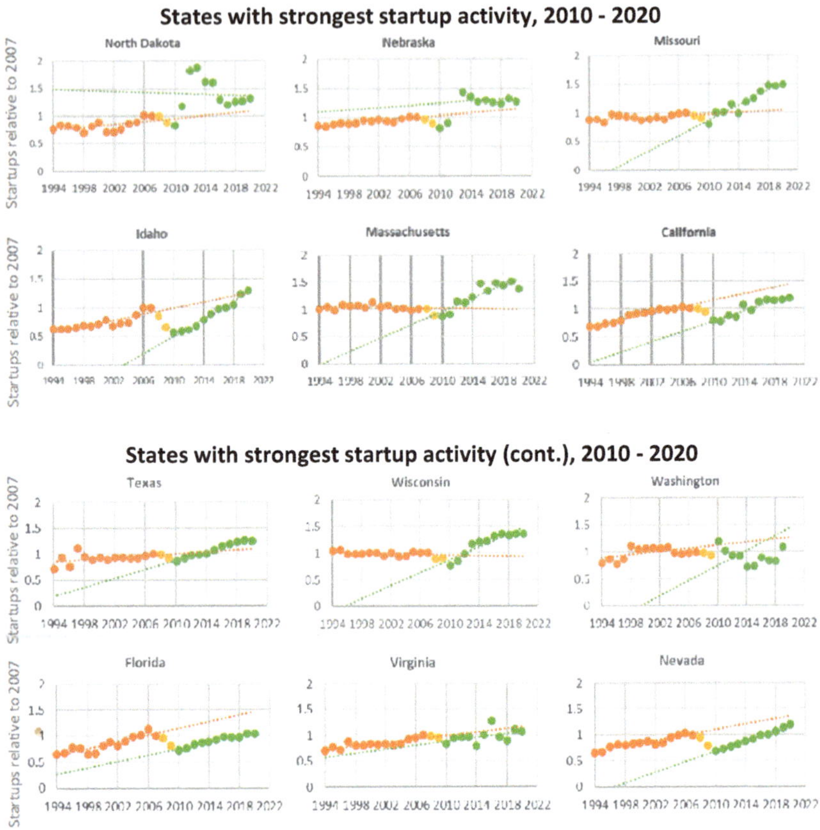

Fig. 3.13 State details, top 12 states: 1994–2020 (*Source* Business Employment Dynamics Data by Age and Size, BLS)

and Nebraska exhibit a sharp upturn in startups in 2011–2013, followed by an equally sharp downturn. This U-turn is anomalous as no other state exhibits this dramatic a switch.

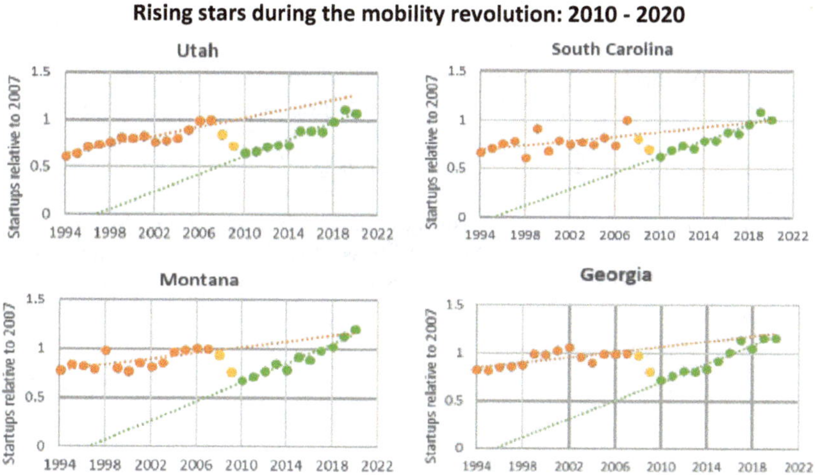

Fig. 3.14 State details, Rising stars: 2010–2020 (*Source* Business Employment Dynamics Data by Age and Size, BLS)

Bibliography

1 History of Netflix. 2022. Wikipedia. https://en.wikipedia.org/wiki/Netflix.
2 Gertner, Jon. 2012. *The Idea Factory: Bell Labs and the Great Age of American Innovation*. The Penguin Press.
3 Casner, Stephen and Stephen Deering. 1992. First IETF internet audiocast. *ACM SIGCOMM Computer Communication Review* 22(3): 92–97. https://doi.org/10.1145/142267.142338.
4 Mbone. 2022. Wikipedia. https://en.wikipedia.org/wiki/Mbone.
5 Lewis, Peter. 1995. Peering Out a 'Real Time' Window. *New York Times*. https://www.nytimes.com/1995/02/08/business/business-technology-peering-out-a-real-time-window.html.
6 Streaming Before Netflix. 2017. *Tedium*. https://tedium.co/2017/01/05/first-streaming-service-itv-hong-kong/.
7 Bloomberg Businessweek. 2006. https://www.bloomberg.com/news/articles/2006-02-12/this-is-the-face-of-broadband-tv.
8 Global Recorded Music Revenue from 1999 to 2020. 2022. https://www.statista.com/statistics/272305/global-revenue-of-the-music-industry.
9 Mathur, Priyamvada and Jordan Rubio. 2022. Mapping Africa's Growing Venture Capital Landscape. https://pitchbook.com/news/articles/mapping-africas-growing-venture-capital-landscape.

10 World Population Review. 2022. https://worldpopulationreview.com/states.
11 Sauter, Michael. 2022. The Largest Employer in Every State. https://247wallst.com/special-report/2018/04/18/largest-employer-in-every-state-2/11/.
12 U.S. Census. 2022. https://www.census.gov/quickfacts/fact/table/US/PST045221.
13 U.S. Census. https://www.census.gov/dataviz/visualizations/043/.
14 Governor Ige's State of the State Address. 2016. https://governor.hawaii.gov/newsroom/governors-office-news-release-governor-iges-state-of-the-state-address/.

CHAPTER 4

The Impact of the Great Recession

The 2008–2009 Great Recession could have severely and negatively impacted entrepreneurial culture. It is a measure of the robustness of the economy that there was significant resilience in multiple states. Not only was there a reversal but there was a meaningful change in new startups after the great recession, as for example in the state of Wisconsin.

An example of how technology has ignited this turnaround is a startup in Wisconsin. Using social media and direct-to-consumer sales, Leslie Svacina started Cylon Rolling Acres in 2013 in Deer Park, Wisconsin. This unique farm business sells pasture-raised goat meat and has not only publicized the business but also educated potential customers on nutritional and cooking aspects of goat meat on social media as well as the company website. Leslie writes on the blog "I bet you'll never guess what my favorite tool is for the farm! It's my iPhone!" [1]

A community-based business is the startup Adventure Games, founded in 2012 by Teddy Alecos. While deployed in Afghanistan with the U.S. Army, he imagined and developed the idea of tabletop games and a meeting place for people to play these games. He purchased a 6000 square foot building in downtown Oshkosh and walk-in traffic increased as the business became part of the local community. Growth and visibility have come via the company's Facebook page, which served as the company's face to the world until the development of the website [2]. The Oshkosh Herald calls this "A store that puts devices aside and lets the

S. Bhatt, *Entrepreneurship Today*,
https://doi.org/10.1007/978-3-031-11495-3_4

imagination wander" and that "board, tabletop, and demo games have become a viable option in the digitalized gaming age because it fosters more community engagement and social interaction" [3].

The Turnaround States

Many states were declining or stagnant in new business activity during the desktop revolution of 1994–2007 but rebounded dramatically following the economic downturn. The turnaround states are those that had the largest change in startup activity in period II relative to period I, with a whopping surge during the mobility revolution of 2010–2020. The top 10 states are Wisconsin, Massachusetts, Missouri, Washington, Idaho, Ohio, Vermont, Kentucky, South Dakota, and Georgia. The next 5 are states that had practically zero startup activity during the desktop revolution but stepped up after the Great Recession were Montana, Tennessee, Texas, Rhode Island, and Alabama.

Differentiating states by their overall trend line, we get two categories of resurgence. The first is the states that had a small upward trend during the desktop revolution and then powered ahead in the later years. The second category comprises states that had a flat or downward trend but showed some renewal after the recessionary years of 2008–2009.

In the first category, we have Washington, Idaho, Georgia, Montana, and Texas. All of these states end up ranking among the high performers during the subsequent years, as discussed in Chapter 3.

In the second category are the states of Wisconsin, Massachusetts, Missouri, Ohio, Vermont, Kentucky, South Dakota, Tennessee, Rhode Island, and Alabama. Ohio had declining rates of new businesses per year of 2% in the early decade and then pivoted to a positive 2% after the economic dislocation of 2008–09. Of these states, only Washington, Wisconsin, Massachusetts, and Missouri rise to the top ranks in the mobility revolution, that comprises the years 2010–2020.

The main point is that the recession either did little harm or energized the states of Washington, Wisconsin, Idaho, Massachusetts, Missouri, Georgia, Montana, and Texas catapulting them into the higher strata of the entrepreneurial atmosphere. In fact, Idaho, Missouri, and Massachusetts are exceptional since they are also among the high-ranking states across the entire 24 years, as shown in the left panel of Fig. 4.1.

Not all states recovered or reacted to the structural changes occurring elsewhere in the country. States with negligible change in new business

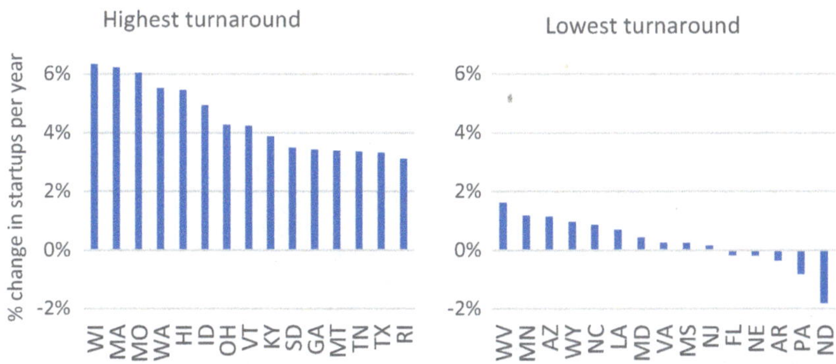

Fig. 4.1 States with highest/lowest turnaround in start-up activity post Great Recession (*Source* Business Employment Dynamics Data by Age and Size, BLS)

formation between the two periods, and with roughly stagnant overall activity, were North Dakota, Pennsylvania, Arizona, Nebraska, Florida, New Jersey, Mississippi, Virginia, and Maryland, as shown in the right panel of Fig. 4.1. Virginia is unique in that it never saw a downturn so there was no resurgence required. As mentioned earlier in Chapter 3 North Dakota actually saw an unusual upturn in 2011–2013 followed by a slow decline. Texas, for example, showed a 3% change. The trend rate of startups in Texas was 0.09% during 1994–2007, which then jumped to 4.25% during 2010–2020.

States that exhibited desultory activity in new business formation are best characterized by the fact that the peak in startups reached around 2007 is not matched in subsequent years. In fact, Ohio and New York peaked much before. These states exhibited a sharp upturn in new business creation in the early 1990s for Ohio and around 2000 for New York. South Carolina and Florida have been climbing rapidly in the post-2010 period, and just about matched the 2007 level during recent years.

Correlation Between the Two Periods

From an empirical perspective, without attributing any kind of causality, it would be useful to see if there were any correlation between the two periods delineated as period I and period II. The issue of responsiveness to the new business environment during the years following the depressed years of 2008–2009 raises the question. It is quite possible

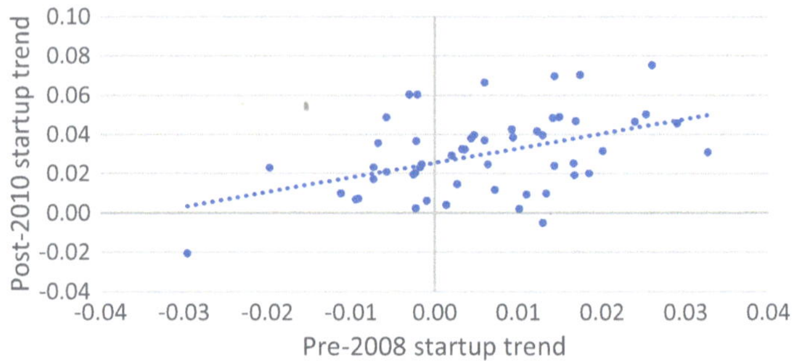

Fig. 4.2 Correlation between pre-2008 and post-2010 startup trend by state (*Source* Business Employment Dynamics Data by Age and Size, BLS)

that the momentum built up during period I sustained activity in the following period, despite the intervening recessionary years. Did the states that had robust entrepreneurial activity during the desktop revolution years continue along this trajectory? Is there a correlation between performance during the two periods for each state and could one conclude that a given state, say Idaho, that demonstrated strong new business activity during the desktop revolution shared similar growth during the mobility revolution?[1]

The results, shown in Fig. 4.2, suggest that startup activity in the later decade was positively, but weakly, correlated with that in the earlier period. More precisely, if a state was entrepreneurial prior to 2007 then it was likely to continue along this trajectory, but at a *slower* rate. The data show that for a 1% increase in startups in the pre-2008 period there was a 0.75% increase in startups in the post-2010 period. This is a weak correlation, and in fact suggests that much of the power behind the second digital revolution did not emanate from that occurring during the previous decade.

The Great Recession was a sort of turning point, not just in terms of employment and jobs, but also in terms of life choices. Much like the recent response to the pandemic, in terms of individuals' reassigning

[1] To answer this question, we calculated the correlation between DR I and DR II, in the following simple linear regression: DR II = $a + b$ *DR I, with coefficients $a = 0.03$ and $b = 0.75$. DR I stands for the desktop digital revolution and DR II stands for the mobility digital revolution.

their priorities and voluntarily changing jobs, there might have been some personal restructuring which led to the powerful resurgence of business formations in the decade following the downturn of 2009.

Per Capita Results

As a check on the ranking of states by their trends over the two decades, a population normalization might reveal additional differences. Migration, both from within the U.S. and from abroad, has altered the face of the country over the past two decades. Since the focus is on new business activity and entrepreneurship, the relevant population is bounded by the ages of 18 and 64. By this definition, Texas added the highest number of working age individuals during the period, 2010–2019, with 240,230 being added per year. Florida and California added over 100,000 people per year over the past decade.

A cursory investigation can be done by visually comparing a population map with startup map, Figs. 4.3 with 4.4. The map in Fig. 4.3 shows the top 15 states by working age population growth. Arizona, Washington, Georgia, North Carolina, and Colorado added around 45,000 new residents per year. Utah, Nevada, and South Carolina added 28,000 to 20,000 people per year during these years. The map in Fig. 4.4 shows startup trend by state.

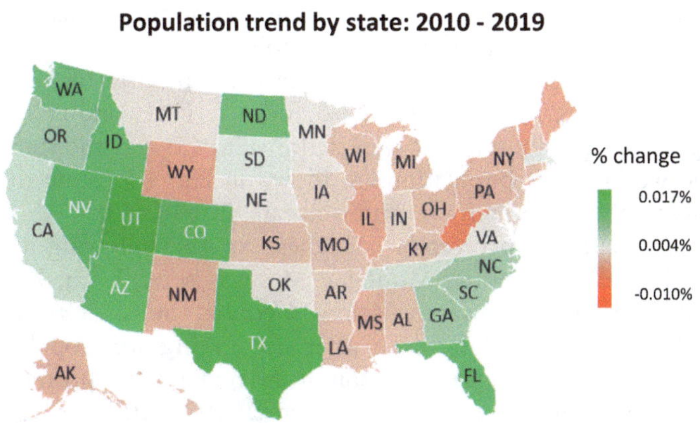

Fig. 4.3 Map of population trend by state: 2010–2019 (*Source* Business Employment Dynamics Data by Age and Size, BLS)

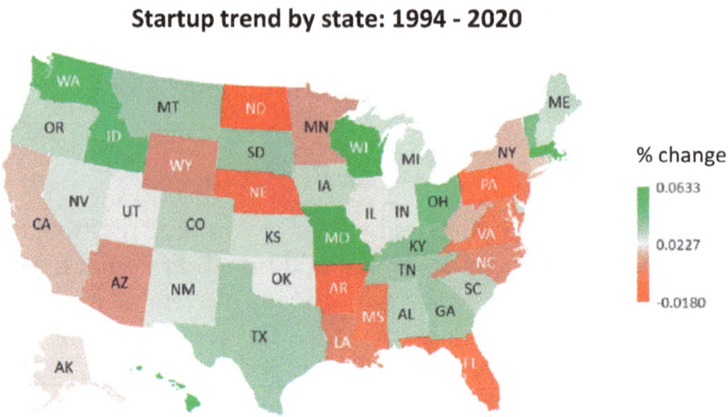

Fig. 4.4 Map of startup trend by state: 1994–2020 (*Source* Business Employment Dynamics Data by Age and Size, BLS)

Finally, the map in Fig. 4.5 puts the two together, depicting the per capita startup trend over the years 2010–2019, the years covering the mobility revolution. From the perspective of economic dynamism and new businesses, Wisconsin, Idaho, Massachusetts, Missouri, and California stand out as the dark green states, the states with the highest per capita startup trend. Texas and most of the South looks weak, with the exception of Florida and South Carolina, the rising star. Interestingly, the strong states in both the mobility revolution continue to maintain their ranking even when considered on a per capita basis.

Using the underlying data to compute per capita startup trends, we obtain the accurate picture in Figs. 4.6 and 4.7. The working age population growth rates by state are depicted in Fig. 4.6 and the startups per 100,000 working age population are shown in Fig. 4.7. Note that these data cover only the mobility revolution years, 2010–2020.

The startup trend per capita is highest for the following 15 states: Idaho, Missouri, California, Montana, Massachusetts, Utah, Wisconsin, Vermont, Nevada, Delaware, Maine, Georgia, South Carolina, and Rhode Island. Significantly, even after accounting for population, all the NUWMIC states, except Washington, retain their prominence in the entrepreneurial world during the years 2010–2020. Normalizing by population alters the composition of the top 15 states by entrepreneurial activity during these years with Washington, Texas, and South Dakota

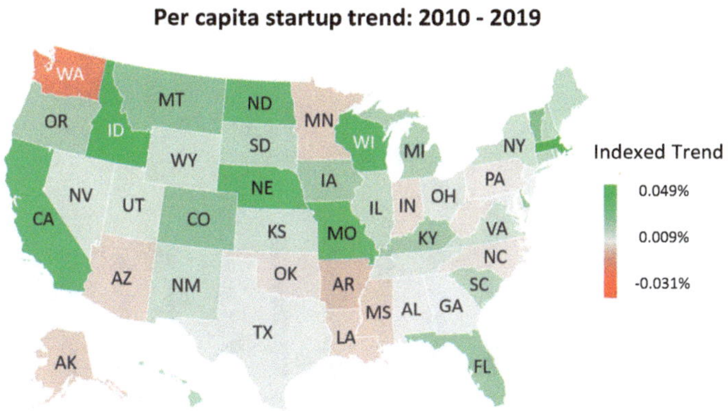

Fig. 4.5 Map of per capita startup trend: 2010–2019 (*Source* Business Employment Dynamics Data by Age and Size, BLS)

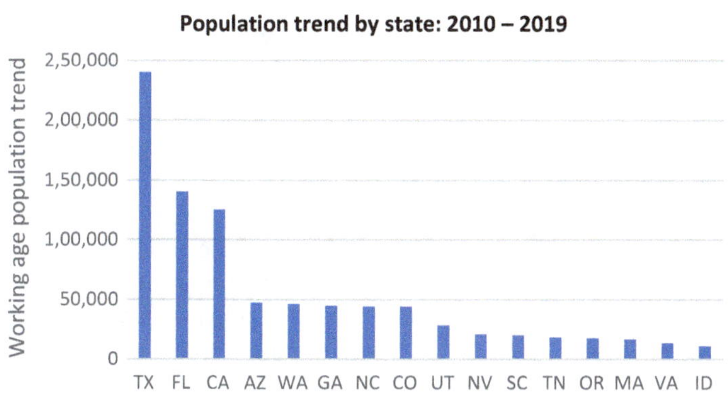

Fig. 4.6 Population trend by state: 2010–2019 (*Source* Business Employment Dynamics Data by Age and Size, BLS)

dropping out of the top echelons and being replaced by Vermont, Delaware, and Maine.

Idaho, Massachusetts, and Missouri are the phenomenal states. Not only do they rank among the top 10 across the entire period, 1994–2020, but they also rank in the top 10 in per capita terms. In addition, they can be counted in the top 10 during the mobility revolution. There indeed

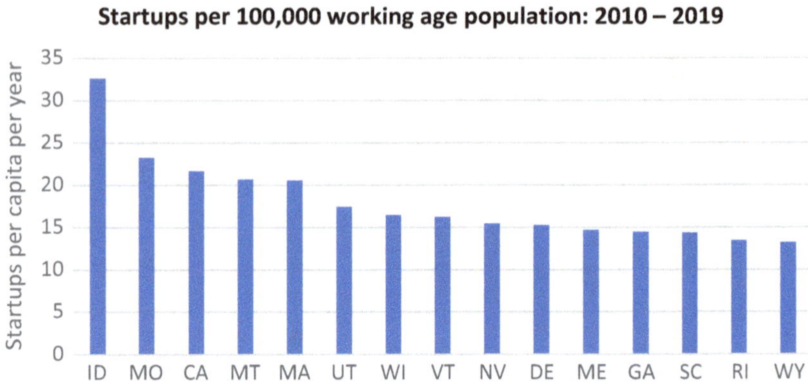

Fig. 4.7 Per capita startup trend: 2010–2019 (*Source* Business Employment Dynamics Data by Age and Size, BLS)

is something special about this particular triumvirate of states. It is not proximity.

Addressing the Unique Nature of Resilient States

Washington

Home to companies like Amazon and Microsoft, and Silicon Valley transplants such as Google and Facebook, Washington is unique. One would think that the state is buoyed by the strength of the overall tech industry with spillover effects. It also hosts a nationally ranked computer science program at the University of Washington. Technology sector employees looking to start their own business would have found the support structure useful, as the state is ranked a national leader in business incubation [4]. Washington ranks at #10 in startup activity during the desktop revolution and #3 in the mobility revolution. It does not rank high, however, in per capita terms.

It may be worth noting that less than 10% of Washington's population has access to 3 or more internet service providers. The percent of a state's population that has access to high speed broadband might play a role in the startup trajectory. A larger number of providers would imply a greater choice of data plans with higher speed and lower latency. At the national level 8.29% of the population has no providers, 56% of the national population has access to 2 or more providers and 13.38% has access to 3 or more providers. Broadband includes both fixed and wireless with speeds of 100Mbps download and 10Mbps upload. Data from the FCC show that the percent of the state's population that has access to 3 or more providers is the highest in the following 15 states: DC, Colorado, Arizona, Utah, Nevada, California, Michigan, New York, Nebraska, Massachusetts, Wyoming, Texas, and Kansas—all have over 15% of their population with this generous access, much above the national average of 13.38%.

While competition in the broadband provision is not a sufficient indicator of startup activity, it appears to be necessary as a fair fraction of the top startup states have 3 or more providers. Washington, Missouri, Idaho, Montana, Wisconsin, North and South Carolina are the anomaly—less than 10% of the states' population has access to 3 or more providers. Approximately 30% of Montana's population has no providers, while at least 30% of the population of the other states listed above have access to 2 or more providers. The Western division is marked by expansive territory, mountainous terrain, and deep rivers. It would be prohibitively expensive to have multiple providers [5].

California

While not a turnaround state, California presents an interesting hypothesis—that the resurgence during the post-recession years were driven by implementation of technology-based businesses. A study done at the Bureau of Labor Statistics, shows that, in California the technology sector had the strongest recovery following the 2008–2009 recession. Employment in the technology sector has grown at rate high enough to support recovery of all non-farm jobs in the state. Defining the technology sector as the group of businesses in professional and business services, information, leisure and hospitality, and education and health services, the study compares employment levels in January 2014 with those in January 2008. Calculating the recovery ratio as 2014 employment divided by 2008 employment, the highest recovery ratios were in the San Francisco—San Jose corridor, with some spillover into the Oakland region, and the San Diego—Los Angeles corridor. Information recovery ratios were highest in the San Francisco location (recovery ratio of 1.31), as were the professional and business services ratio (1.19) and leisure and hospitality (1.16). Education and health services were equally high in both the San Francisco and Los Angeles corridor (recovery ratio of 1.29 and 1.25 respectively)[2] [6].

Idaho, Massachusetts, and Missouri

Recessions and the corresponding stretches of unemployment faced by many can prompt changes in career paths. Rather than allowing resumes to be scarred by periods of joblessness, people may switch to self-employment or start their own business. Together with new technologies at their disposal it could be tempting to consider this sort of career change. Quite remarkable is the fact that not only did Idaho, Missouri, and Massachusetts change paths so dramatically, but they also responded forcefully in period II. Whether it was the recession itself that precipitated change or a delayed uptake of technology, or more likely a blend of both, is debatable.

Extrapolating from this study, one could posit that Idaho, Missouri, and Massachusetts had a technology-driven rebound, with a likely predominance of the professional, scientific, and technical subsector. In fact, the professional and business services sector is the second largest employer in Massachusetts, growing by 31.3% between 2010 and 2020. This sector is the third largest employer by sector in Idaho and Missouri, with growth of 32.8% in Idaho and 22.9% in Missouri between 2010 and 2020. Biotechnology employment grew by 4.9% in Massachusetts, matching the rate in 2008.

According to recent data, employment in the education and health sector ranked the highest at 21.7% of the total employed labor force in Massachusetts, while professional and business services were the second largest employer with 17.5% of the state's total employment, as of December 2020. Idaho had 12.6% of its employed labor force in the professional, scientific, and business services in December 2020. Missouri had, in December 2020, 17.1% of its employed labor force in education and health services, followed by 13.2% in professional and business services. To be clear, the largest employer was trade, transportation and utilities at 18.9% in Missouri, while in Idaho this sector employed 19.4% of the employed labor force [7].

[2] The professional, scientific, and technical subsector did exceptionally well in terms of recovery ratios and is responsible for 50% of all jobs in the professional and business grouping.

Transportation equipment is the largest export of Missouri, at 22.6% of total exports, followed by chemicals and rare earth metals (19.4%) and food (10.4%), with the top markets being Canada, Mexico, and China, as of 2020 [8]. Idaho's top export is semiconductor devices, with integrated circuits comprising 14.2% and computer parts and accessories 7.4% in 2018. No agricultural commodity made it into the top 10, although Idaho ranks second nationally for its production of sugar beets [9].

According to the U.S. Census, Massachusetts' top three exports were unwrought gold, comprising 5.7% of the state's exports, machinery for making semiconductors (5%), and medical/dental/veterinarian instruments (4.3%) [7].

Bibliography

1 Svacina, Leslie. 2022. Blog. https://grazingwithleslie.com/.
2 Accessed from https://www.facebook.com/AdventureGamesOshkosh/?ref=page_internal. Many of the small business stories in Wisconsin can be accessed at https://wisconsinsbdc.org/client-successes/page/4/.
3 The OshKosh Herald. 2022. https://oshkoshherald.com/wp-content/uploads/2020/02/February-26-2020-Oshkosh-Herald.pdf.
4 Schlosser, Kurt. 2021. We're No 1 (Again). Washington Takes Top Spot in 'Best State' Rankings as Tech Fuels Economic Engine. *Geek Wire*. https://www.geekwire.com/2021/no-1-washington-takes-top-spot-best-state-rankings-tech-fuels-economic-engine/.
5 Fixed Broadband Deployment, Federal Communications Commission. 2022. https://broadbandmap.fcc.gov/#/area-comparison?version=dec2019&tech=acfosw&speed=100_10&searchtype=state&searched=y.
6 Nicole Havins. 2014. Technology Industries Helped Post-Great Recession Jobs Grow Faster in Northern Than in Southern California. *Monthly Labor Review*. U.S. Bureau of Labor Statistics, December 2014. https://doi.org/10.21916/mlr.2014.39.
7 Bureau of Labor Statistics. 2022. Geographic Information. https://www.bls.gov/regions/economic-summaries.htm#ID.
8 The Missouri Economic Datebook. 2020. *The Beige Book*. https://www.kansascityfed.org/.
9 Morrison, Ryan. 2019. Idaho's Biggest Exports and Products. *Idaho News*, December 26. https://idahonews.com/news/local/idahos-biggest-exports-and-products.

CHAPTER 5

The Mature Startups

The community and local support structure should be ranked among the highest order of importance for the survival of startups. This chapter examines the patterns created by the intersection of mature startups across states, industries and working age population, as well as the sustainability of these older startups. This broader perspective will allow us to better understand the life-cycle of entrepreneurship.

There are multiple milestones or stages for a new business. The idea stage is first, where the problem is discovered. Second, a possible solution is imagined and third, it is tested among an initial group of users. It is at stage four, the mature startup phase, where customer acquisition becomes the focus. The fifth stage is the expansion stage where new markets are explored.

Mature startups are defined as those in stage four, new enterprises 1–4 years in existence with less than 500 employees. More precisely, the data for mature establishments comprise businesses that were around for over a year, may have temporarily shut down and were now starting up again, less businesses that have closed (or been acquired) and reported zero payroll. These businesses had reported a positive payroll sometime between 1 and 4 years ago.[1] Therefore, a mature startup is a business that went from idea stage to product development and launch, expanded its

[1] This includes reopening after temporary and seasonal shutdowns.

S. Bhatt, *Entrepreneurship Today*,
https://doi.org/10.1007/978-3-031-11495-3_5

workforce sometime in the past four years, has now had survival issues and had to temporarily shut down. The evidence suggests that the majority of startups do not survive beyond the first year, either due to acquisition by larger incumbents and private equity firms or due to exit in the wake of insufficient support, both technical and marketing. Remarkably, the states that ranked high in early-stage startup creation were precisely those that saw the most exits or acquisitions. Correspondingly, the weakest states had the least number of exits or acquisitions since there were few startups in the first instance.

Consider the example of BioNTech. The life-saving anti-COV 2020 vaccine, marketed by pharmaceutical giant Pfizer, was invented by BioNTech, a small firm using mRNA technology. It was the second collaboration between the two companies, following the influenza vaccine collaboration in 2018. This collaborative agreement, rather than outright acquisition, is a partnership for research and development as well as commercialization; the two trade as separate entities with Pfizer trading on the New York Stock Exchange and BioNTech on the NASDAQ exchange. BioNTech has multiple pharmaceutical collaborators, including Sanofi, Genentech (a member of the Roche Group), and Regeneron [1].

As businesses mature, they could expand their workforce or remain microbusinesses. In a 1979 study of businesses operating between 1969 and 1976, Birch showed, using detailed industry data, that "about 50% of all jobs are created by independent small entrepreneurs. Large firms (those with over 500 employees) generate less than 15% of all net new jobs".[2] This altered the collective wisdom that large corporations were the big job creators. Small firms, despite their higher exit rates, are the engine of job creation. Importantly, Birch finds that "[y]ounger establishments clearly generate the great majority of jobs, particularly in the growing service sector. Job generation falls off sharply after four years of age and declines steadily thereafter. Our economy thus counts on younger as well as smaller businesses to provide most of its replenishment jobs" [2]. *This means that jobs are created by startups in the acceleration stage, which is beyond the first year, but less than four years.*

Following that reasoning, policy directives aimed at *mature startups,* ranging from tax breaks to regulatory exemptions to procurement favors, may be justified. To be clear, all startups should be nurtured,

[2] Birch used novel Dun & Bradstreet data comprising 5.6 million records about small businesses for the years, 1979, 1972, 1974, and 1976.

whether they are creating jobs or not, in contrast to past research which suggests that the remedy for declining business dynamism was to target job creating young firms—a conclusion derived from defining startups as young firms that create jobs. The firms that need to be targeted are "the most difficult to identify and the most difficult to work with. They are small. Then tend to be independent. They are volatile. The very spirit that gives them their vitality and job generating powers is the same spirit that makes them unpromising partners" for the local government administrator [2]. Detailed knowledge of the local culture, as with "rifle shooting" works better than "shotgun shooting" where large budgets are devoted to providing general, but weak, incentives, such as tax cuts. New businesses tend to locate in regions of the nation where, not only are costs of production lower, but the quality of life is higher—where the business climate, to put it succinctly, is pleasant. This topic is discussed in more detail later in Chapter 6.

Fifty years later, technology has become an integral part of new businesses, replacing a large workforce. More pertinently, the point of efficiency-enhancing new methods of production and service is to increase output per worker, which is productivity. New tech-driven businesses don't need a large employee base. The "rifle shooting" policy nudges appear to have worked. In 2019, 44% of the employed population worked for businesses with less than 400 employees, while 35% worked for businesses with greater than 5000 employees and 24% worked for establishments with more than 20,000 employees. Looking at the number of establishments, the fraction of all the establishments in the U.S. that had fewer than 100 employees was 78%, while the establishments with greater than 20,000 employees comprise a mere 7% of total establishments. Over three quarter of establishments had fewer than 100 employees and they captured 44% of the employed population. Small businesses are no small change [3]. Returning to the job creation aspect, a Kaufmann Foundation study of startups and job creation in 2010 found that "net job growth in the U.S. comes from firms less than one year old, formally defined as startups. ... it lies at the three- to nine-month point after firm founding" [4].

It must be recognized, however, that the effects of *young* small businesses, i.e. startups, may be different from that of *older* small businesses, the two not necessarily being the same. Most young businesses are likely to be small, but not all small businesses are young. As discussed in Chapter 1, a startup *starts* as a small business with an idea and a few employees. The exact moment of job creation varies by the idea, the market, and the environment. At the very early stage, a startup is a small business. As it matures, it adds workers in a process that could be swift or long-drawn. A young small business is a startup even if it exhibits gradual and cautious job creation, but an older small business may remain small in employee size. Local mom-and-pop outfits are small and could have been started a generation ago. Stories abound, such as that of a young person preserving a tailoring establishment started by their grandfather.

The notion of startups as being engines of job creation does not imply that founders care about job creation or scaling the enterprise rapidly. Rapid expansion by hiring large numbers of workers is not the goal of founders. Focusing on the universe of small employer establishments with less than 19 employees, researchers find that most such businesses are either restaurants, skilled professionals (physicians, lawyers, dentists, accountants, architects, consultants), skilled crafts-persons, professional service providers, general service providers, and small retailers (grocery stores, gas stations). The owners are more interested in preserving a lifestyle than becoming a behemoth and conquering vast markets. "It is not true that most new businesses generate employment growth" [5].

One could argue that ignoring the job creation aspect of startups can be costly and decrease productivity. First, they are a cost for the public sector. When the job creation benefits of supporting small businesses are missing and the costs incurred in promoting small businesses via subsidies are large, there can be a net loss. Second, there are limited benefits as the local economy, and perhaps the national economy, "becomes less productive, given that individuals respond by choosing to work in small (subsidized) self-owned firms rather than establishing larger firms that can produce at lower average cost by exploiting the returns to scale". These subsidies are also regressive, in that "the subsidy is just a plain reward for charting a course they would have undertaken in any case". Attracting high wage workers with subsidies (low-cost credit) to deflect their higher opportunity costs of leaving regular employment is not a recipe for success. However, there may be "other social virtues to non-innovative small businesses, such as supporting communities and neighborhoods" [5]. The last statement is the most important aspect of startups and ranks as high as job creation and the exploitation of economies of scale, which often leads to the creation of behemoths, a matter that would be of concern on anti-trust grounds.

The idea that young, small businesses are not entrepreneurial simply because they do not employ large numbers of workers is unjustified. They may, in fact, generate employment in complementary or ancillary markets within their respective regions. Most small business owners care for work flexibility rather than income, and at least a third of business founders "wanted to create a new product or had a very good business idea". Innovation means a new way of solving an old problem, so new ideas and products may not suggest invention, but they do flag innovation. The point is that growth incentives, job creation incentives, are not the first order reasons for startup creation—creating a culture of risk-taking is of the first order. Debates about aggregate labor productivity have been creating ambiguity in policy decisions. Perhaps it is time to think in new ways—development of the community and business climate might be more important.

Mature Startup Survival

Examining data from the Bureau of Labor Statistics, I define mature startups as the net change in establishments 1–4 years in existence, with less than 500 employees. Also analyzed is data on the over 500 employees size class.

Across the 26-year span of this analysis, a meaningful result is the slow death of average startup activity as firms age into the older category. Consider Fig. 5.1, which shows the net change in mature startups—opening establishments minus closing establishments—from 1 to 4 years in existence, with under 500 employees. There is a decline of approximately 966 mature establishments per year, which can be interpreted as the death of young firms that have aged beyond one year, or acquisition by incumbent behemoths or private equity firms. The net change in establishments that have scaled up to over 500 employees within the same age group, is essentially zero. Few establishments have scaled to over 500 employees in under 4 years.

Indexing the data by the peak year, 2012, is one way of standardizing or normalizing the data. Recall a similar indexing was applied to the data on young startups in Chapter 2. Figure 5.2 makes plain the slowdown in startup activity. There is a statistically significant decline in business activity in the mature firm category. The average rate of decline, the slope of the trend line in Fig. 5.2, is **−0.38%,** which means that there was a decrease in mature startups over the entire period—more startups closed

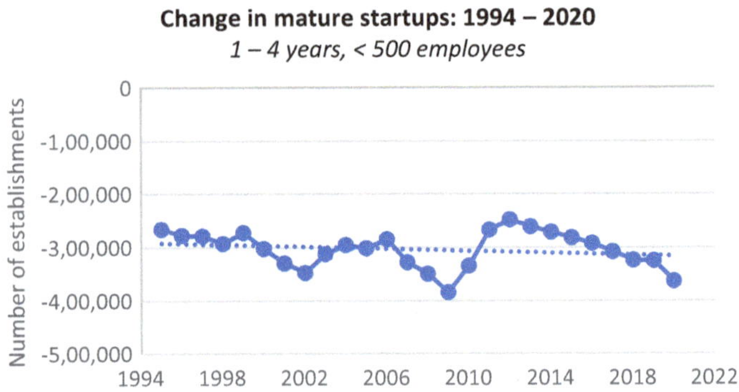

Fig. 5.1 Change in mature startups, 1–4 yrs, less than 500 employees: 1994–2020 (*Source* Business Employment Dynamics Data by Age and Size, BLS)

than were created. Recall from Chapter 3 that the average startup trend for firms under 1 year in existence was **0.6%**. Startup activity has shown a statistically significant change from a year-over-year increase of 0.6% in young startups to a year-over-year decrease of 0.38% of firms that have crossed the one-year mark. There is a marked slow attrition of firms aged 1–4 years.

Is there a difference between the two time periods, the desktop revolution and the mobility revolution? Consider Figs. 5.3 and 5.4. The trend in period I is −1.4% per year while the trend in period II is −2.6% so

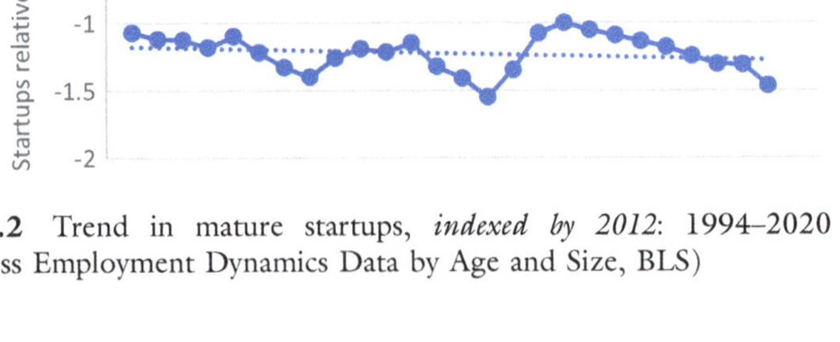

Fig. 5.2 Trend in mature startups, *indexed by 2012*: 1994–2020 (*Source* Business Employment Dynamics Data by Age and Size, BLS)

there is a faster exit rate in the more recent decade. Effectively, mature startups are dwindling progressively over the two decades examined. This result may be due to a faltering entrepreneurial spirit as the business grew or due to the weak business climate following the economic slowdown, where ancillary and complimentary markets are either non-existent or dysfunctional.

A weak supply chain is an example of an unstable business climate. Consider the trucking industry, a vital element in the supply chain of inputs such as raw materials, labor, and capital to final output. The recession could have weakened a local trucking firm which is unable to consistently provide stable flour supplies for a budding new bakery. This new business cannot bake its daily bread and croissants without a reliable

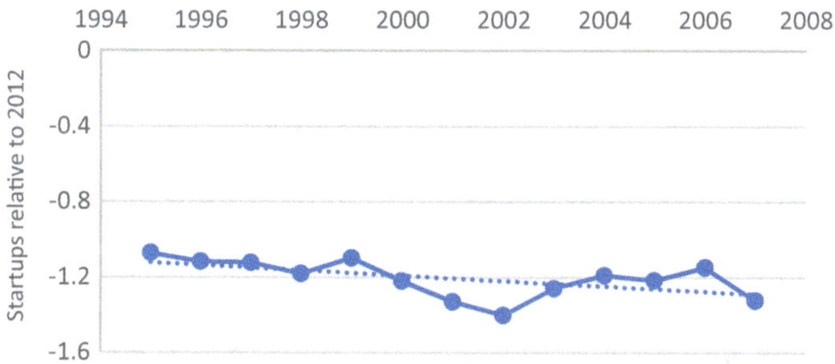

Fig. 5.3 Trend in mature startups, *indexed by 2012*: 1994–2007 (*Source* Business Employment Dynamics Data by Age and Size, BLS)

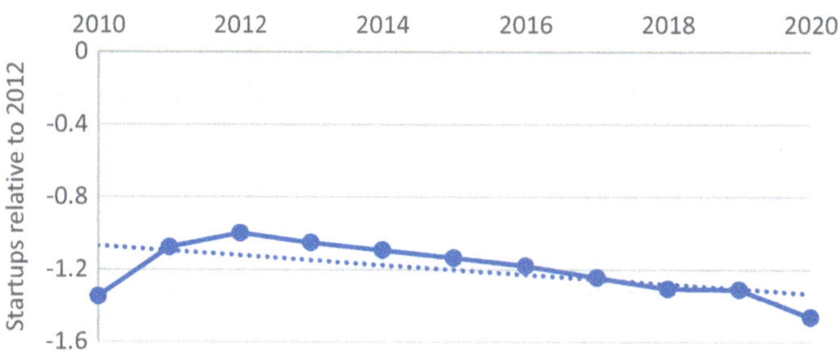

Fig. 5.4 Trend in mature startups, *indexed by 2012*: 2010–2020 (*Source* Business Employment Dynamics Data by Age and Size, BLS)

supply of flour. The fragility of the supply chain spells doom for such new businesses. In general, complementary markets, such as trucking, are vital to a startup. The crucial fact is that most trucking firms are themselves small businesses, with over 90% of the firms operating less than 6 trucks in 2019. A just-in-time inventory system has put even more emphasis on the trucking industry. This industry consists of the use of road transportation, such as semi-trailers and light trucks, to move goods across overland routes. Trucking is responsible for most of the overland freight in the U.S. In 2020, there was a huge deficit of truck drivers leading to driver wages skyrocketing [6]. Driver shortage has been simmering since 2015 when aging truck drivers began to retire—the average age of current truck drivers is high, and many are due for retirement. Long hours on the road coupled with hard working conditions have reduced the supply of drivers. Increase in motor vehicle crashes involving large trucks has caused a spike in insurance premiums for trucking companies [7].

The Delay Hypothesis

Exit of mature startups is suggestive of Robert Gordon's hypothesis that technological progress may not immediately be evident in the path of U.S. GDP growth and productivity.[3] "Overall, growth in output per capita exhibits a stunning seven-fold decline from 2.46 percent per year in 1920–70 to a mere 0.35 percent per year in 2006–16" [8]. Productivity growth is growth in the ratio of output to hours worked.[4]

The productivity paradox is the slowdown in productivity growth in the U.S. from the 2000s to the 2020s. While the desktop revolution improved supply-chain and back-office operations, the mobility revolution was expected to generate improvements in front-office operations and yet-to-be introduced new products. This downshift in growth of output per hour is due to a decline in hours worked and 40% of this is due to a

[3] "The growth rate of real GDP decelerated modestly from 3.71 percent during 1920–70 to 3.17 percent during 1970–2006 ... The second phase of the slowdown in GDP growth occurred after 2006, from 3.17 percent for 1970–2006 to a mere 1.35 percent during 2006–16" [8].

[4] Formally, the percentage change in productivity growth in any given time period is the difference between the percentage change in output growth and the percentage change in labor force growth.

decline in population growth. Without adequate labor, technology alone cannot generate output.

One factor inducing population decline is the increased mortality rate of white adults aged 35–54 with a high school or less education from 1999 to 2015. The loss of job opportunities for the cohort born around the 1980s, particularly for those with limited education, results in what Anne Case and Angus Deaton call "deaths of despair" due to suicide, drugs, and alcohol [9]. Social isolation and mental distress, accompanied by poor health, in middle-aged white non-Hispanic Americans with less than a bachelor's degree helps explain the rise of suicides. A simultaneous trend of non-participation in the labor force, in religious institutions and the institution of marriage eliminates protective institutions that may have provided much needed succor. The authors attribute these social trends not to the Great Recession but to earlier years, starting in the 1970s when median wages became stagnant for all men, and even declining at 0.2% for white men during the past 50 years.

The lack of access to public healthcare services, together with unscrupulous pharmaceutical manufacturers that promoted OxyContin, "a legalized heroin" or opioid painkiller, is cited as a cause. The total number of deaths during 2000–2017 exceeds the number that died during the two world wars. The key point is the absence of adequate support structures, both at the public and community level, as well as the presence of special interest groups that seek to enrich themselves over the needs of the less educated [9].

Plant closings and labor strife in the manufacturing sector contributed to the employment problems for this cohort of white males, with the prime working age of 35–54 during 2000–2017. These are the years that comprise some part of the time horizon considered in my analysis, which shows a slow, but steady, growth of startups during 1994–2020. However, these young businesses, lacking mentoring support and appropriate incubation, didn't survive beyond the first year.

As new technologies were implemented in the workplace, workers were replaced in various tasks due to automation. But automation also increased the efficiency of production, as workers, aided by technology, could now produce more output. If workers took home higher wages, spent more on consumption across a variety of goods and services, demand would increase. Workers then get "reinstated into a broader range of tasks" where labor has a comparative advantage. But the data show otherwise, supporting Case and Deaton's analysis. There was a "deceleration in the creation of new tasks", in particular new tasks where labor had an advantage, resulting in a stagnant labor demand over the years 1987–2017, with stagnant or even declining wages [10].

This is exactly where the creation of a new business would be the reentry point for these displaced workers. Why did this not happen and instead lead to the deaths of despair? Was there sufficient support at the grass-roots level to accommodate this "reinstatement" of displaced workers? These years also saw increased female labor force participation which is not reflected in new task creation.

In fact, "the U.S. tax code aggressively subsidizes the use of equipment (for example, various tax credits and accelerated amortization) and taxes the employment of labor (for example, via payroll taxes)" [10].

A second factor exacerbating the population growth slowdown is declining fertility rates and resistance to immigration. The impact is an increase in the age-dependency ratio of retired people plus non-working children to younger workers, suggesting a larger fiscal burden for working adults.

Third, declining labor force participation is yet another factor reducing hours worked. Lower participation for men between the ages of 25 and 54 continues a long downward trend that has taken their labor force participation rate from 98% in the 1950s to 88% today [10]. See the discussion in Chapter 9 about the implication of low participation rates and high quit rates among workers between the ages of 25 and 44.

Gordon argues that the digital revolution generated a lift to productivity only during 1996–2006 but faltered after that. New inventions are unlikely to "boost productivity growth by the same order of magnitude as the transition from typewriters and card catalogues to the personal computer and internet. ... Progress thus far suggests that the impact on productivity growth and job destruction will be gradual and evolutionary, not sudden and revolutionary" [8]. The benefits of free Internet services that arrived during 2006–2016 do not compare favorably with the social benefits created by "electric light, refrigeration and air conditioning, the replacement of scrub boards by washing machines, the replacement of horse by motor cars, the replacement of water pails by running water and of outhouses by waste removal pipes, the replacement of carrying wood and coal for heat by central heating fueled by natural gas, the arrival of free entertainment on radio and TV, and the conquest of infectious diseases and infant mortality" [8]. The innovations between 1870 and

1970 untethered women from the home and allowed entry into the larger workforce. This was the huge social welfare improvement.

The social welfare impact of digital technology cannot be weighed against past technologies such as electricity. At least, not yet. Invention of new technologies is quite different from implementation of technology and the high failure rate of startups could be due to the difficulty in fording the wide chasm between the two.

State Level Description

Since the time horizon is 26 years and the geographical dispersion is vast, a state level analysis might reveal patterns that are obliterated by the larger national picture. National measures might eclipse variation among states and present an overly dismal picture.

Three significant observations can be made upon examining the Business Employment Dynamics dataset from the Bureau of Labor Statistics. Figures 5.5 and 5.6 show the top-ranking states among mature startups during the years 1995–2020 and 2010–2020 respectively.

First, the survival rate is negatively correlated with young startup rank. Consider the states of California, Massachusetts, Missouri, Idaho, and Wisconsin, which ranked among the top 10 in both time periods for young startups. During 1995–2020, California lost 206, while Massachusetts lost 50, Missouri lost 122, Idaho lost 28, and Wisconsin lost 57 startups per year. On the other hand, Ohio, New York, Indiana,

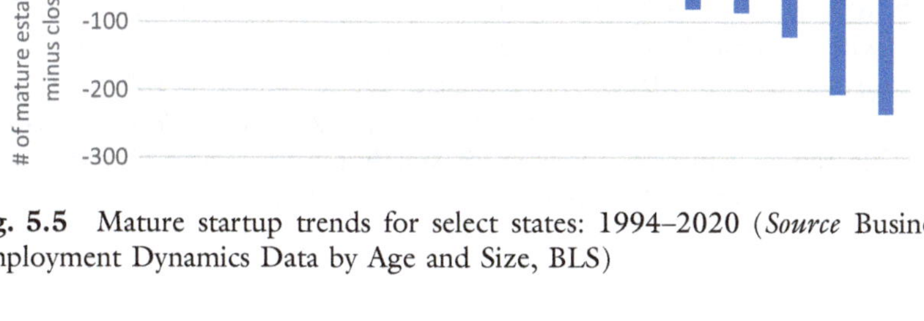

Fig. 5.5 Mature startup trends for select states: 1994–2020 (*Source* Business Employment Dynamics Data by Age and Size, BLS)

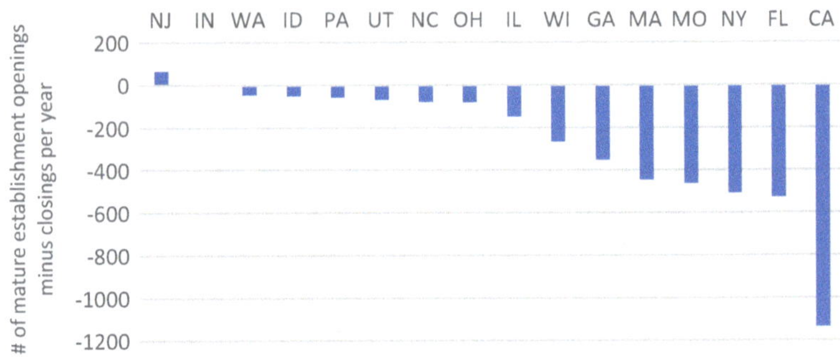

Fig. 5.6 Mature startup trend for select states: 2010–2020 (*Source* Business Employment Dynamics Data by Age and Size, BLS)

and Illinois, which had the weakest young startup trends, had positive mature startup rates of 165, 146, 64, and 21 per year, respectively—mature startups in these states were either not being acquired or were steadily surviving. Putting these numbers into perspective, consider that these states saw a young startup trend during 1994–2020 of 1703 new establishments per year in California, 202 in Massachusetts, 248 in Missouri, 80 in Idaho, and 109 in Wisconsin. Amongst startups created in these states, 12% died in California, 24% in Massachusetts, 35% in Idaho, 49% in Missouri, and a whopping 52% in Wisconsin. By contrast none died in the states with weakest early startup trends.

During the mobility revolution years of 2010–2020, Massachusetts was sixth in the ranking of startups, with 783 startups per year, while California ranked seventh with 5490 startups per year (Fig. 3.10). During these same years, Massachusetts lost 466 mature startups while California lost 1134 for an exit rate of 60% and 21% respectively. More startups are being acquired or are dying in period II compared with period I, in two of the most entrepreneurial states. Missouri, Wisconsin, and Idaho, three other top-ranking states during the mobility revolution also saw high exits, with 464 establishments vanishing in Missouri, 264 eliminated in Wisconsin and 50 in Idaho. While the exit rate dropped to 13% for Idaho, they increased during the recent decade to 57% and 52% for Missouri and Wisconsin. Almost a quarter of startups were being eliminated in California and over half in Massachusetts and Missouri.

There are two possible explanations. A state that generates much entrepreneurial activity also becomes the hunting ground for acquisitions. Deep pocketed incumbents find it more efficient to buy a new business than to create one. In the time it would take to assemble the appropriate workforce, these existing firms could absorb multiple startups. Whether the integration proceeds smoothly is questionable as organizational cultures differ and a startup mindset is uniquely different from that of an older firm. The other explanation is that the mature startup simply disintegrates for lack of direction and support, a result of flying off the wrong airstrip.

Second, the hard charging NUWMIC states in the West rank among the highest in exits.[5] These western states ranked in the top 10% among young startups during the mobility revolution with over 4% growth of new businesses, as shown in Fig. 3.10. As the startups matured, these were among the states that saw the largest acquisitions or exits as shown in Fig. 5.6. Effectively, 1134 mature startups were eliminated per year in California, 87 in Nevada, 69 in Utah, 50 in Idaho, 46 in Washington, and 19 in Montana, during period II.

Third, states east of the Mississippi that performed well among the young startups, such as Georgia and South Carolina, also had negative mature startup rates which means that startups were being acquired or simply exiting at these rates. During period II, for example, Georgia lost 351 mature establishments, South Carolina lost 147 while Virginia lost 52, for exit rates of 34%, 31%, and 14% respectively. The first two states ranked among the top 10 while Virginia was in the lowest decile among young startups.

Per Capita Results

These states differ in population which suggests that normalization by population, in addition to indexing by year, would make the results comparable. Since there is great population variation across states, it could be argued that larger states, by population, are more likely to have greater startup activity.

If we define the working age population as being those between the ages of 18 and 64 years, we can construct per capita mature startups.

[5] Recall, from the discussion in Chapter 3, that NUWMIC is the acronym for Nevada, Utah, Washington, Montana, Idaho, and California.

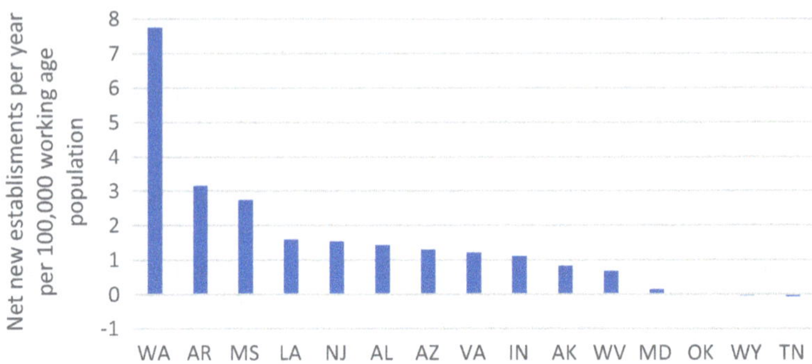

Fig. 5.7 Per capita mature startup trend: 2010–2019 (*Source* Business Employment Dynamics Data by Age and Size, BLS)

A ranking of states by mature startups for every 100,000 individuals is shown in Fig. 5.7. This diagram should be interpreted with caution. Reflecting the large exit rates in the more entrepreneurial states, the per capita numbers simply suggest that regions with low population and weak young startup activity rank higher in per capita terms. However, the state of Washington is the exception in that despite its high ranking among young startups, it saw a decreasing exit rate. Fewer mature startups were being acquired or exiting in the state. This could be the effect of young businesses moving from California to Washington, as founders escape the higher costs of living in the Silicon Valley area.

Acquisition by the Behemoths or Absence of Support Architecture

What are the factors that encourage startups or inhibit their development? Do technological innovations, and improvements impounded into new products and services, new ways of organizing a business, have little capacity for persistence? Or is there an absence of support architecture?

The slow disappearance of mature startups could be attributed to their acquisition by larger, well-established firms, as in the case of Pfizer and the startup BioNTech discussed earlier in the chapter. In the case of an innovative new businesses with a patent in hand, the lure of distribution and marketing at scale is compelling. Strategic partnerships have long been an important source of drug discovery. Big pharmaceutical companies have been forming partnerships and alliances with smaller biotech innovators to market, and in some cases increase research productivity or drug discoveries due to deeper resources. From the smaller biotech startup's perspective big pharma expands the geographical distribution network of the drug by managing later-stage development and commercialization.

Biotech startups are comprised of researchers in academia and other organizations who can specialize in more diseases and afflictions. The level of scientific expertise in biotech is extremely high today and is better financed than previously. Venture capitalists are looking to fund biotech, so early stage financing is not scarce. Moreover, the research tools and expertise that were once the exclusive domain of large pharma are now widely available. While biotech may acquire the patent protection, they lack the resources for preclinical development that would weed out toxicity issues. Big pharma has the infrastructure in most countries to conduct clinical trials. "There's data out there showing that of the recent molecules many big pharma companies launched over the past five years, often around 90% of them have a very significant component that came from the outside" [11].

What other factors could inhibit the development of young firms? The logistics can be costly. Administrative and labor costs could swamp the financial resources that startups raised during their first year, and additional funding from venture capitalists might not be forthcoming.

New businesses have to cross several administrative hurdles such as choosing a name and location, registering the business, getting federal and state tax ID numbers, applying for licenses and permits where applicable, opening a business bank account, and getting business insurance. Some states make this process less cumbersome than others by having a centralized directory and advisory. In addition, local business expenses such as minimum wage laws, business insurance rates, utilities and government licenses and fees can add up to a sizable amount. Additionally, there may be local zoning ordinances and state and local taxes and incentives.

Could minimum wage laws be holding up business development? Among the top 10 startup states, Washington has the highest minimum wage at $14.49 per hour, with Massachusetts following at $14.25 per hour and California at $14 per hour for establishments with less than 26 employees and $15 for larger than 26 employee-businesses. Missouri has $11.15, Virginia has $11, Nebraska has $9, while Idaho, North Dakota, Texas, and Wisconsin are at $7.25 per hour which is the current federal minimum wage. New York has $13.20 and Florida has

$10. Clearly, state minimum wage laws appear to have little correlation with startup activity [12].

Unlike large companies that can access public stock markets for financial resources, startup or private companies must access private equity funding. Startup funding can come from multiple sources, such as family and friends to professional "accelerators" or "incubators" that provide mentorship to fledgling businesses.

Recent data show an unbalanced distribution of venture funding across states. Much like the distribution of income, the venture dollars spent on the top three states accounted for three quarters of the total funding for all states: California, New York, and Massachusetts [13].

California's ranking among the top states appears to confirm general expectations of Silicon Valley as historically being the hub of new businesses. According to data from Statista, California led way in 2020 with $84 billion, followed by New York at $18 billion, Massachusetts with $17.3 billion, Washington and Texas with $4.8 billion each, North Carolina with $3.6 billion, and Michigan, Colorado, Illinois, Pennsylvania, and Georgia with $2–3 billion [13]. Of these, the eastern states New York, Michigan, Pennsylvania, and Illinois have very little entrepreneurial activity.

Only 5 of the top 15 states with high young startup activity during 2010–2020 received over $1 billion. This suggests that there is little overlap between huge venture funding in a state and that state's ranking in either young or mature startups.

Industries and Sectors

What are the drivers of the economy in these states? What are the sectors and industries that provide the pasture for startups in these states? Prominent contributors to the output of a given state could provide a signal as to the location of entrepreneurial activity. Deducing from broad sectoral drivers one can form a sketch of the budding new ventures that might have sprouted within these sectors, which are defined on a wide enough canvas so as to encompass a range of new enterprises. The rationale is that if certain sectors contributed significantly to a state's economy, then startups are quite likely to be related, either directly or indirectly via the supply chain or are ancillary to these industries.

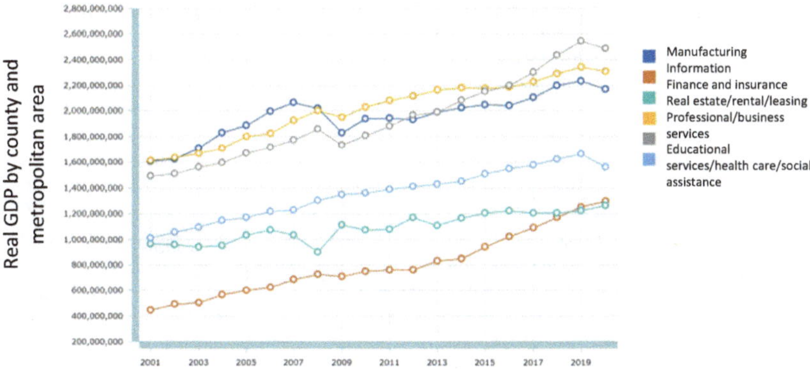

Fig. 5.8 U.S. value added by industry as a percent of GDP (*Source* U.S. Bureau of Economic Analysis)

Before detailed state analysis, consider the sectors that have contributed most to national economic growth in recent years: professional and business services (PBS); real estate, rental, and leasing (RRL); education and health services (E&H); finance and insurance (F&I) and information. The category professional and business services comprises (i) professional, scientific, and technical services (ii) management of companies and enterprises and (iii) administrative and support and waste management.[6]

PBS and RRL have overtaken manufacturing at the national level [8]. As shown in Fig. 5.8, PBS strikes out on an upward trend, overtaking manufacturing and RRL around 2015 to position itself as the top contributor to national output. Taking second position is RRL and third in the ranking of contributors to the national economy is manufacturing. Education and health services are fourth and rising rapidly, since 2013, to the fifth place is information. The state level diagrams are shown in Fig. 5.9 for select top-ranking states.

These sectors comprise large and small businesses, young and old. Buoyed by the strength in these economic groups, new businesses would emerge, firstly because there are direct economic opportunities and, secondly, there is demand for complementary services and products.

Colby Thrift and Adam Haney are co-founders of Mora Technologies in Warrensburg, Missouri. This startup, opened in January 2021, focuses

[6] These sectors correspond to the 2-digit NAICS codes, 54, 55, and 56.

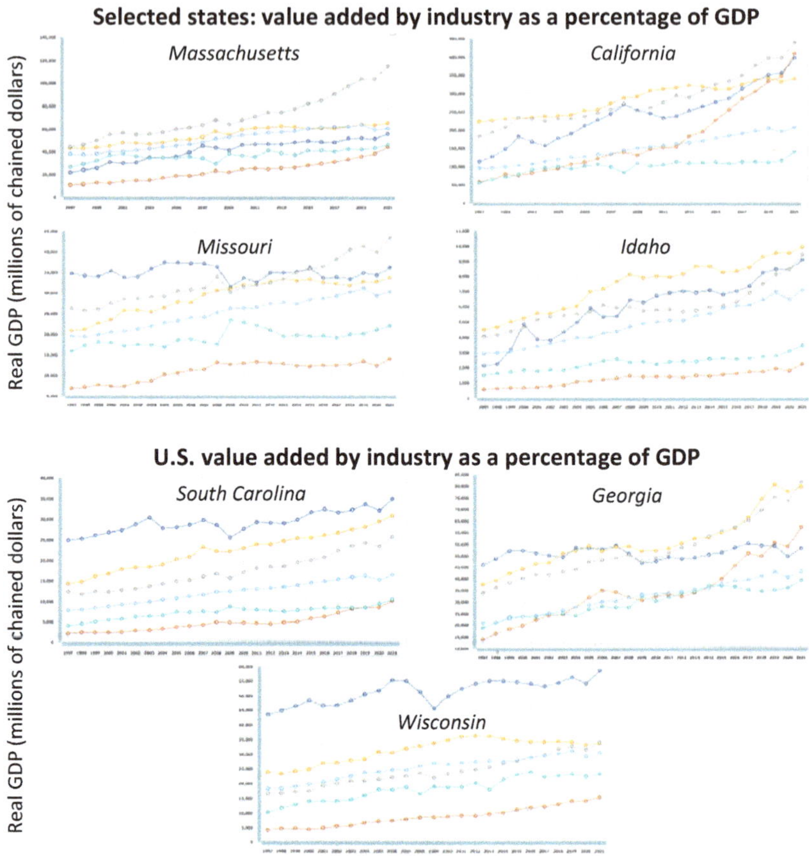

Fig. 5.9 Value added by industry, select states (*Source* U.S. Bureau of Economic Analysis, https://apps.bea.gov/itable/iTable.cfm?ReqID=70&step=1&acrdn=1)

on business automation, with higher level programming. One of their products is hand-held and stationary code scanners which can read traditional bar codes, QR codes and Optical Character Recognition (OCR), enabling inventory management and order fulfillment [14].

In many cases, the startups may not share the same NAICS code as professional and business services but apply business matching platforms to grow their fledgling enterprise. Jennifer Hart started her own design-build company in 2010, Hartline Construction in Kansas City, Missouri, focusing on carpentry packages. Carpentry, trim, painting, and tile at Kansas City International Airport's modernized terminal, to be completed by 2023, is being done by Hartline. Hart enrolled in the Elevate program offered by the Missouri Small Business Development Center, which matched the business founder with mentors and consultants across the nation using digital communication technologies. Listening to peers share their experience, gave Hart the overall vision for her business [15].

Similarly, using the tools of digital technology, such as social media, Tameka Stigers, leveraged the social media presence and launched the beauty supply company, Locs of Glory, in 2009, catering to the demand for natural hair care for Black people in St Louis, Missouri. The vast reach of the social platform allowed Tameka to create the business with minimal marketing expenditures, friends tweeted to friends generating membership closure around the new business. Initially, the business was run from the basement, then moved to a remodeled back porch, and later expanded to Black Beauty Supply, which delivers products to salons and barbershops [16].

These examples reveal a larger pattern, the widespread application of existing digital communication technologies to new business ventures. Startups can be invention-based, innovation-based, and implementation-based. The Covid vaccine invented by BioNTech is an example of the first, while innovation and implementation, which involve solving old problems in a new and better way by applying existing technologies, is illustrated by Jennifer Hart's business as well as Tamika Stigers' startup.

This model is best elucidated by looking at the state level trends in the top performing sectors. State data cover the period 1997–2021, and in general, these patterns are persistent throughout those years, but one trend that occurs is meaningful. The preponderance of services in the digital economy is revealed by the dominance of professional and business services, real estate, rental, and leasing services, and education and health services. All three rank among the top 3 drivers of the economy of high-ranking states in the mobility revolution, as well as that of many states during the desktop revolution (see Fig. 5.9).

The professional and business services sector is not only among the top three contributors across all years comprising the digital revolution but overtakes other sectors around the year 2015 in several states, such as Massachusetts and Missouri to become the top contributor to the state's GDP. We examine the dominant sectors and then the states in the following sections.

The Professional and Business Services Sector

This sector was not only dominant in the national economy in 2020 but was the principal driver of the economies of several states ranking among the top in both period I and period II. The professional and business services sector, PBS, aggregates professional, scientific, and technical services; management of companies and enterprises; and administrative and waste management services.

Professional and business services dominated the state economies, ranking among the top 3 contributors, of all the states that played a large role in both of the digital revolutions. In other words, this sector was either the most important contributor, or the second or third contributor, to the top startup state economies during the entire period, 1997–2020. These rankings provide some evidence that the startup trends were, to a very large extent, in the professional and business services sector.

Massachusetts, Virginia, and Nevada were supercharged by the professional and business services sector throughout the period 1997–2020. This sector was the second driver in the states economies of Nevada and Florida; and the third driver in South Carolina, Washington, Utah, and Montana for the entire period, 1997–2020. In the years after the Great Recession, between 2012 and 2015, this sector began to dominate the economies of California, Texas, Georgia, North Carolina, Colorado, and New Jersey.

Real Estate, Rental, and Leasing Sector

The real estate, rental, and leasing sector dominates as the principal contributor to several states' GDP and is prominent in all the states that rank high during the mobility and desktop revolutions. This sector consists of activities related to real estate, automotive equipment rental and leasing, consumer goods rental, commercial and industrial machinery rental and leasing. It also includes lessor of non-financial intangible assets (except copyrighted works) such as patent buying, licensing, and leasing.

Consistently across the top states and across the time period 1997–2020, RRL ranked first or second. In Idaho, Montana, Nevada, and Florida, the sector was consistently the principal driver of the economy.

Across all the years, the sector was the second most important in the states of Massachusetts, Washington, Wisconsin, Virginia and South and North Carolina, Colorado, and Nebraska. In Texas and Missouri, it was the third-ranking sector in importance.

In the years prior to the Great Recession, this sector was the most important in California, North Dakota, Idaho, Florida, Georgia, Utah, Montana, and Nevada but then dropped to second place during the mobility revolution. In the years after the Great Recession, RRL was the major driver of the economies of Idaho, Nevada, Montana.

The real estate, rental, and leasing sector also includes industries such as professional employer organizations or PEO. These firms lease employees and manage all the human resources, payroll and employee benefit functions for their clients, who retain the daily management of these workers. Employee leasing is a valuable organizational tool for firms with seasonal swings in their workforce, as in agriculture. Rather than temporary layoffs, the business can lease workers for the required time period. This organizational format is also valuable to small businesses which cannot provide worker benefits, such as the employer share of FICA, Medicare, and unemployment insurance withholdings. Contractors or independent workers can be classified as leased employees by a small business, rather than temporary employees, if the small business does not pay the benefits but manages the daily operations of the workers.

The leased workers are counted as employees of the PEOs for tax purposes. For example, in 2018 Florida ranked first in PEOs with 520 such organizations that employed 1.3 million workers with an annual payroll of $62.5 billion. Note that these workers would have been leased to other businesses and hence not worked in Florida itself. However, they are counted as employees of the PEO in Florida. Nationwide, in 2018 there were 451 PEOs with more than 1000 employees and these had 88% of the 3 million employees in the PEO industry [17].

What does the prominence of RRL signify for startup activity? This sector is primarily concerned with operators involved in the management, sale, purchase, and rent of real estate. The sector also includes the renting and leasing of tangible goods, such as equipment, and intangible goods like patents and copyrights, as Americans replace ownership of assets with rental contracts. The former would impose large costs at the front end, requiring cash-on-hand or borrowing capacity. The latter depends upon short-term liquidity since rental payments are made on a monthly or quarterly, and perhaps in some instances, annual basis. The purchase contract is more likely to lead to a liquidity problem should cash flow not cover interest payments on the original borrowed amount and spiral the firm into bankruptcy to reorganize the financial structure of firms. Like wages and salaries, rental payments constitute an on-going cost of running the business. The PPP program instituted in March 2020 as part of the CARES ACT, was meant to provide a shortstop for payables, due to the pandemic emergency.

Also, under RRL is the "Cowboy Cocktail", a financial arrangement consisting of a trust and private companies with hidden ownership [18]. These trusts were identified in The Pandora Papers, an investigative report filed by The International Consortium of Investigative Journalists (ICIJ) and The Washington Post that exposes the movement of private family wealth around the globe. This financial arrangement has three ingredients. (i) A Wyoming trust and a nested group of private companies with hidden ownership, (ii) The trust owns another company, a limited liability company, where the families place their assets, and (iii) Some families create another company to oversee the trust.[7]

Individuals who work for these trusts as their agent are known as company representatives, and they do the routine job of filing incorporation documents and annual reports. More often, they are unaware of the exact business, usually incorporated as a limited liability company (LLC), that is paying them the nominal fee. The business places a private company at the center of the trust, and often a second company holds financial assets. The sprawling industry—comprising attorneys, part-time participants, and multistate specialty operations representing thousands of businesses—is a weak point in the U.S. financial system.

Wyoming, Delaware, and Nevada have been at the forefront of a national debate about whether to ramp up oversight of registered agents. Those states and a handful of others are havens for hidden wealth, prized by company owners for their low incorporation fees, scant regulation and offers of anonymity. Wyoming's state lawmakers approved, in 1977, the formation of limited liability companies that would locate in the state and

[7] The offshore financial system allows people to follow the financial laws of a country different from the country of residence. They can shelter their wealth in these offshore financial centers in entities called trusts or holding companies or shell companies. These trusts reduce the tax revenue of their home countries. The owners of these offshore entities include Jordan's King Abdullah II, the Czech Republic's prime minister and the president of Ukraine, among others.

add to its declining state revenues formerly from taxes on fossil fuels. The laws were amended until finally, in 2011 the Cowboy Cocktail took off. "A Cowboy Cocktail is a double-barreled approach to asset protection that may be the best thing since sliced bread" according to one estate planner [19]. There are a few regulated trusts and hundreds of unregulated trusts with assets of $100 million or more. Wyoming is ranked ahead of North Dakota, another international tax haven, along with Alaska, Delaware, and Nevada. Sioux Falls, South Dakota now rivals locations in the Caribbean, when a financial firm called Trident Trust set up an office in Sioux Falls, South Dakota, relying on the state's laws that were tax-friendly.

In October 2021, a bipartisan group of lawmakers proposed federal legislation that would require registered agents to scrutinize clients and report suspicious transactions. They drafted a measure called the Enablers Act, following publication of the Pandora Papers, a global investigation by the International Consortium of Investigative Journalists (ICIJ), The Washington Post and other media partners exposing how the global elite shield their riches from taxing authorities, criminal probes, and public accountability. Congressman Tom Malinowski, a key sponsor of the legislation, feels that states have not acted responsibly in laundering money. Since Russia invaded Ukraine, governments have hastened to freeze assets held by Russian oligarchs, such as Igor Makarov, who held real estate and a private jet through an LLC and trust in Wyoming, one of the most secretive tax havens [20].

Education and Health

Education services and health care and social assistance are aggregated as E&H, and provide public or privately-owned education, inpatient and outpatient health care services, nursing care and social assistance for individuals. Not only is this sector the fourth largest contributor to national output, but state universities are the largest employers in California, Wisconsin, Michigan, North Carolina, New York, Nebraska, New Mexico, Iowa, and Vermont. For example, the University of Wisconsin at Madison employs 39,000 people or 1% of the state's working age population.

The pandemic has, of course, altered market interactions substantially and it would be fair to expect education and health services to be on the upward trend in all states during the past few years. This is not born out by the data. E&H ranks at third place in Massachusetts and Nevada, while remaining at the fourth or even fifth level for all other states that are spurring the startup revolution. The same could be said for the Finance and Insurance industry as well as Information.

Information includes the publishing industries (except software); the motion picture and sound recording industries; broadcasting and telecommunications; data processing; digital publishing and other information services.

Finance and Insurance includes Federal Reserve banks, credit intermediation and related services; securities and commodities contracts; insurance carriers; funds, trusts and other financial vehicles.

Manufacturing

Manufacturing used to be the lifeblood of the economy until the digital revolution, marked by the introduction of the computer and the World Wide Web. Across the entire period under consideration, manufacturing has retained its prominence in Wisconsin, Utah, Nevada, Nebraska, North and South Carolina.

It was the second most important sector in Idaho and the third most important in Virginia. In the years preceding the Great Recession, manufacturing was the primary sector in Missouri, Georgia, and Washington. As mentioned earlier, PBS became important in Missouri after 2014, RRL and PBS took over in Georgia after 2007. The information sector took off on an exponential path in the state of Washington after 2015.

In California, manufacturing is equally important to the state's economy as information, and is, in fact, a rising sector in the state. Manufacturing is not the old-fashioned kind which uses lots of machinery and levers and pulleys; it is automated, with software controlling the hardware, combining artificial intelligence with robot movement.

In fact, manufacturing today is vastly different from the assembly-line technology used in the past. The integration of multiple manufacturing devices can be seamlessly achieved by equipping them with sensors, identification, processing, communication, and networking capabilities. For example, the connectivity between smart machines, warehousing systems, and production facilities can facilitate autonomous information exchange, initiate actions, and control the system independently. Sensors on Internet of Things systems generate huge data sets upon which algorithms can be trained for predictive maintenance purposes. Radio-frequency identification uses electromagnetic fields to transfer data for the identification and tracking of tags attached to objects. The tags contain information about the object allowing improved supply chain management and production scheduling. Wireless sensor networks also provide connectivity by sending their data to the base station for processing [21].

It is estimated that the U.S. manufacturing industry spends $200 billion on maintenance of plant equipment and facilities. For example, predictive maintenance uses machine learning to define the actual condition of the system and equipment and forecast its future states, predicting when it will require maintenance. This is a pro-active process, not a reaction to machine breakdown. As such, the deliberative maintenance prevents unforeseen delays. Utilizing data from past performance of the machines, the algorithms can predict faults and signal maintenance schedules, all the while preventing random breakdowns which deplete resources [22].

Oil and Gas

Wyoming, Montana, North and South Dakota are home to over 500,000 acres of oil and gas wells on federal lands. The data show the total number of acres of land covered by producing leases as of the last day of the fiscal year. The states with the highest average acres under production during 2001–2020 are Wyoming and New Mexico (both with over 3.5 million acres), Utah (1 million acres), Montana (over 700,000 acres), and North Dakota (450,000 acres) [23].

The Wyoming territory covers both Nebraska and Wyoming with 42 million acres of fluid mineral estate and 10 million acres of oil and gas leases, the largest of any state in the nation. The New Mexico territory, comprising New Mexico, Oklahoma, Texas, and Kansas covers two of the most prolific oil and gas basins in the U.S.—the San Juan Basin in the northwest corner and the Permian basin in the southeast. This four-state area has over 45 million acres of mineral estate.

The Rocky Mountain Region around Utah holds large reserves of onshore oil and gas deposits. The conflicts between multiple stakeholders in the regions rich in oil and gas resources are illustrated by the Moab Master Leasing Plan. This plan covers over 700,000 acres of public lands in Utah's Grand and San Juan counties, home to Arches and Canyonlands National Parks, and also to the Ancestral Puebloans who once called it home. The plan includes protection of high-use recreation areas and those with "high scenic quality" [24].

The Montana area covers North and South Dakota as well as Montana. Note that oil and gas extraction has blossomed at the national level since 2010 and the corresponding path for this industry is matched by North Dakota, Utah, and Montana, which rank highest, after Texas, in terms of the real dollar value of output in mining, quarrying, and oil and gas extraction industry (NAICS 21) [25].

Surprisingly, the oil and gas extraction sector is dominant only in the states of North Dakota and Texas. In the former, the sector surpasses manufacturing and education and health in 2013, and real estate, rental, and leasing in 2015. By contrast, in Utah, oil and gas extraction lags behind manufacturing, RRL, PBS as well as information, a sector which is rapidly rising in Utah. In Montana, RRL and E&H dominate the economy. What was special about the year 2015? Congress lifted the ban on oil exports, as discussed below.

State-By-Industry Portrait

Recall the distinction made in Chapter 3 about geography—ten and eleven of the top 15 states in both the revolutions in period I and period II, respectively, were in states west of the Mississippi. Since PBS is a dominant force in most of these states, we can now perceive how the intersection of geography and industry presents itself. The diagrams in Fig. 5.9 illustrate the discussion, for some states, showing the size of each industry in each state's economy in millions of dollars (normalized or chained to 2012).

The Northeast Region

Massachusetts

Associated with the internationally renowned research and educational institutions, Harvard and MIT, it is small wonder that the professional and business sector has been consistently the principal driver of Massachusetts' economy since 1997. In particular, the sector, professional, scientific, and technical services (PST), overtook real estate, rental, and leasing (RRL) and education and health care (E&H) around the year 2015 to become the top sector in terms of its contribution to state

GDP. The two sectors, RRL and E&H, are roughly equal contributors to Massachusetts' economy, tying for second place.

Wisconsin

Professional, scientific, and technical services do not rank high in Wisconsin's GDP. The largest contributor to GDP in Wisconsin is manufacturing followed by RRL. Kohl's is the state's largest private employer, but overall, the University of Wisconsin at Madison is the state's largest employer [26]. Until 2017 E&H ranked third, but was then overtaken by PBS, which is clearly on an upward trend in the state.

The Southern Region

Georgia and South Carolina

Home Depot, UPS, and Delta call the state of Georgia their home. And, of course, the old favorite, Coca-Cola in Atlanta. A steady upward trajectory of three sectors delineates the economic picture for Georgia. PBS, RRl, and Information strike out around 2010, and land in first, second, and third place, respectively by 2020. In 2007, PBS ranked second and RRL ranked first. Information was a distant fourth as manufacturing still retained its number 3 ranking. Overall, PBS has been a strong contributor to Georgia's economy, employing just under 60% of the state's workers [27].

South Carolina differs, in that PBS drops to third place. The state has a very consistent pattern that prevails during the entire period 1997–2020, with manufacturing leading, followed by RRL and then professional and business services as a steady third place contributor. Michelin Tire is the largest company headquartered in South Carolina.

Texas

Oil and gas extraction overtook manufacturing around 2015, perhaps related to legislations enacted by Congress in 2015, to become the leading provider for the state. PBS is also on a strong upward trend, tying with oil and gas at the top. In 2007, PBS was second, just ahead of RRL, but behind manufacturing which was dominant until the mid-teens.

The Midwestern Region

Missouri

Sitting on the west bank of the Mississippi river, the Gateway Arch monument in St Louis, Missouri, stands as a gateway to the west and commemorates the Louisiana Purchase of 1803 and the subsequent opening of the West following the Lewis and Clark Expedition of 1804–1806. It became the crossroads of westwards travel and the start of the Santa Fe, California and Oregon trails, and the center of fur-trading. The St Louis Symphony Orchestra is one of the oldest in the U.S. [28]. Missouri follows a pattern similar to the national trends, with PBS leading, followed by manufacturing, RRL, E&H, and F&I. It was not always so. In 2007, manufacturing ranked higher than PBS, which crossed over in 2015 to become number one.

Nebraska and North Dakota

Berkshire Hathaway leads as the state's largest employer by factor of 10 compared to the second largest employer, Union Pacific Railroad [29]. Finance and insurance play a dominant role in Nebraska. F&I has a jagged trajectory starting at the fifth rank but becoming the biggest contributor to the state's GDP around 2015, followed by manufacturing, PBS and RRI.

Oil and gas come tearing into North Dakota's economy, rising to the dominant sector around 2015. RRl and E&H follow in second and third place. Recall that oil and gas extraction demonstrated a similar trajectory in Texas' economy around 2015.

Since Congress lifted the ban on oil exports in 2015, all U.S. drilled oil and natural gas have been sold on the international markets. Geopolitics now sets the price of oil and gas in the U.S. The average U.S. price for regular gasoline was around $4 at the pump in July 2008, falling to a low of $2 in February 2015. It has since gradually risen, reverting to its previous high of $4 in March 2022. In 2020, the U.S. had 20% of the world share of oil production, dwarfing Saudi Arabia's 12% and Russia's 11%. But the grim humor in this market is that the U.S. also accounts for 20% of total world oil consumption in 2019, followed by China (14%) and India (5%) [30].

The vast majority of oil production comes from tight formations that necessitates the use of hydraulic fracturing technology and up to 95%

of new well drilled today are hydraulically fractured. However, environmental groups are blocking the development of critical infrastructure, due to concerns over freshwater use and wastewater disposal, ground water contamination, and other disturbances. "Despite these challenges, an unprecedented opportunity has emerged for the U.S. Vast new reserves of unconventional domestic oil and gas have been opened up over the last five years, using recent advances in hydraulic fracturing and horizontal drilling. U.S. production of natural gas has increased by 35% since 2005, eliminating the need for gas imports. Oil production has increased by 45% since 2010, restoring the U.S. as the second largest oil producer in the world for the first time since 1991", according to a report by Michael Porter et al. [31]. The unintended impact of this surge in U.S. oil production is cheap gas, shifting the demand for bigger, less fuel-efficient cars upward. This demand shift and corresponding increase in oil revenues spills over to foreign providers of oil, such as Russia and Saudi Arabia [32].

The Western Region

Idaho and Montana

Both states have RRL as their dominant driver. Home to Panera Bread, Albertson's and Micron Technology, Idaho's economy, in 2020, was dominated by the real estate, rental, and leasing industry (RRL), followed by manufacturing, PBS, E&H, and F&I. This pattern was persistent across the years 2001–2020, except that manufacturing rose from third to second place over the two decades. PBS is creating an upset with a strong upward trend and could become the top contributor in 2022.

Montana has a clear consistent picture throughout the years, with RRL dominating, followed by F&I and then PBS. Manufacturing comes in at fourth place. Home to Glacier National Park, Sklar Bikes and Simms Fishing Products, Montana has unparalleled outdoor recreation opportunities. But most of the recent growth is in the PBS sector. Following the Oracle purchase of Bozeman-based cloud-software company RightNow Technologies in 2012, former workers are funding technology startups, attracting workers from California and the East.

Colorado, Nevada, and Utah

All three contiguous states have PBS as the second largest contributor to state GDP. Natural beauty is the hallmark of these states. Between them, these states have 11 national parks, 19 national forests, and at least 30 world-renowned skiing areas. Utah alone has 5 national parks, 6 national forests, and 10 ski resorts.

Colorado, home to Coors Brewing Company as well as Dish Network, is strongly supported by RRL and PBS during the entire 20-year period. The third largest contributor is E&H. Nevada has a steady pattern, with RRL dominating, followed by PBS in second place throughout the 25-year period. E&H follow in third place. In Utah, manufacturing and RRL run neck-and-neck upward in a narrow band from 1997 until 2019, when PBS, which was number three in 2007 pulls ahead to the number two spot.

California and Washington

Both of these states have been lifted by the searing upwards trajectory of the information sector, with Walt Disney being the fifth largest employer in 2021 in California. Westcon-Comstor, a global technology provider, first founded in an upstate New York garage is the state's second largest employer, after Wells Fargo [29]. This sector comprises newspaper publishers, software publishers, the motion picture and video industries, sound recording industries, radio and television broadcasting, wireless and satellite communications carriers, data processing and other information services—both the physical and digital side of information transmission.

The Information sector strikes an upward path in California's economy starting in 2012, becoming the second largest contributor to the state's GDP in 2021. PBS, which was second most important in 2007, rises to the top spot by 2020, barely keeping ahead of information. Manufacturing is the third largest contributor with RRL in the fourth place.

Home to Starbucks and Costco, Washington is remarkable in that Information pulls ahead after 2010 and is the number one sector in the state by 2015. Manufacturing and RRL are the second and third—until 2020 when PBS creeps ahead, just slightly. In a state that houses Amazon and Microsoft, it is perhaps Boeing, and complimentary sectors servicing the aerospace industry, that takes the larger slice of the state's GDP. Despite Boing's departure—Boing left its Seattle headquarters in September 2001, following its 1997 merger with St Louis, Missouri-based McDonnell Douglas in 1997—fixed wing aircraft are the state's leading export. Paccar, a leading manufacturer of light, medium, and heavy duty trucks is the seventh largest company based in Washington.

Taxation

Most states tax at least some types of business income derived from the state. As a general rule, the details of how income from a specific business is taxed depend upon its legal form. In most states, corporations are subject to a corporate income tax, while income from pass-through entities such as S corporations, limited liability companies (LLCs), partnerships and sole proprietorships—which is the principal organizational format for startups—are only subject to a state's tax on persona income.

Taxable income from an S corporation or an LLC is passed through to the individual shareholders, and each individual shareholder is subject to federal tax on his or her share of the corporation's income. The corporate rates vary from 4 to 10%, but personal rates vary depending upon the amount of income.

Six states do not have a corporate income tax—Nevada, South Dakota, Wyoming, Washington, Texas, and Ohio. All these states, except Ohio, also have no personal income tax. Florida and Alaska also have no personal income tax. Note that of these six states, Washington and Nevada rank among the top 10 startup states in both the desktop digital revolution as well as the mobility digital revolution. Could the low tax rates on personal income, which is the appropriate consideration for a startup, be a cause?

Bibliography

1 Pfizer website. 2022. https://www.pfizer.com/news/press-release/press-release-detail/pfizer-and-biontech-sign-new-global-collaboration-agreement.
2 Birch, David G.W. 1979. *The Job Generation Process*. University of Illinois at Urbana-Champaign's Academy for Entrepreneurial Leadership Historical Research Reference in Entrepreneurship. Available at SSRN: https://ssrn.com/abstract=1510007.
3 U.S. Census Bureau. 2019 SUSB Annual Data Tables. https://www.census.gov/data/tables/2019/econ/susb/2019-susb-annual.html.
4 Kaufmann Foundation Report. 2010. The Importance of Startups in Job Creation and Job Destruction. https://www.kauffman.org/wp-content/uploads/2019/12/firm_formation_importance_of_startups.pdf.
5 Hurst, Erik and Benjamin Wild Pugsley. 2011. What Do Small Businesses Do? *Brookings Papers on Economic Activity, Economic Studies Program* 43(2 (Fall)): 73–142.
6 American Trucking Association. 2022. Economics and Industry Data. https://www.trucking.org/economics-and-industry-data.

7 Kearny, John. 2019. Big Rig Safety Tech and Trucking Insurance Hikes. NJ Property Casualty 360. https://www.propertycasualty360.com/2019/01/22/big-rig-safety-tech-and-trucking-insurance-rate-hikes/.

8 Gordon, Robert. 2018. Why Has Economic Growth Slowed When Innovation Appears to Be Accelerating? *NBER Working Paper 24554*. https://doi.org/10.3386/w24554.

9 Case, Anne and Angus Deaton. 2020. *Death of Despair and the Future of Capitalism*. Princeton University Press, ISBN: 9780691190785

10 Acemoglu, Daron and Pascual Restrepo. 2019. Automation and New Tasks: How Technology Displaces and Reinstates Labor. *Journal of Economic Perspectives* 33(2). https://doi.org/10.1257/jep.33.2.3.

11 Brown, Noel and Grea Wiederrecht. 2021. Biotech and Big Pharma: Blueprint for Successful Partnership. RBC Capital Markets, October 5. https://www.rbccm.com/en/gib/biopharma/episode/biotech-and-big-pharma-blueprint-for-successful-partnership?utm_source=pitchbook&utm_medium=en&utm_campaign=rbccm_biotech_2021_amer_united_states_of_america_awareness&utm_term=299004261&utm_content=dailypitch_partnershipnewrules.

12 State Minimum Wage Laws. 2022. https://www.dol.gov/agencies/whd/minimum-wage/state.

13 Statista. 2022. https://www.statista.com/statistics/424167/venture-capital-investments-usa-by-state/#:~:text=In%202020%2C%20the%20state%20which,dollars'%20worth%20of%20VC%20invested.

14 Mora Technologies. 2022. https://www.moratechusa.com/vision.

15 Missouri Small Business Development Center. 2021. Hartline Construction. https://sbdc.missouri.edu/news/self-performing-woman-owned-construction-business-pushing-it-forward-hartline-construction-kansas-city-mo-5330.

16 Small Business Development Center of Missouri. 2022. https://sbdc.missouri.edu/news.

17 Hait, Andrew. 2021. Number of Workers of Employee Leasing Firms Soared 686% from 1992 to 2017. U.S. Census Bureau. https://www.census.gov/library/stories/2021/05/businesses-lease-cars-office-space-furniture-and-workers.html.

18 Cenziper, Debbie, et al. 2021. The Cowboy Cocktail: How Wyoming Became One of the World's Top Tax Havens, The Pandora Papers. *The Washington Post*, December 20. https://www.washingtonpost.com/business/interactive/2021/wyoming-trusts-finance-pandora-papers/.

19 Cenziper, Debbie, et al. 2022. The Gatekeepers Who Open America to Shell Companies and Secret Owners, The Pandora Papers. *The Washington Post*, April 5. https://www.washingtonpost.com/business/interactive/2022/tax-havens-wyoming-pandora-papers/.

20 Bureau of Land Management, Energy and Mineral Development. 2022. https://www.blm.gov/programs/energy-and-minerals.
21 Yang, C., W. Shen and X. Wang. 2018. The Internet of Things in Manufacturing: Key Issues and Potential Applications. *IEEE Systems, Man, and Cybernetics Magazine* 4(1): 6-15. https://doi.org/10.1109/MSMC.2017.2702391.
22 Amruthnath, Nagdev and Tarun Gupta. April 2018. A Research Study on Unsupervised Machine Learning Algorithms for Fault Detection in Predictive Maintenance. https://doi.org/10.13140/RG.2.2.28822.24648.
23 BLM National NEPA Register. 2022. https://eplanning.blm.gov/eplanning-ui/project/68430/560.
24 Bureau of Economic Analysis, GDP-by-Industry. 2022. https://apps.bea.gov/iTable/index_industry_gdpIndy.cfm.
25 Bureau of Economic Analysis, New Release. December 22, 2021. https://www.bea.gov/sites/default/files/2021-12/gdp3q21_3rd.pdf.
26 Slater, Sauter. 2018. The Largest Employer in Every State. https://247wallst.com/special-report/2018/04/18/largest-employer-in-every-state-2/2/.
27 Georgia Small Business Economic Profiles for 2018. 2022. https://www.sba.gov/sites/default/files/advocacy/2018-Small-Business-Profiles-GA.pdf.
28 Gateway Arch. 2022. https://www.britannica.com/topic/Gateway-Arch.
29 Statista. 2022. https://www.statista.com/statistics/1018670/leading-companies-headquartered-california-number-employees/.
30 U.S. Energy Information Administration. 2022. https://www.eia.gov/tools/faqs/faq.php?id=709&t=6.
31 Porter, Michael, David Gee and Gregory Pope. 2017. America's Unconventional Energy Opportunity. *Harvard Business School*. https://www.hbs.edu/competitiveness/Documents/america-unconventional-energy-opportunity.pdf.
32 Meyer, Robinson. 2022. America Is the World's Largest Oil Producer. So Why Is Losing Russia's Oil Such a Big Deal. *The Atlantic*, March 8. https://www.theatlantic.com/science/archive/2022/03/us-oil-natural-gas-price-surge-energy-independence/626979/.

PART II

Entrepreneurship and Community - Creating a Culture of Risk-Taking

CHAPTER 6

Is It About Technology?

Quantum computing has arrived. Sandbox, a startup spun off from Alphabet officially announced its birth on March 22, 2022 in Palo Alto, California. Sandbox will develop quantum computing applications for financial services, computer security, healthcare, and other sectors. In the short term, it is introducing software that runs on classical computers but can block quantum computers from unlocking encryption and allowing quantum-secure communications. Quantum sensing technology is being tested at many pioneering hospitals around the country, such as New York's Mount Sinai Health System, to improve drug development and improve medical imaging with data obtained from quantum-based sensors. The startup will be able to raise the capital to hire the skilled engineers, and scientists in diverse fields such as physics, chemistry, AI, neuroscience, mathematics, and other areas [1].

"The first quantum revolution brought us the great technological advances of the twentieth century—the transistor, the laser, the atomic clock, and GPS, the global positioning system. A second quantum revolution is now underway, changing how we store, process, and communicate information using quantum hardware that is neither analog nor digital, data is no longer in the form of bits, which are represented by a discrete number of possible states, 0 or 1. In a quantum computer, the information is stored in quantum bits or qubits. Qubits have an infinite number of possible states. Think of a qubit as being able to be on and off at

S. Bhatt, *Entrepreneurship Today*,
https://doi.org/10.1007/978-3-031-11495-3_6

the same time", according to Steve Girvin, Professor of Physics at Yale University [2].

Rigetti Computing has graduated into the public sphere when it merged with a special purpose acquisition company, SPAC, in March 2022 as this book was going to press. In October 2021, IonQ followed a similar strategy, becoming the first in commercializing quantum tech. D-Wave, which collaborated with CaixaBank in Spain, combined the power of quantum computing and classical computing in D-Wave Leap's quantum cloud service and quantum hybrid solvers to improve the hedging strategies of investment portfolios. "What normally took the bank several hours of compute time was reduced to just minutes via quantum computing technology".

Emerging biotech companies like Menten AI are exploring how quantum hybrid technology can expedite drug design and development. Protein design research has been a trial-and-error process, and Menten is in the process of designing anti-viral binders to battle the COVID-19 disease. The firm used the D-Wave Advantage quantum computer to explore the vast combinatorial space and design a peptide that binds with the SARS-CoV-2 spike glycoprotein, preventing it from messing with the receptors on human cells and infecting them with the virus [3].

Yes, indeed, it is about technology. But not yet, not for these glamorous technologies. Chetan Nayak, Distinguished Engineer and Principal; Research Manager of Microsoft Station Q, believes that while "the underlying physics is demonstrated, the next step is a topological qubit' which will ultimately power a fully scalable quantum machine in the future." [36] Andrew Houck, Professor of Electrical and Computing Engineering at Princeton, and leading researcher for the NSF Quantum Leap Challenge Institute for Robust Quantum Simulation, believes that "large scale quantum computers remains a distant goal." [37] The chasm between invention and implementation is wide, and deep with treacherous undercurrents [4].

The premise of this book is that the past two decades have seen a resurgence of small, young businesses in technology-driven markets. The examples described above are in the professional and business services sector, are all located in California and have emerged during the mobility revolution, the digital revolution during the second decade of this century, 2010–2020. The data validate this premise for startups under 1 year in existence with fewer than 100 employees but find low survival rates beyond 1–4 years. In general, a startup may not necessarily have invented the technology, but it will have utilized the technology in a manner that gives it merit in a socio-economic context. These new ventures show great promise with a first-year survival rate of 80% bringing forth a creative application of new technologies, associated new products and services, and enhanced versions of old products and services to consumers [5]. But a focus on rapid expansion of the startup with limited attention to the nature of the technology or the users is a recipe for disaster.

Since the invention of the transistor in 1947, many magnificent technologies in the digital communication and information universe have made their appearance, but their application for the business startup appears to be some distance away. Research laboratories are in the race for generating inventions, with a goal of shooting for the stars, most of which remain far removed from actual implementation. At the funding level there is a belief that *glamour* takes precedence over *user-friendly*. Money is pouring into the venture capital space, and especially the seed and angel stage where funding for early-stage businesses is the goal. The practical fulfilment of this "shooting-for-the-stars" objective leaves much unexplored new venture terrain on earth.

Transmission of basic research and its development into user-friendly services or products creates ripple effects from the technologies into consumer facing businesses. Using the number of startups as a measure of inventiveness of the nation can be misguided since new business follows the path laid out by application of science into know-how. The last chapter illustrated the sluggish performance of mature startups, those that persisted beyond the first year but failed somewhere between one to four years. There are three possibilities for this failure. One, many grand technologies require enormous upfront fixed costs which are beyond the pale of most small businesses. If a startup is located in a state with a higher proportion of larger technology firms, then proximity and spillover effects influence the nature of new businesses. Two, there is insufficient attention paid to implementation, as would happen when the goal is solely to accelerate sales, disregarding other factors. A third, related rationale, is the absence of non-financial support for new enterprises, such as mentoring, networking and the presence of role models in the community. The first two arguments are explained in this chapter, while the second is explored in Chapter 7.

Fundamentally, I take issue with the belief that small businesses are not entrepreneurial simply because they do not employ large numbers of workers. They may, in fact, generate employment in complementary or ancillary markets within their respective regions. Most small business owners care for work flexibility rather than income, and at least a third of business founders "wanted to create a new product or had a very good business idea". Innovation means a new way of solving an old problem, and while new ideas and products may not suggest invention, they do signal innovation. The point is that growth incentives, job creation incentives, are not the first order reasons for startup creation—creating a culture of risk-taking is of the first order. A singular focus on macroeconomic measures of labor productivity has been misleading policymakers all these decades. Perhaps it is time to think in terms of micro foundations—development of the community and business climate might be more important.

The Technologies

Application of existing technologies is more likely to be the engine that powers startups than an inventive, new technology. Inventions, the creation of something new, such as the iPhone, are infrequent and while they create far-reaching ripple effects, they are not the only generator of technological change. In practice, resurgence of young enterprises reflects three possible paths: **innovation** or a **new** way of solving an old problem; **improvement**, which is a **more efficient** way of solving an old problem, and **implementation**, which is applying existing technologies to a new problem.

Following this line of reasoning, what were the technologies that were developed during the time period under consideration? The years 1994–2020 can be split into two logical periods, separated by the Great Recession. Period I comprises the years 1994–2007 and period II the years following the economic downturn, 2010–2020. As was discussed earlier in Chapter 2, the economic environment of 2008–2009 together with the introduction of the smartphone in March 2007 motivated this division into two periods. In this vein, what other major technology breakthroughs were predicted at the beginning of the second period in 2010? The breakthrough technology predictions according to the 2010 issue of *The MIT Review*, an alumni magazine, at that time, were [6]:

i. Real-time search
ii. Social TV

iii. Duel-action antibodies
iv. Cloud programming
v. Mobile 3-D: Smartphones will provide images that change from 2-D in the vertical orientation and switch to 3D in the horizontal orientation. Mobile games and video could take this technology to the customer, but modern online video games are still desktop versions.
vi. Engineered stem cells: Mimicking human disease in a petri dish.
vii. Solar fuel: A renewable fuel, based on lab created photosynthetic microorganisms that use sunlight to convert carbon dioxide into ethanol.
viii. Light-trapping photovoltaics: Nanoparticles make solar power more functional, but this technology is based on cadmium telluride, which is a rare material.
ix. Green concrete: Carbon dioxide stored in cement.
x. Implantable electronics: Devices dissolvable in the body are based on an implanted silk sensor, which is also combined with flexible silicon electronics.

While all these technologies are in the public domain, which among them have actually been launched on a wide scale during the mobility revolution? The first four are already on the global radar screen, and none are the creation of young startups.

One, real-time search is parsing social networking information in the sense that every tweet, is deconstructed for data. Ephemeral info-nuggets are the Web's new currency and sifting through them is a challenge for search engines. Facebook and Twitter sell their data feeds directly to search providers such as Google's computers. The challenge lies in interpreting those bits of data. This successful and now controversial technology is perfected by Douyin, a startup launched in China in 2016 by Byte Dance. The platform hosts short-form videos and, soon after buying another similar app Musical.ly, was released in Shanghai in 2014, and globally as TikTok in 2017. The application's patented algorithm accurately and, practically instantly, predicts user preferences based on their viewing style [7].

Two, social television is where the watching experience is shared over broadband connections or interactive TV devices. In a felicitous twist, the functionality of social television is possible via Twitter, where chatter with

280 characters has replaced the need for physical proximity and banter across the living room couch.

Three, a duel-action antibody is the basis of the drug Kadcyla, which received FDA approval in 2013. Dual action antibodies combine the action of two antibodies, Avastin and Herceptin, in one molecule, making it more effective in treatment for metastatic breast cancer, as well as cheaper relative to the purchase of two drugs. It is not the product of a small startup, however. It is the work of Genentech, which is the maker of Avastin and Herceptin. Genentech, the first biotech startup, was launched in 1976, and was acquired in 1990 by the Swiss pharmaceutical giant Hoffmann-La Roche.

And four, cloud computing has also been implemented, by technology behemoths, Amazon Web Services, Microsoft's Azure, Google Cloud, and Alibaba Cloud (the primary option in China). Information technology startups are using cloud-computing as the go-to model in prioritizing services over traditional goods.

Note that all four successful breakthroughs are the creation of industry behemoths, not startups. The prevailing story, where a new invention first located in a lab or university is then absorbed by a firm with deep pockets and resources spanning the entire business space from finance, legal, and networking with the decision-makers in ancillary markets, doesn't appear to hold. Genentech was nurtured through the multiple years of its growth phase by money and connections. Bold, path-breaking inventions are costly and time-consuming. Hoffmann-La Roche fostered the new invention by actually being at the center of the research arena from the very start, as in the case of dual action antibodies and Genentech. TikTok was nurtured by deep-pocketed Chinese behemoth, Byte Dance.

Putting It All Together

In the past few chapters, we examined the intersection of startups and states and the industries that have dominated various states to generate a topography of entrepreneurship. This resulted in a relatively accurate and detailed delineation and description of how many, when, where, and how startups are being launched. Consolidating the results obtained in Chapters 3, 4, and 5 such as the two digital revolutions, the overwhelming dominance of the mobility revolution across most states, the importance of the professional and business services sector, the weaker evolution of mature startups and the resilient response of some states to the Great Recession, I summarize with a few keen observations.

First, young as opposed to mature, startup is a more revealing metric of entrepreneurship. Software and technology startups are emblematic of the lean startup idea that has become the iconic representation. Rapid expansion with minimal overhead costs is the goal of founders. However, most startups do not fit that icon. Launching a startup requires the digital infrastructure to support online sales, payments, ordering, and customer relationships. It takes time to be recognized and acquire legitimacy in the business world. Do entrepreneurs need a strategy compass with a "systematic evaluation of four competing go-to-market strategies: protecting the startup's intellectual property, disrupting competitors, working within the existing value chain, or creating an entirely new value chain"? Or can they "learn by doing, a practice rooted in phenomenology, [which posits that] people learn about the world through their experiences of it … and on the basis of what they discover they engage in new experiences, building up an understanding of their world as they proceed" [8]?

This suggests two views. The academic view would place more weight on mature startups as a measure of entrepreneurial activity since that would prove their legitimacy. This would coincide with the product launch stage where the 1st, 2nd, and 3rd rounds of venture funding might be forthcoming. On the other hand, policymakers view would consider the young startup as more indicative of where the helping hand of public infrastructure needs to be targeted in order to enable better launching of the young startup. This would be the idea and product development stage corresponding with angel and seed funding. Taking the side of policymakers, young startups are the appropriate metric [9].

Second, consider the table in Fig. 6.1 which brings together all the state rankings. The first three columns depict the state rank for startups over the entire period, 1994–2020, startups in the years 1994–2007 and post-2010 startups respectively. Column 4 ranks states by young entrepreneurial activity per capita. Column 5 depicts mature per capita startup activity and column 6 ranks the states by working age (ages 18–64) population growth trends.

Moving to the divided time periods, the presence of the following states in the first four columns in Fig. 6.1, is noteworthy: Wisconsin, Idaho, Massachusetts, Missouri, and California. The only column they do not <u>all</u> enter is that of young startups during the early period, 1994–2007, where Massachusetts and Missouri are absent. The very fact that

	Young startup trend	Young startup trend: desktop revolution	Young startup trend: mobility revolution	Young startup trend per capita	Mature startup trend per capita	Working Age Population Trend
Time Period	1994 - 2020	1994 - 2007	2010 - 2020	2010 - 2019	2010 - 2019	2010 - 2019
States	ND	FL	ID	ID	WA	TX
	NE	CA	DC	DC	AR	FL
	DC	ID	WA	MO	MS	CA
	MO	NV	MO	CA	LA	AZ
	ID	UT	WI	MT	NJ	WA
	MA	AZ	MA	MA	AL	GA
	CA	NJ	NV	UT	AZ	NC
	TX	DC	MT	WI	VA	CO
	WI	VA	HI	VT	IN	UT
	WA	NC	GA	NV	AK	NV
	VA	MT	UT	DE	WV	SC
	NV	WA	CA	HI	MD	TN
	FL	WY	TX	ME	OK	OR
	UT	GA	SC	GA	WY	MA
	SD	AR	SD	SC	TN	VA

Fig. 6.1 Summary of trends (*Source* U.S. Census and author's calculations)

these states ranked high in overall terms, in per capita terms and particularly during the later period of the mobility revolution suggests that the Great Recession had little effect in dampening new ventures and that the states were resilient. It could be that the governments in these states were proactive in easing the regulatory framework for new businesses after 2010.

Third, as discussed in Chapters 3 and 5, the high-performance western states, which I have termed the NUWMIC states capture the top spots among all young startup rankings, with the exception of Montana in the overall category and Washington in the per capita category. California is the home of Silicon Valley so its appearance is to be expected.

However, what makes Nevada, Utah, Washington, Montana, and Idaho so supercharged?

Most of the Washington state's workforce is composed of employees of Microsoft and Amazon, which have their headquarters in Seattle. In 2021, Amazon overtook Boing as being the largest employer, abetted by the plunge in the travel industry as the pandemic took charge of the nation's economy. Boing and Amazon are two opposing models of the U.S. economy: one is the giant of manufacturing and the other is the giant of consumption. Washington, with its large population growth, declines in the per capita rankings. Admittedly, California is ranked third but still prevails among the top five in per capita terms, testimony to the state's powerful entrepreneurial surge during the early desktop revolution.

Four of the six NUWMIC states ranked among the top 10 in working age population growth trends: Of these NUWMIC states, only Montana, and Idaho did not have high population growth over the past decade. The presence of larger numbers of working age people may have a role in generating creative energy.

Montana is present among the top-ranking young startups both during the desktop and the mobility revolution. The years of the Great Recession cratered the economy explaining the state's absence in the overall rankings, which covers the entire period 1994–2020 and therefore includes the recessionary years. Work has begun, in 2022, on installing Montana's first fiber optic network, Yellowstone Fiber. This project will provide fast internet connectivity to the city of Bozeman and all rural areas and ranches deep into Gallatin County. Montana remains one of the least-connected states in the nations and a third of this county's residents lack access [10].

Nevada, an important player in the national security business, is home to Nellis Air Force Base, Creech Air Force Base, the Naval Air Station Fallon, and the Hawthorne Army Depot. The publicly funded Desert Research Institute studies the use of technology for desert combat settings. Businesses that are born and develop would be related to the defense industry, a stable industry. In response to the recent slowdown in new businesses, the state has launched, in March 2022, a nationally-ranked small business and startup accelerator in Las Vegas, as well as one in the Reno-Tahoe corridor to provide mentorship and financial support to new ventures in Nevada [11].

Fourth, the South makes a huge splash in the young startup revolution. Florida, North Carolina, and Georgia are among the top 15 states during the early years of the desktop revolution. But there is some weakening during the later years, as only Georgia remains among the top-ranking states, with North Carolina being replaced by South Carolina. Florida is absent during the recent decade. The Great Recession weakened the economies of Florida and North Carolina, in the sense that these states dropped out of the ranks during the mobility revolution.

One can summarize with the projection that Georgia and South Carolina are the rising stars among young startups.

Of the southern states, Florida, Georgia, North and South Carolina rank in the top quintile in population growth trends nationally and Georgia and South Carolina retain their ranking among the top 15 states in per capita startups. Despite that fact that the working age (ages 18–64) population in Florida and North Carolina was growing at a rapid clip, startup activity during the recent decade didn't keep up with the population growth.

Fifth, Texas entered the startup scene with a flourish during the mobility revolution among young startups. As with South Carolina, there was an enormous growth of new businesses during 2010–2020. Similarly, Wisconsin was not active in the entrepreneurial picture until the second decade of the digital revolution, 2010–2020 and then became supercharged ranking high in per capita terms as well. Massachusetts and Missouri sweep into the picture during the decade of the 2010s ranking high both in nominal and per capita terms, which propels them into the top overall spots. However, both states are absent during the desktop revolution. They woke up to the race pretty late, but more than made up.

This brings us to the most important question. What factors contributed to the resilience and strength of these states in the recent decade? In order to understand the development of Wisconsin, Idaho, Missouri, Massachusetts, California, and South Carolina as the leading states in startup activity consider the industries that are dominant in these states. Complementary businesses will likely sprout up to support this dominant industry which would allow us to understand the source of entrepreneurial activity in the state. Is there a correspondence between the glamorous technologies and the dominant industries? Industries dominant in a particular state could presage the emergence of startups in their image. New opportunities for business tend to arise in complementary or affiliated sectors so it would not be misleading to provisionally conclude that the dominant industries in each state provided the leadership for all newcomers.

Earlier, in Chapter 5, we examined which sectors were dominant in the leading states and confirmed that professional, scientific, and technical services remained among the top 3 drivers of economic systems across states in all columns in the above diagram. The industry leading growth in Wisconsin and Idaho is real estate, rental, and leasing, RRL, while it is professional and business services, PBS, in California, Massachusetts, and Missouri. PBS is the third most important driver in Wisconsin and Idaho. There would likely sprout an economy of support services alongside these principal sectors which would imply that startups would also be located somewhere within the same PBS sector. New ventures would be part of the dominant sector, both in leading economic growth and also in supporting economic growth.

The state result is corroborated at the national level, as seen in Fig. 5.9 in the last chapter, which shows how businesses in various industries contributed to national GDP. Professional and business services, real estate, rental, and leasing and manufacturing added the most value to the U.S. economy over the 2010–2020 period. By comparison, the information industry which comprises the publishing industries, motion picture, broadcasting and telecommunications, and data processing and internet publishing represents a smaller contribution to national economic growth, and finance and insurance were lesser contributors, tying for the fifth place. Education and health services are the fourth contributor. It is remarkable that these rankings have remained persistent over the past two decades.[1]

Looking at the number of establishments across all major industries in 2020 we find that of the 7.99 million establishments in the U.S., 1.03 million are in the retail trade, 0.94 million in the professional, scientific, and technical services sector, and 0.93 million in the health care and social assistance sector. Real estate, rental, and leasing has 0.44 million establishments. These numbers cover establishments of all sizes, but their relative establishment numbers illustrate the importance of the professional, scientific and technical services sector. Health care and social assistance rank high in terms of paid employees, which is consistent with the fact that

[1] The NAICS classification system is a production-oriented concept which groups producing units rather than products or services, making it a production-oriented system rather than a market-based system.

it was in 2020, when the World Health Organization had declared, on March 11, that COVID-19 was a global pandemic. Workers were needed in the healthcare sector [12].

Idiosyncratic Aspects of States

Wisconsin

From a political economy perspective, the Badger State of Wisconsin is considered a swing state, together with Ohio, in U.S. Presidential elections. In both the 2000 and 2004 elections Wisconsin went Democratic with a 0.22% and 0.38% margin, respectively. In the 2016 election, however, Wisconsin flipped to the Republican candidate with a 0.77% margin, returning to the Democratic candidate in 2020 with a 0.63% margin. The low margins of victory as well as the pivot from one party to another and back again suggest shifting ideas and demographics in a complex socio-economic interaction.

From an education and skills perspective, not only is the University of Wisconsin at Madison one of the finest state educational institutions in the country, but also, according to the National Assessment of Educational Progress Report Card, the reading scores for fourth and eighth grade public school students from 1992 through 2019 were consistently above the national average [13].

While exhibiting a sluggish response to technology in the first decade of this century, Wisconsin raced ahead in the second decade to host increasing numbers of new businesses. Taking the pulse of the startup climate in a state depends mostly on anecdotal evidence, and local newspapers are often the best source. In the Kauffman Foundation's Rate of New Entrepreneurs, which is a measure of the fraction of a state's population that starts a new business (of all sizes) in a given month, Wisconsin's rate was 0.22% in 2020. The U.S. average rate was 0.38%. On the other hand, looking at the universe of firms with less than 100 employees, the per capita trend calculated in this book, shows 16.48 startups per year per 100,000 working age people across the years 2010–2019. [See Fig. 4.7]. The national average is 9.89 startups per 100,000 working age people. The measure of population is working age adults between the ages of 18 and 64.

Idaho

Noted for its spectacular natural beauty such as the Sawtooth National Recreation Area, the 25-mile-long Lake Coeur d'Alene, the 212-foot Shoshone Falls created by the turbulent force of the Snake River and also known as the Niagara of the West, and world famous ski slopes in Sun Valley, outdoor recreation accounted for merely 2.1% of the Idaho's economy. Nevertheless, these sites lend Idaho a rank in the upper echelons of the national recreational landscape. In 2020, the outdoor recreation economy accounted for 1.8% or $374.3 billion of current dollar GDP at the national level, and the top five states in terms of outdoor recreation value were: 4.3% of Montana's state economy, 3.7% in Vermont, 3.4% of Wyoming, 3.3% in Maine, and 2.7% in Idaho [14].

While Idaho is the nation's leading exporter of potatoes, Gen Z favorites like Chobani and Cliff Bar, beef (Agri Beef Co), trout production and cheese, food and agriculture are not the leading employers in the state, nor do they provide the largest fraction of tax revenues or contribute to GDP. Notably, all of the state's nearly 500 dairies are family owned.

And yet, there is another side to the state. Idaho is home to the Idaho National Laboratory, designated by the Department of Energy as the nation's leading nuclear research facility. Micron Technology, the only US-based memory chip maker, is located in Idaho, which is also the home of Hewlett-Packard's imaging and printing group (HP LaserJet printer). Idaho hosts 37 business partners/suppliers for Boeing which is directly linked from Boise and Spokane to Seattle, home of Boing [14].

Massachusetts

Consumer Value Stores, now known as CVS Pharmacy, was founded in Lowell, Massachusetts in 1963 and is currently the largest pharmacy chain in the U.S. by number of locations. In 2018, the pharmacy benefits manager merged with Aetna, one of the nation's largest insurers.[2] Massachusetts' most visible firms, in terms of employee count, are TJX,

[2] The trend for pharmacy benefits managers to merge with other players in the prescription drug pipeline is illustrated by the merger of Express Scripts, a CVS rival, with the big insurer, Cigna in 2018; and OptumRx, a PBM with UnitedHealth Group in 2011. To mitigate burgeoning employee health care costs, Amazon, JPMorgan, and Berkshire Hathaway announced plans to form a new company, Haven, in 2018. But this project failed in February 2021. "Data was a central challenge. Haven struggled to aggregate and

a multinational discount department store, parent to Marshalls and TJ Maxx, General Electric and Stop & Shop, a supermarket chain.

But it is also the base for Thermo Fisher Scientific, a supplier of scientific instruments and software services, and Raytheon Technologies, the world's largest defense manufacturer. It hosts the nation's largest insurance company, Liberty Mutual Insurance and Fidelity Investments, a financial services corporation. Smith and Wesson, the manufacturer of firearms had its headquarters in Massachusetts. The Boston Globe ranked the biotech and technology firms, Alynlam Pharmaceuticals, Akamai Technologies, and Dell Technologies as the top 3 places to work [16].

Missouri

Home of Mark Twain and President Harry S. Truman, St Louis in Missouri was home to the 1904 World Fair. Monsanto, founded in 1901 is located in Creve Coeur, Missouri, and is an agrochemical and agricultural biotechnology corporation. Monsanto faced public relations disasters due to its production of the infamous DDT from 1944 to 1977, which Congress then banned in 1979. In 1968 Monsanto became a pioneer in the field of optoelectronics with its production of LEDs or light-emitting diodes.

After merging in 1999 with the pharmaceutical company, Pharmacia & Upjohn, Monsanto as part of the agro-biotech subsidiary was divested and became the new Monsanto. By 2015, it became the world's largest supplier of seeds, with 26% of the global seed market. In September 2016, the German chemical company Bayer acquired Monsanto in an all-cash deal, which was finally approved by the European Union in March 2018 and the combined firm is now under the name Bayer. Notably, Monsanto was a major donor for scientific research at Washington University in St. Louis [17, 18].

California

While California may not have played host to John Bardeen, who invented the transistor, the invention that started the digital revolution, it did play host to Robert Noyce, who co-founded Fairchild Semiconductor and

analyze information on health-care costs for the three companies' employees". Lack of transparency in healthcare costs is a major hurdle for technology-based reform [15].

Intel Corporation, along with Gordon Moore of Moore's Law. Noyce and Moore created the integrated circuit, the silicon microchip. Jack Kilby simultaneously created his version, the germanium microchip, while at Texas Instruments in 1958, for which he won the Nobel prize in 2000 (Noyce died in 1990 and hence could not be nominated for the prestigious prize). Today, Intel is the world's largest semiconductor chip manufacturer by revenue.

Sizzling Patent Is Not a Startup

The word startup conjures a business that is capitalizing on a "sizzling patent", which can now be commercialized and scaled, bringing vast riches to those inventors. Imagining "organizations formed to search for a repeatable and scalable business model" as opposed to small businesses which are "looking for a business model that works from day one", these potential founders want to disrupt industries and change the world—at scale [19]. They dream of providing a needed, but as yet unrealized, product or service, generating enormously large valuations that lead to a quick exit through an initial public offering in the public stock markets. The business should scale rapidly, in a few iterative steps that involve testing the skeletal product or service followed by consumer feedback and usage data, and subsequently improving and revising until the final release.

Role models are famous startups such as Facebook, Amazon, Apple, Netflix, and Google. They started as ideas about unique products or services that were brought to market and made irresistible and irreplaceable for customers (e.g. how to connect students across a vast campus, as Mark Zuckerberg did with the early version of Facebook at Harvard). Rooted in innovation the goal was to remedy deficiencies of existing products or create entirely new categories of goods and services, disrupting entrenched ways of thinking and doing business for entire industries. Amazon changed the way books were purchased, Netflix changed the way entertainment was obtained, and Google changed the information acquisition process, and importantly, created the concept of on-demand information. There is no disagreement that cannot be solved with a quick swipe on Google.

The thinking is that regular companies duplicate what has been done before using an old template. A startup, on the other hand, creates an entirely new template, like Instacart and WebVan in the food industry and WeWork in the business space industry. The outcome for these two was diametrically opposite. Instacart survived and WebVan failed.

Webvan was launched in 1996 in Oakland, California and by 2001 it had signed a $1 billion deal with the giant construction corporation Bechtel to build out distribution centers, much like today's Amazon's centers in multiple U.S. cities. Was it moving fast and breaking the business model of established grocery chains? Were people ready to purchase groceries online? Note that this was before Amazon had purchased Whole Foods, and two decades before the pandemic. There were other online grocery stores that were ready for customers, like Peopod, that had launched around 1990.

What were the missteps taken by Webvan? Was home delivery not on customers' radar screen? Webvan bundled the quality and variety of Whole Foods together with the low prices of Safeway which sent an obfuscating message to customers. Was this for upmarket customers or price sensitive customers? Whereas, in fact, Webvan was selling a luxury service - sushi and organic foods delivered to your home. There was little clarity in defining the appropriate client and their problem.

Furthermore, initial software development costs to synchronize distribution and inventory management were enormous. "Five miles of conveyor belts in the Oakland Distribution Center (DC) transport 10,000 totes around the DC daily. After conveying the item to automated carousel pods, which would spin like jukeboxes to transfer the item in question into the tote, the entire process would repeat until the order was completed and integrated at the shipping dock. Additional real-time inventory management algorithms would make sure that if a customer ordered milk on the website, it was currently in stock; software algorithms would route delivery vans to multiple delivery stops while minimizing drive time; and software on Palm Pilots in drivers' hands would deal with real-time delivery confirmation or returns". Building out the physical infrastructure was also expensive. Webvan spent $1 billion to build state-of-the-art warehouses and distribution centers in 26 cities, with each location costing over $30 million [20]. Rapid cost escalation in order to meet imagined demand was the second mistake.

Instacart, on the other hand, is centered on delivery and customer service, subsuming the delivery fee into a higher markup. Convenience is the real demand, so the markup is unquestioned. Individuals who keep track of the prices in grocery store do not constitute the target market.

The business has been transformed from a product-and-price model to software-as-a service model to satisfy the demand for convenience.

In short, the two most common mistakes made by startups were made by WebVan: a lack of clarity on the minimally viable product, an error on the demand side, and an emphasis on excessively fast growth in sales with a concomitant explosion of costs, an error on the supply side.

Clarity About the Product and Customer Feedback

To start, what is a minimally viable product (MVP)? It is an experiment in assessing whether the product or service will remain aloft. It means listening to customers and grasping the crux of their problem and developing a tentative solution. This is the experimental part. Then follows a methodical dance with the market as customer feedback is incorporated into the MVP and a revised version is introduced into perhaps other market segments. With a series of back-and-forth dance steps, the new product or service is ready for national, and possibly global, markets.

An example of this process is the case of Ceres Imaging. Precision agriculture was the area looked into by a group of Stanford University students in 2013. Using drones equipped with a spectral camera, images could be captured and inform farmers about diseases, fertilizer, and water levels. Farmers could make improved forecasts about yield and precise treatment locations. The startup would be a data service provider. Did they actually talk to the farmers? Yes. It turns out that, indeed, farmers not having this level of detail was a problem, but they could not afford to pay for drone and sophisticated spectral cameras. The farmers told them they frequently used crop dusters to spray pesticides—their version of drones and that version was cheaper. The startup, now called Ceres Imaging, mounted their cameras on the crop dusters, acquired data and their principle contribution became the specialized algorithms designed to process this data. Communication and awareness of the market was the magic [21].

Customer feedback and its incorporation into the business takes time, during which competitors might gain the upper hand. Take the case of Bolt, a startup valued at $11 billion, which develops one-click payment software. This market is ripe for entrants since Amazon's patent on the technology expired in 2017. Stripe and Shopify are in the same markets, as competitors, which may account for the fall in Bolt's merchant accounts during 2021. To stem the fall in accounts, Bolt dropped fees, reducing revenue further. "But signing up customers doesn't immediately translate into new revenue because the integrations can take months, particularly larger merchants". Testing new markets, obtaining customer feedback, redesigning the product or service, and returning to the customer are all time-consuming processes. They involve individuals making choices, evaluating alternatives, and introspecting about their own preferences. These processes are unlikely to be altered by technology alone [22].

The Demand Side—Awareness of a Problem

Disintermediation is the lynchpin of startups with digital connectivity untethering product/service production and consumption decisions from intermediaries. There has been a trend toward organizational restructuring leading to granularity and disintermediation on an economy-wide scale. Rather than relying on some retailer to provide the appropriate smorgasbord of services and products, new businesses have sprung up to tailor the purchase experience to the person. Food delivery apps have split fine dining into the gastronomic experience and convenience, with delivery and on-demand services, untying the link between the restaurant or intermediary and the food. Uber has split car ownership from transportation-as-a-service. The early disrupters in the airline industry attempted to unbundle the air transport experience into flight plus seat plus food plus luggage.

Airbnb is the story about perceiving a problem and using technology to implement the solution, disintermediating the hotel industry. Brian Chesky, the founder, was in San Francisco during an international design conference in 2007 and noticed that all hotel rooms in the city center were booked up. He developed a rudimentary website listing his own apartment as being able to accommodate three visitors, provided they slept on inflatable air beds. Thus, began the concept of unused apartment space being pivoted toward unmet hotel demand by tourists. In 2008, during the Democratic National Convention in Denver, anticipating excess hotel room demand, Chesky roped in Obama supporters as hosts on the Airbnb platform. The name itself is a play on the origins, air mattresses. Chesky's awareness of the environment, of the problem, noticing the excess demand in San Francisco and the anticipating a similar situation in Denver, was the key driver. Chesky started with the problem, not with the digital communication technology that would eventually catapult Airbnb into winner category.

The mission of a startup is not directed toward scaling up and quickly exiting via an initial public offering, an IPO. That is the investor's perspective. The founder, on the other hand, cares about the company and the early employees and the market—the people who buy the product or service. The growth-at-all-costs mentality has led to the demise of too many startups. Creating focus groups of potential customers is not entirely reliable since that would assume that people are aware of the exact nature of their problem, that they know what they want. According to the scarcity principle, when individuals are deeply engaged in addressing some constraints, either resource or time, they develop tunnel vision, becoming unable to visualize anything outside of the immediate obstacle. At this point, articulating the nature of the underlying predicament can become a fuzzy account. When potential customers cannot effectively communicate their problem to the founder, rapid growth in the absence of careful attention and awareness of market demand, is a short-sighted strategy. How can you assist the customers in articulating their needs? What problem is the startup aiming to solve?

According to data from the Bureau of Labor Statistics, establishments that opened in March of 1994 had an 80% survival rate at the end of the first year. This means that 80% of the 1994 startups survived beyond one year. By March of 1997, 60% of these businesses had survived, suggesting that 40% of businesses failed after 4 years. In March of 2004, the ten-year mark, 33.6% of the same starting cohort had survived. Consider the cohort of startups that opened in March of 2007. These establishments had a 1-year survival rate of 77%, 4-year survival rate of 50%, and 10-year survival rate of 33%. And, finally, for the cohort of businesses started just after the Great Recession in 2010, the 1-year survival rate was 78%, the 4-year rate was 56%, and the 10-year rate was 34%. Across all three cohorts of new business starts, 1994, 2007, and 2010, fully 2/3 of businesses did not survive past 10 years, while 40–50% did not survive beyond 4 years and about 20% of businesses failed after 1 year, consistent with the results obtained in Chapter 5. More recently, for businesses that commenced operations in March 2017, 2018, 2019, and 2020 the 1-year survival rate hovered around 80% [23].

While finance makes up 38% of the causes cited, poor market awareness causes 74% of failures (no market need, got outcompeted, flawed business model). It seems obvious, upon thinking, that if a founder lacks perceptiveness about consumer needs and problems, the startup is likely to be flying off the wrong runway. Quibi, a startup with famous founders Meg Whitman and Jeffrey Katzenberg, shut down in October 2020, 6 months into the new venture. They had raised $1.8 billion. Meg Whitman wrote to employees that a stand-alone streaming service was not what the market needed[3] [24]. In addition, regulation, as it happens, can be devastating and unforeseeable, causing 18% of startup failures. The smart luggage manufacturer, Bluesmart, had to close after most U.S. airlines banned checked luggage with non-removable lithium ion batteries.

Emphasizing time-to-market has the odor of a Ponzi scheme: start with copious funding, rapid product launch and expansion, and then a quick exit via an IPO or acquisition. In the past two years, founders have been receiving reverse pitches. "For Daniel Perez, a co-founder of Hinge Health, a provider of online physical therapy programs, the unsolicited emails from investors started in late 2020.They contained pitch decks packed with elaborate research that investment firms had done on Hinge. ... These reverse pitches ... were meant to persuade Mr. Perez to take money from the investment firms. ... Three different investors sent Mr. Perez videos from celebrities they had hired on Cameo to make their case" [25].

There is no concern in this startup cycle for product viability over the longer horizon nor whether the fundamental consumer dilemma was solved. Consumers incur search costs for replacement and repair when inferior goods are brought to market. This obvious waste is not an environmentally sustainable path to solving a human predicament or improving peoples' lives. There are other effects of scaling.

Scaling and Rapid Cost Escalation

Speed is the other demon as startups are also looking to rapidly expand their customer base. Startups are typically online businesses, either in existing markets or in an entirely new market. The emphasis on quickly scaling-up is often fueled by investors who want a quick exit and a high

[3] Based on an analysis of 111 startup post mortems since 2018 [5]. The reasons cited were: Ran out of cash/failed to raise new capital (38%); no market need (35%), got outcompeted (20%), flawed business model (19%), regulatory/legal challenges (18%), pricing/cost issues (15%), not the right team (14%), product mistimed (10%), poor product (8%), disharmony among team/investors (7%), pivot gone bad (6%), and burned out (5%).

return. This helps them establish larger market shares, inspiring more funding with higher valuations. The cycle continues with faster scaling of the products and the audience. All of this rapid growth and improvement is typically, implicitly or explicitly, in the service of an ultimate goal: going public.

With a focus on speed and growth, Steve Blank, entrepreneur and Stanford professor, believes “many startups fall into the trap of building a ‘mission’ rather than a minimally viable product.. However, solely focusing on your mission is the same as being unfocused” [19]. Very soon, ambition hits a hard constraint of resource limitation which requires making tradeoffs, giving up part of the mission in order to gain traction with the viability of the new product or service.

Multiple startups have arisen under the umbrella term on-demand or just-in-time customer experiences. These models often parlay quality and functionality for time and convenience, encouraging customers to place value on efficiency. Speed in information transmission is grafted onto all aspects of consumption and all products regardless of whether customers care about speed and time. A sense of urgency and immediacy is being felt across all businesses such that a higher value is placed on technologies that reduce latency and increase the speed of various services. This is realistic, for example, when it comes to platforms such as Netflix and streaming where buffering and delayed signals can ruin a movie, but not in the case of WeWork—the demand for office space doesn’t grow that fast.

WeWork was a startup that obtained huge funding but failed to deliver since it grew too quickly. The idea behind the startup was to lease buildings from developers, chop them up into functional spaces, and rent out on a short-term basis. The real innovation was leasing space rather than buying square footage. And the second innovation, which proved damming, was the flexible rental policy. This means that while WeWork’s revenue could be volatile due to changing demand for office space, lease payments remained constant. By renting short term and leasing long term WeWork was following the conventional financial institution model of borrowing short term and lending for the long term, so when short-term interest rates suddenly swerve upward, the banks are paying more in interest than receiving on the fixed-rate loans. Such an asymmetric balance sheet could be sustained only with generous funding which in the case of WeWork came from SoftBank’s Saudi-backed Vision Fund which placed $4.4 billion into WeWork in 2017. The Vision Fund may have confused companies with large funding requirements with companies that offer rewarding opportunities.[4]

Dog-walking as a startup might sound exciting and innovative, as in the 2015 entry of Wag which received $300 million from SoftBank's Vision Fund. In the frenzy of on-demand startups, initiated by Uber connecting passengers with car owner-drivers and Airbnb connecting travelers with homeowners, Wag connected pet owners with walkers, renting out their services as independent contractors. With a focus on growth, the thorny aspect of dogs simply not liking all strangers was their nemesis. Dogs getting off leash and lost dogs was a common problem.

In short, SoftBank's Vision Fund had almost $100 billion available for investing and a global network of connections. Juxtaposed on funding, entrepreneurs, in the wake of the Great Recession, sprinted to create all manner of on-demand app-based services. Some have made the case that geopolitics diverted the idea of technology implementation into creating wealth for large corporations, a visionary Japanese phone entrepreneur, and the Saudi treasury [26].

Unintended Effects of Rapid Scaling

Scaling in various industries can have unintended consequences. It may, for example, change the picture for the labor market, in the sense that the labor share of that industries' income falls. Firms that dominate their respective industries in terms of sales revenues are more productive—a given quantity of labor produces more output. This could be due to increased (and improved) application of technology as well as better organization of the enterprise.

Autor et al. [27] find that certain firms, in manufacturing, retail and wholesale trade, services, finance and utilities, that capture a higher proportion of the sales in their sector have higher productivity. The output per worker is higher in these larger firms. For example, in finance, larger firms have higher sales per worker. The increase in sales could be due to organizational changes, in addition to technological changes.

4 The transformation of WeWork from investor favorite to castaway is due to elements of misogyny and mendacity. WeWork's greatest legacy could be the financial gymnastics that led to creating a new metric called Community Adjusted EBITDA, which measures earnings stripped of all costs incurred to open new locations. This is, of course, eclipsed by the "entitled frat-boy culture that permeates WeWork from the top down" [26].

Firms that dominate a certain industry attract workers. But if that firm has a lower proportion of workers relative to other firms, there will be a trend toward lower labor share overall. "[t]he growth of concentration is disproportionately apparent in industries experiencing faster technical change ... suggesting that technological dynamism, rather than simply anticompetitive forces, is an important driver – though likely not the only one – of this trend" toward higher productivity in more concentrated industries [27]. Scale is an outcome of superior organizational and technological skills in a firm's workforce, not an objective.

The focus on growth at all costs suggests a misunderstanding of the concept of scaling. "Scaling simply refers, in its most elemental form, to how a system responds when its size changes" [19]. Since firms are "continuously evolving complex adaptive systems" the outcome of simply growing subscribers or customers is not well understood. Continuous monitoring is required to maintain the processes of the startup and the consequence of this continuous monitoring might actually be disorder. This is entropy or disorder, which, according to the Second Law of Thermodynamics, inevitably increases "[w]henever energy is used or processed in order to make or maintain order within a closed system". As a startup applies technology and superior organization it will see an increase in sales, but in the absence of continuous feedback and monitoring, this scaling may lead to bankruptcy or entropy.

Increasing the scale of organizations often relies on linear thinking. For example, if Missouri had 17,890 young startups and a state population of 3.7 million in 2019, then a state with double the population, say Pennsylvania with 7.7 million will have double the number of young startups, or 35,780 young establishments. In fact, in 2019, Pennsylvania had 21,574 startups which is 20% more than Missouri. Most economic measures that involve social organization scale non-linearly, which means that "the characteristics of a system generally do not simply double when its size is doubled" [24]. There are, in general, decreasing returns to scale, or *sublinear scaling* to use the physicist's jargon.

Human organizations are complex adaptive systems which means that the whole is different from the simple sum of its elements. This outcome is called emergent behavior and is a characteristic of many social and biological systems, which self-organize by adapting and growing in response to changes in the environment. The mathematical structure of scaling is the power law, and the scaling component refers to the exponent on a power law. When the exponent is less than one, there are economies of scale. For example, when a mammal doubles in weight, its cell count also doubles but its metabolic rate increases by only 75%, not 100%[5] [24].

The infrastructure of cities scales sublinearly with size, so the number of gas stations and length of roads have a scaling component of 0.85. Most socio-economic variables involving human interaction scale superlinearly. Cities have superlinear scaling due to agglomeration economies. "The dynamics of social networks underlying wealth creation and innovation leads to the opposite behavior, namely, the systematically increasing pace of life as city size increases: diseases spread faster, businesses are born and die more often, commerce is transacted more rapidly and people even walk faster" [24].

Humans have risen to the top of the food chain not because of our superior intelligence or technological capabilities, but because of our ability to cooperate at scale, according to Yuval Harare [28]. As bands of humans grew in size, cooperation became key to survival and that key unlocked Homo Sapiens' potential.

Researchers suggest that tool-making and mental sharpness enabled the ascent of Homo Sapiens. But the genus Homo were already superior technologists, with their Stone Age tool-making skills, some 2.5 million years ago, and yet they didn't overtake the physical world. The species Homo Sapiens emerged around 200,000 years ago, and, with the onset of the cognitive revolution, starting around 70,000–30,000 years ago, developed language and began to share information about the world, and gossiping. It is this feature that promoted cooperation in large numbers, and coordination of abilities to master the environment. Language allowed not only communication but also thinking, the ability to imagine. "That's why Sapiens rule the world, whereas ants eat our leftovers and chimps are locked up in zoos and research laboratories" [28].

Cooperation and the Human-Centered Anthropocene

Scaling or increasing the size of socio-economic variables, such as size of startups, mandates cooperation in order to avoid the unforeseen

[5] "The pace of life systematically and predictably slows down with increasing size, and this is accompanied by increasing economies of scale" [24].

bankruptcy or failure. The time-line of our planet can be divided into geologically determined epochs, marked by changes in the state of the planet. Human activity is the dominant cause of changes to the Earth's geology and environment. Therefore, we are living in the human-centered geological epoch, the Anthropocene, after the Holocene epoch, dated about 10,000 years ago. The bane of this human-centered epoch may well be a demise of cooperation. This is the most potent argument against rapid scaling [29].

Some philosophers conjecture that individuals are primordially individualistic and enter into society as a rational calculation that social cooperation will enable people to attain their individual aspirations. But, survival of the individual is superseded by survival of the individuals' gene pool which means that there is natural cooperation among kin. There is also reciprocal altruism due to repeated interactions. People will encounter each other in various avenues, signifying that cooperation today will be met with cooperation at a later date, while discord will engender further strife. So also, mutual gains can be perceived when the startup is small, and all stakeholders see value in the project. When the new business begins to grow, its network spreads and all nodes in this larger community may not regard strategy and outcomes in a similar manner.

Building brand image has been the strongest tool for sustaining the firm as it scales. Constructing a unique corporate identity motivates employees and customers, as firms like Apple have demonstrated. The guiding star for Apple has been privacy when it turned down federal requests for the password to unlock an iPhone belonging to the perpetrators of the San Bernardino shooting in 2015. Apple was branding itself as the company that sold privacy via communication devices and infrastructure. This lofty ideal became the firm's bonding mechanism as it grew larger. A firm's values are incorporated in its mission which is what motivates employees and fosters cooperation across the behemoth firm. The synchronized belief system supersedes mere survival, it ensures cooperation at scale.

Does a startup need to create a synchronized mission statement across all its constituents prior to scaling or does the very process of scaling create a homogeneous, shared reality and hence cooperation? Perhaps ubiquitous connectivity, due to digital communication technology, produces a business and social network with relatively similar belief systems. A bunch of individuals working long hours at a startup are quite likely to influence one another, and this influence can spread to new employees. As the firm begins to fill out the employee roster, triadic closure, a kind of social influence, will become pervasive. The firm and its culture are intertwined in the wider world. Shared beliefs, shared stories, will engender the sort of cooperation vital for success. Storytelling gives meaning to most people's lives and can be the glue that binds the particular new firm.

The story could be that startups become successful by capturing ever larger market share. All believe in it and then work toward it without thinking of the larger picture, the ensuing transactions costs. The belief that economic growth is fundamental almost becomes a religion since it now purports to solve any, if not most, of our ethical dilemmas. Institutions arise to embed these beliefs and behavior patterns in rules, which, facilitate human collective action since rules last well beyond the short-term interactions and eliminate renegotiation between parties as the business landscape changes. Thus, venture capitalists set growth targets as a condition of lending.

Costs of Coordination

In 1992, Paul Milgrom and John Roberts wrote in their seminal book, "A fundamental observation about the economic world is that people can produce more if they cooperate, specializing in their productive activities and then transacting with one another to acquire the actual goods and services they desire.[6] The problem of organization then arises because when people are specialized producers who need to trade, their decisions and actions need to be **coordinated** to achieve these gains of cooperation, and the people must be **motivated** to carry out their part of the cooperative activity" [30]. Coordination and motivation face a common hurdle—adequate information. Information must be complete, with no missing pieces, and symmetric across all parties. In competitive markets, this problem is believed to be solved by prices.

In the world of markets coordinated by prices, workers are motivated by their own individual welfare and will select "training, career and jobs where their talent and energy are most valuable", producers will sell goods and services that consumers value the most and produce these

[6] Paul Milgrom, along with his colleague at Stanford, Robert Wilson, subsequently went on to win the Nobel Memorial Prize in Economic Sciences in 2020 for their contributions to auction theory.

goods at the lowest cost. Owners of resources, both physical and financial "seeking only to increase their own wealth will deploy these assets in socially desirable ways" [30].

This model of competition ignores the reality that large firms may have more power in pricing and product decisions, incentives for producers and consumers may not align with social objectives and the markets for some goods may not exist. This reality adds up to **transactions costs**. For startups, when a specific investment has to be made to ensure a transaction, when certain kinds of transactions occur more frequently and over a longer period of time, when the measure of performance in the transaction is both unclear and unobservable and the interconnectedness of transactions across time and space, the solution costs multiply. It therefore becomes imperative to pay special attention to the organizational form of the business.

The organizational form of the business is set up to minimize these transaction costs. A startup may remain private and small if that minimizes some of these transaction costs, or go public and scale. In the early years, remaining privately owned rather than having to answer to outside shareholders might be more efficient. If transactions costs can be eliminated by private dialogue and coordination, then the solution is efficient. The efficiency principal is the idea that if individuals can "bargain together effectively and can implement and enforce their decision, then the outcomes of economic activity will tend to be efficient (at least for the parties to the bargain)" [30]. If any party could do better, it would not be part of the agreement. Efficiency is a positive concept in that it can explain and predict, but it is also a normative concept since it could be used as a prescription. Note that the definition of efficiency applies to outcomes (or resource allocation more generally) not prices.

Organizational form matters, and business failure is not a sustainable way of running the economy. It is not about speed and scale and get-rich-quick—peoples' livelihoods are at stake. It is about recognizing and solving problems, of scaling if, and when, coordination allows an efficient allocation of all resources. Yes, the take-over-the-market slogan is pervasive in the startup world. But that is not an accurate picture of startups. Most young firms start out with a plan to make a difference, a small impact, not disrupt the market. How can you envision disruption unless the plan has worked itself out over a number of years?

Founding a firm is not unlike an Antarctic exploration that is based on lots of careful planning, but where the outcome and impact is uncertain. In 1909 Norwegian explorer Ronald Amundson had planned to drift across the North Pole when he learnt that American Robert Peary had already made that trip in April 1909. He started his expedition in June 1910, informing his crew and the public that they were headed to the North Pole. Only when their ship was leaving the last port of call in the Madeira Islands, off the coast of Morocco, did he reveal the true destination. In fact, Amundsen, arrived at the South Pole on December 1911, after three months of traversing through the vast expanse of the continent.

Appendix

In a book about the startups and new business ventures, it is appropriate to take a glimpse at the predictions made about the future of technology from a business perspective as well as a science and development perspective. In that context, I list below the forecasts from the consulting firm, McKinsey, made in 2021, and forecasts for 2021 and 2022 from the *MIT Technology Review. The MIT Review* is wholly owned by MIT but is editorially independent and targeted at senior business executives, researchers, and policymakers.

McKinsey Technology Forecast

In a report from September 2021, McKinsey lists 10 technologies that are attracting the attention and funds of technologists and investors [32]. They are also the ones most likely to feature in the changing face of the modern work environment. They may not be the most cutting-edge but they are the ones that could provide a competitive edge and embody basic technologies such as cloud computing, quantum computing, 5-G connectivity, 3D printing, virtual and artificial reality, natural language processing and computer vision and distributed ledger technologies such as blockchain, which comprises trust architecture.

Looking at the next three decades, the top trends in technology "that matter the most" are:

i. Next-level process automation and virtualization with robotics, industrial internet-of-things, 3-D printing. Efficiency enhancing technologies.

ii. 5G broadband cellular networks combined with the Internet-of-Things. Faster connectivity across longer distances, increasing download speeds and reducing latency.
iii. Distributed infrastructure which brings together cloud and edge computing to move computing power to the edge of companies' networks so as to reduce latency for data-hungry devices spread out spatially. This trend will increase efficiency in the sense of speed of decision-making.
iv. Next generation computing or quantum computing which could enhance cybersecurity.
v. Applied AI where computers are trained to decipher and interpret patterns in real-world data using computer vision and natural language processing.
vi. The future of programming where programmers are replaced by neural networks that use machine learning to develop software. This development would automate low-level programming. The danger is the inadvertent creation of bias as well as making programming redundant as a skill.
vii. Trust architecture which includes distributed ledger technologies such as blockchain. This technology records transactions across a distributed public or private architecture with hash function encryption. The transaction is verified using consensus mechanisms across multiple nodes in this architecture of nodes, at which point the transaction is added to the ledger.
viii. Bio Revolution with personalized medicine, combining genomics and artificial Intelligence.
ix. Next generation materials based on research in materials science are exploring graphene and molybdenum disulfide with uses in aerospace and medicine.
x. Future of clean technologies in power (smart grids, energy-storage solutions), transport with electric vehicles, buildings with automation and water treatment and desalination.

MIT Review Technology Forecast

The 10 breakthrough technologies, listed by the *MIT Technology Review* in **March 2021**, that will play a role in our "collective future" are [32]:

i. Messenger RNA. The rapid deployment of the two most potent vaccines against the coronavirus was possible due to this 20-year-old technology. It is likely that this technology will be a transformative tool in fighting infectious diseases. In an interconnected world disease transmission is almost a certainty making this technology vital.
ii. GPT-3, a natural language processing model.
iii. TikTok's recommendation algorithms which are "particularly adept at feeding relevant content to niche communities of users who share a particular interest or identity".
iv. Lithium metal batteries, currently developed in beta mode by startup Quantum Scape.
v. Data trusts or an organization, authorized by law, to agglomerate and manage individuals' data on their behalf.
vi. Green hydrogen, a possible replacement for fossil fuels.
vii. Digital contact tracing based on GPS and Bluetooth technology.
viii. Hyper-accurate positioning, an improvement over currently used GPS. China is the leader here with its BeiDou global navigation system, available since 2020, has precision of 1.5–2 million around the globe. GPS, the U.S.-based global position satellites are expected to launch new satellites and be in orbit by 2023.
ix. Remote everything or work-and-play from home technologies.
x. Multi-skilled AI with computer vision and speech recognition.

According to the *MIT Technology Review* in **March 2022**, the 10 breakthrough technologies which will have the most impact on our collective future are [34]:

i. The end of passwords. We will have biometric scans, or a link sent via email and push notifications. How will this be leveraged into a startup? It might make the operational side of startups easier.
ii. Covid variant tracking via better surveillance.
iii. A long-lasting grid battery.
iv. AI for protein folding making it possible to create drugs for various diseases,
v. A malaria vaccine, the first for a parasitic infection, with potential benefits for countries in tropical climates.

vi. Proof of stake for cryptocurrency mobilization without lavish energy usage. Ethereum plans to use this system in 2022.
vii. A pill for Covid from Pfizer, providing better protection against the virus and new variants.
viii. Practical fusion reactors, which would aid in the phasing out of fossil fuels.
ix. Synthetic data for AI, which would mitigate the privacy issues surrounding consumer tracking.
x. A carbon removal factory to assist in abating climate change.

North American Industrial Classification System (NAICS)

The U.S. Census Bureau classifies industries into 2-digit sectors, 3-digit subsectors, 4-digit industry groups, the 5-digit code designates the NAICS industry, and the 6-digit code designates the national industry.

For example, sector 54 is professional scientific and technical services, which "comprises establishments that specialize in performing professional, scientific, and technical activities for others".[7] They include activities such as legal services; accounting and bookkeeping services; architectural and engineering services; computer services; consulting services; research services and other professional, scientific, and technical services. Back office operations, such as bookkeeping, are not included. **Subsector 541** is professional, scientific, and technical services, which has the same name, but has human capital as the dominant input in the production process. These establishments provide expertise along a variety of dimensions and quite likely require college education.

The 4-digit industry group 5413 is architectural, engineering and related services, which breaks down into the 5-digit NAICS industry 54132 for landscape architectural services and finally into the 6-digit code 541320 for golf course or ski area design services.

Located under 4-digit code 5415, computer systems design and related services, is the 5-digit code 54151, computer design and related services (again the same name), which consists of expertise in the field of information technology. Nested in this category, is the 6-digit code, 541511, for

[7] The NAICS is a classification system by the U.S. Census Bureau, which has establishment as the statistical unit of interest. "An establishment is the smallest operating entity for which records provide information on the cost of resources—material, labor, and capital—employed to produce the units of output" [34].

custom computer programming services, which would include software design and development.

Management, scientific, and technical consulting is located under 4-digit code 5416 and management consulting services alone is 5-digit code 54161.

Scientific research and development is the 4-digit code 5417, within the broader category of PST. The 6-digit code 541713 comprises research and development in nanotechnology, 541714 is the code for R&D in biotechnology and 541715 includes basic research in physical, engineering, and life sciences. Marketing research is also grouped under this category as 541721, R&D in the social sciences and humanities.

Advertising agencies (541810), public relations agencies (541820), media representatives (541840), direct mail advertising (541860), and marketing research and polling (541910) are all included under the general heading of professional, scientific, and technical services.

The point is that the industry group is diverse and multiple varieties of startups and small businesses can fall under this broad category. The technologies listed at the beginning of this chapter all fall under NAICS category 541, professional, scientific, and technical services. In fact, they also mostly can be grouped under NAICS code 5415, computer systems design and related services, and 5417, scientific research and development services.

Bibliography

1 Manson, Katrina. 2022. Sandbox AQ Gets Backing from CIA's Venture Capital Arm. *Bloomberg*, May 2. https://www.bloomberg.com/news/articles/2022-05-02/google-spinoff-sandbox-aq-gets-backing-from-cia-s-venture-arm?sref=m0aVO2qb.
2 Girvin, Steve. 2022. Progress and Prospects for the Second Quantum Revolution. Donald R. Hamilton Lecture at Princeton University, April 21, 8 pm.
3 Unlock the Power of Practical Quantum Computing Today. D-Wave website. https://www.dwavesys.com/.
4 Menard, Alexandre, I. Ostojic, M. Patel and D. Volz. 2020. A Game Plan for Quantum Computing. *McKinsey Quarterly*, February. https://www.mckinsey.com/business-functions/mckinsey-digital/our-insights/a-game-plan-for-quantum-computing.
5 Hecht, Jared. 2017. Are You Running a Startup or Small Business? What's

the Difference. *Forbes*, December. https://www.forbes.com/sites/jaredhecht/2017/12/08/are-you-running-a-startup-or-small-business-whats-the-difference.

6 Breakthrough Technologies. 2010. *MIT Technology Review*. https://www2.technologyreview.com/tr10/?year=2010.

7 Tidy, Joe and Sophia Galer. 2020. TikTok: The Story of a Social Media Giant. BBC News, August 5. https://www.bbc.com/news/technology-53640724.

8 Schramm, Carl. 2018. It's Not About the Framework. *Harvard Business Review*, May–June.

9 Gans, Joshua, Erin Scott and Scott Stern. 2018. Do Entrepreneurs Need a Strategy? *Harvard Business Review*, Reprint R1803B, May–June.

10 Internet Service Providers in Montana. 2022. https://www.highspeedinternet.com/mt.

11 Nevada Governor's Office of Economic Development. 2022. https://goed.nv.gov/nationally-ranked-startup-accelerators-to-locate-in-las-vegas-and-reno/.

12 U.S. Census, 2020 County Business Patterns First Look. 2022. https://www.census.gov/data/tables/2020/econ/cbp/2020-first-look.html. This dataset, County Business Patterns faces the problem of under coverage since it excludes data on self-employed persons.

13 The Nation's Report Card. Results for the 2019 Reading Assessment. https://www.nationsreportcard.gov/reading?grade=4.

14 Idaho Commerce. 2022. Key Industries. https://commerce.idaho.gov/site-selection/key-industries/.

15 Herrera, Sebastian and David Benoit. 2021. Why the Amazon, JPMorgan, Berkshire Venture Collapsed: Health Care Was Too Big a Problem. *Wall Street Journal*, January 7. https://www.wsj.com/articles/why-the-amazon-jpmorgan-berkshire-venture-collapsed-health-care-was-too-big-a-problem-11610039485.

16 Top 30 Largest Employers in Massachusetts in 2021. *Boston Globe*, December 1. https://www.bostonglobe.com/2021/12/01/magazine/top-30-largest-employers-massachusetts-2021/.

17 *The Economist*. November 19. https://www.economist.com/briefing/2009/11/19/the-parable-of-the-sower.

18 Dewey, Caitlin. 2018. Why Monsanto Is No More. *Washington Post*. https://www.washingtonpost.com/news/wonk/wp/2018/06/04/why-monsanto-is-no-more/.

19 Blank, Steve. 2014. How To Be Smarter Than Your Investors—Continuous Customer Discovery. https://steveblank.com/2014/02/19/how-to-be-smarter-than-your-investors-continuous-customer-discovery/.

20 Relan, Peter. 2013. Where Webvan Failed and How Home Delivery 2.0 Could Succeed. TechCrunch, September 28. https://techcrunch.com/2013/09/27/why-webvan-failed-and-how-home-delivery-2-0-is-addressing-the-problems/.
21 Blank, Steve. 2021. A Path to the Minimum Viable Product. https://steveblank.com/2021/04/20/the-secret-to-the-minimum-viable-product/.
22 Morris, Malique. 2022. Bolt, a Checkout Startup Worth $11billion, Lost Customers as Revenue Stalled. The Information, April 24. https://www.theinformation.com/articles/bolt-a-checkout-startup-worth-11-billion-has-been-losing-customers-as-revenue-stalls.
23 Bureau of Labor Statistics. Survival of Private Sector Establishments by Opening Year. 2022. https://www.bls.gov/bdm/us_age_naics_00_table7.txt.
24 West, Geoffrey. 2018. *Scale: The Universal Laws of Life, Growth and Death in Organisms, Cities and Companies*. Penguin Books.
25 Griffith, Erin. 2022. It's All Just Wild: Tech Startups Reach a New Peak of Froth. *New York Times*, January 19. https://www.nytimes.com/2022/01/19/technology/tech-startup-funding.html.
26 Zeitlin, Matthew. 2019. Then We Came to the End: WeWork's Contradictions. *Nplusone Magazine*. https://www.nplusonemag.com/online-only/online-only/then-wecame-to-the-end/.
27 David Autor, David Dorn, Lawrence F Katz, Christina Patterson and John Van Reenen. 2020. The Fall of the Labor Share and the Rise of Superstar Firms, *The Quarterly Journal of Economics* 135(2 (May)). https://doi.org/10.1093/qje/qjaa004.
28 Harare, Yuval Noah. 2015, *Sapiens: A Brief History of HumanKind*. Penguin Random House.
29 Lewis, S. and M. Maslin. 2015. Defining the Anthropocene. *Nature* 519: 171–180. https://doi.org/10.1038/nature14258.
30 Milgrom, Paul and John Roberts. 1992. *Economics, Organization and Management*. Prentice Hall.
31 The Top Trends in Tech. 2022. McKinsey Insights. https://www.mckinsey.com/business-functions/mckinsey-digital/our-insights/the-top-trends-in-tech.
32 *MIT Technology Review*, February 24. https://www.technologyreview.com/2021/02/24/1014369/10-breakthrough-technologies-2021/.
33 The 10 Breakthrough Technologies 2022. *MIT Technology Review*, May/June. https://www.technologyreview.com/.
34 For details see https://www.census.gov/naics/reference_files_tools/2022_NAICS_Manual.pdf.
35 https://www.microsoft.com/en-us/research/blog/microsoft-has-demonstrated-the-underlying-physics-required-to-create-a-new-kind-of-qubit/.

36 https://ece.princeton.edu/people/andrew-houck.
37 https://ece.princeton.edu/people/andrew-houck.

CHAPTER 7

The Entrepreneurial Culture

The creation of an entrepreneurial culture is the objective of many nations, states, and regions. Culture is a mental model of decision-making based on underlying values and beliefs. The values and beliefs that foster a risk-taking, entrepreneurial culture are marked by connectivity and embeddedness in a strong community. It is a belief system where risk taking is applauded and even encouraged. Like birds who sense an increase in barometric pressure in the aftermath of a storm and leave the safety of tree branches to soar into the sky, founders not only perceive the opportunity, they take the plunge and embrace risk.[1]

Business organizations shape their space and also form the environment for their employees, influencing their experiences and their beliefs. This influence works the other way around as well. People, the employees of these organizations, take these experiences home to their communities, their family and friends spreading the ideas, influencing job selection and career choices. Small changes in the composition, size, and age of these organizations alter the experience of their employees and therefore can have large effects on their ideas and beliefs, changing the entrepreneurial culture and, therefore, the organization itself. The entrepreneurial ecosystem is the environment encompassing a

[1] Barometric pressure declines predictably before a storm and animals change their behavior to conserve energy. A common hypothesis is that birds perching on power lines are a sign of an impending storm.

S. Bhatt, *Entrepreneurship Today*,
https://doi.org/10.1007/978-3-031-11495-3_7

vast support system and infrastructure to nurture emerging organizations. Rapid expansion of the enterprise, fueled by massive amounts of venture capital, coupled with a lack of awareness of the markets, the people who will ultimately use the product or service, is the bane of entrepreneurial culture.

It is not About Finance

Let me explain by clarifying what this culture is not. First, it is not about finance. At the private sector level, venture financing can be preferential toward certain regions and sectors. On the public sector side, financing options and tax incentives proliferate as policymakers attempt to promote innovation and job creation. Despite being offered $3.4b in tax breaks by New York City, Amazon withdrew plans to locate its HQ2, second headquarters, from Queens to the DMV—the DC, Maryland and Virginia area—making it a haven for tech startups. As part of the generous incentives offered by the state, if Amazon created 25,000 jobs in New York State by 2028, it would receive $1.2billion in tax credits for the Long Island City location. Interestingly, these behemoths are still expanding in New York City but without the taxpayer subsidies. The advent of the large technology behemoth, exemplified by Amazon's purchase of the iconic Lord & Taylor building on Fifth Avenue, is expected to create multiple jobs in complementary sectors.

Long before the pandemic, the tech behemoths had made plans to expand their presence in New York City, bringing with them complementary businesses. There is an entire technology corridor from Pennsylvania Station on 34th Street to Battery Park in Lower Manhattan. To support these behemoths, smaller tech companies such as Salesforce, LinkedIn, and Spotify have also established their offices in the neighborhood. Facebook has increased its presence in New York City in the 107-year-old former main post office complex near Pennsylvania Station. Google has developed a large technology campus around the Chelsea neighborhood [1].

There are non-financial factors that influence the location choice of firms, whether they are established technology behemoths, or more pertinent to this discussion, startups. Why do some regions have more entrepreneurs than others? Are there accommodations that encourage and support female entrepreneurship? These factors might play a major role which could be unearthed by investigating the patterns across time and geography revealed by our previous analysis of states and time periods. Some of these factors are along non-economic dimensions which would suggest an important explanatory role for socio-cultural factors.

In a recent paper, David Card finds that there are agglomeration effects arising from location.[2] "[T]here is an important geographic component in wage setting that adds a roughly constant pay premium for workers in all industries" and that these agglomeration effects arise from location. These "meaningful CZ effects" arise due to employers in these locations paying a fixed premium over and above the national wage for their respective industry. CZs are commuting zones, regions where workers commute, and cover both urban and rural areas, making it more comprehensive than metropolitan statistical areas. All workers migrate to high wage zones so that there is an earnings premium or meaningful commuting zone premium, not related to industry clustering, where two-thirds of the variation in these earnings differences across CZs are due to human capital and one-third to the CZ itself. So high earning capacity (higher skilled) workers drift (assortative matching) to high wage CZs [2]. These agglomeration effects are reflected in higher wages, but not the startup culture directly, in the sense that population density was not found to be an important factor, as discussed in chapter 3. However, spillovers may manifest in the form of peer effects, as will be discussed below.

It is not the Gold Rush Model

The risk taking culture is not the gold rush model in which founders crowd into pastures where others have already grazed. Would-be founders do not follow the trail left by others; in fact, they perceive an opportunity which no one else has observed. These opportunity-perceivers encourage the development of complementary businesses, other risk-takers, and in doing so found a local ecosystem. In several years, if successful, these startups form the germ of an emerging local industry. As a result, startups create emerging industries rather than the other way around.

In regions with small firms, ambitious individuals opt for founding their own firms for career advancement. They don't have the possibility of

[2] David Card received one half of the 2021 Nobel Prize in Economic Sciences for his empirical contributions to labor economics, with Joshua Angrist and Guido Imbens sharing the other half.

promotions and moving up the "corporate ladder" as would be possible in large firms. They also work across multiple tasks, gaining proficiency in a variety of roles. There is no division of labor as would be the case in larger firms. Covering multiple areas of responsibility prepares individuals to launch their own firms where there is no one other than yourself to handle the demands of a business. These small firms may provide support services, such as legal and administrative services. In one top-ranked state, Idaho, the professional and business services sector grew to support industry in neighboring California.

Connectedness

Third, this culture doesn't develop in isolation. Clustering or geographic concentration of entrepreneurial activity can lead to spillovers in the form of peer effects. A higher proportion of young and small businesses, for instance, could make a difference by influencing beliefs and risk perceptions. Policymakers have sought to promote this agglomeration via the accelerator model. These "academies" gather cohorts of entrepreneurs and provide resources and mentorship. The pathways through which these accelerators work could be direct, through actual participation, and also be indirect, through changing the local culture [3, 4].

The mere presence of an accelerator changes the local ecosystem by attracting more investors, both from outside the region as well through an increase in local funding groups. Even as participants in the accelerator are mentored, their impact in the regional entrepreneurial culture can be felt through peer effects and role models. The presence of an accelerator in a region, increases the number of startups in the region, whether they participated in an accelerator or not, and these startups obtain more than double the funding than they would otherwise have received, absent the accelerator [11]. The budding local entrepreneur is surrounded by encouraging new possibilities and ideas regarding business. Peer effects alter behavioral norms such as risk aversion and trust. It can embolden them to revise their subjective estimates of success. However, when the famous accelerator program, Y Combinator, was launched in Boston, it was met with limited success.

There is an endogenous transformation of the local culture as "regions rich in startups produce individuals better equipped to found firms and to staff startups. They create a climate (culture) in which entrepreneurship becomes 'normal'...and support an infrastructure that reduces the costs of being an entrepreneur". Substantiating the role of peer effects, Sorenson writes that "changing attitudes toward entrepreneurship led to a revitalization of the [Boston] region" [5].

One aspect of connectivity is the emphasis on customer experience. Rather than locking the customer into a particular product or service by a sales contract, short-term rental contracts allow periodic feedback and contact with the buyers. Consider the subscription model, which is defined by customer relationships and experiences in a dynamic context. The experience comprises long-term value, memorable experiences, and on-demand fulfillment with personalized services. This is in contrast to the traditional economy which focused on static offerings, a single branded product and the acquisition of new customers. This model survived due to high search and switching costs in an unconnected world. Today keeping customers engaged over time, in a connected world where multiple products and experiences are available, is the goal. Bringing buyers or the demand side into the picture is suggestive of a network form of business organization where the community of individuals on all sides of the platform interact in the production of a superior, and recurring, experience for all.

The company GoPro, founded in 2002, produced cameras and software tools that made sharing content more versatile. In 2016, GoPro moved to the subscription model, HERO5 Black, with unlimited cloud storage and premium editing tools. The Zuora platform, which enabled this development, is an incubator of sorts since it helps startups merge single time transactions, such as the purchase of a camera, with recurring services such as storage and payments [6].

On the other hand, a less successful example is that of co-working spaces. These spaces aimed to offer open collaborative space for early-stage companies in the form of desks and/or private offices, but did not offer education or training, except through speakers. Moreover, they were motivated to retain members as a revenue source rather than graduating them. Economic development centers managed by the state focused on the creation of jobs and investment in the region, but they do not offer the space or formal training for entrepreneurs.

Consensual Disagreement, and Adversarial Collaboration

The support architecture is the network of connectedness within a community, and these links between individuals and institutions play an important role in the founding process. These interactions represent differing perspectives and are unlikely to be smooth. But consensual disagreement can be strengthening since all players become aware of diverse aspects of the business and its general community. Knowing who to hire, who to get funding from (the angel investors or friends and family), which lawyer would provide legal wisdom at critical junctures—are links in a closely networked community and provide the backing needed for all of these services. Trust is embedded in such networked communities obviating the need for searching and verifying the competence of random service providers in less embedded communities.

A measure of connectivity is the clustering coefficient, which is the fraction of a founder's friends who know each other. Reputation formation or your value in a community is a precious status symbol which is granted by a dense network of people knowing each other and trading insights about various individuals' behavior. This forms the basis of trust. For a founder, it means a lot to know that your friends also know each other so that any one friend would be unlikely to mislead, fearing the sanctions levied by their common friends. Collaboration need not involve bland cooperation; it can be enlivened by varied and contrasting approaches.

Culture has a social element and it is promoted by constant and ubiquitous connectivity. Technology has facilitated sharing and shared experiences. People desire to talk about themselves, describing their interactions with others and with the environment. Conversation brings comfort in knowing that one is not alone and that others have equally dramatic adventures. Personal anecdotes and life stories paint a picture of a world that has some underlying commonality and therefore generates a feeling of solidarity and belonging. The sense of self, the feeling of legitimacy, swells as does a feeling of overall well-being in a world of contrasts.

The app-based sharing economy and the self-esteem it brought to millions of consumers is the result of commercialization of sharing via platforms that bring people together. What these platforms have succeeded in doing, in reality, has had perverse consequences. Let me illustrate with a personal anecdote. Upon describing my morning running routine with friends, we quickly compare miles covered and discover which person has the most stamina or strength. And then we judge. Why some person barely manage only half a mile and that too only twice a week, whereas the average runner in the group does 3 miles a day, every day. My friends are comparing and judging and have negated the whole point of the exercise, which was meant to increase everyone's pleasure.

Comparisons and judgments are distracting, consuming attention resources deployed to allay the discomfort from feeling diminished. Finding that some of my friends run more miles triggers a painful reassessment and recalibration of what had been a reassuring practice. Spreading limited cognitive resources over yet more mentally demanding activities leads to a deficit, an attention deficit. Could this constriction on attention also be a factor in the fragility of startups?

Being constantly measured and ranked can become debilitating and distracting. It consumes scarce cognitive resources. In their discussion of scarcity, Mullainathan and Shafir talk about tunneling. When people are confronted with scarcity in any dimension, the process of managing this deficit leads to tunnel vision where all else is blotted out. The singular aspect of life becomes this scarcity. In an experiment with workers in rural India in 2019, relaxing workers' financial constraints by compensating them after just a week at the work site compared to payment at the end of the two week experiment, increased productivity of the former group by about 10%. The early payments allowed workers to pay off loans to moneylenders. "We find positive evidence of one particular channel, attention. To investigate potential impacts of the Early-Pay Treatment via attentional channels, we collected detailed markers of inattention at work...Mirroring the impact on worker productivity, the early payment increased worker productivity" due to a reduction in errors arising from a lapse in attention, perhaps worrying about forthcoming loan repayments [7].

Quarterly milestones such as revenue targets can lead to tunnel vision. For a new business, with multiple uncertainties on all fronts, focusing on meeting this goal abstracts from recognizing the other constituents in the game. There are employees, consumers, and suppliers who have their own agenda and tunneling past their requirements can in the end diminish the entire startup. Recall the discussion in chapter 6 about the distortionary effects of a singular focus on scaling or increasing revenue. There the very process of scaling was questioned from the perspective of functionality and operations. Here the issue is the impact on individual, the founder's judgment and decision-making apparatus.

Tunnel vision is at one end of the information processing spectrum. At the other end lies an attention deficit due to the tsunami of content. Vast amounts of information about markets, about trends, about local and global resource imbalances, about social and community predicaments pervade the consciousness of the founder. This enormous demand for cognitive bandwidth is set against a fixed mental capacity, leading to an attention deficit.

In fact, information processing has two stages. The first stage involves filtering the relevant information. This process denudes mental capacity of its sharpness even prior to the second processing stage. As the tsunami of content grows, the demand for attention increases while the supply of cognitive bandwidth is depreciated by the initial filtering requirement. There opens up an enormous attention deficit. For the entrepreneur, there are two possible outcomes, both of which may be simultaneously present. First, there may be a tendency to jump to conclusions and make hasty judgments, snap decisions. This short-term focus can lead the startup down an irreversible path. Second, the deficit of systems for balanced, reasonable analysis may lead to cognitive apathy. Founders talk of mental paralysis when accosted with multiple, simultaneous decision-making points.

Mullanaithan and Shafir call this the "bandwidth tax".[3] When we think of having very little (time, money, calories) we focus on the physical implications of scarcity: less time for fun, less money to spend, fewer slices of chocolate cake. The bandwidth tax suggests there is another, perhaps more important, shortfall. We must now get by with fewer mental resources. Scarcity leaves us handicapped in other aspects of our lives. It makes us dumber. It makes us more impulsive. We must get by with less mind available, with less fluid intelligence, and with diminished executive control—making life that much harder. Fluid intelligence, the capacity to think logically, analyze and solve novel problems, independent of background knowledge might be broadly referred to as cognitive capacity, the psychological mechanisms that underlie our ability to solve problems,

[3] "Bandwidth measures our computational capacity, our ability to pay attention, to make good decision, to stick with our plans and to resist temptation. The blanket term bandwidth refers to two broad and related components of mental function", fluid intelligence and executive control [8].

retain information, engage in logical reasoning, and so on. The bandwidth tax diminishes logical reasoning and working memory. It also reduces executive control, to direct attention, initiate an action, inhibit an impulsive action. Much like a central processor in a computer system, executive control is essential to our ability to function well.

However, if there is any slack in the system, if there is more cushioning for failure, then failure itself might not occur. When the pressure of meeting various targets set by either the founder or by the financiers is relaxed, business performance might improve as the individuals involved can now attend to a wider range of issues. When the cost of error falls, there is more room to think as the tunnel is broadened. By reducing cognitive bandwidth, "scarcity not only raises the costs of error; it also provides more opportunity to err, to make misguided choices" [8].

Daniel Kahneman, who won the Nobel Prize in economics in 2012, is the Eugene Higgins Professor Emeritus of Psychology at Princeton University. Kahneman makes the case that there are systematic errors in the thinking of normal people due to the simplifying heuristics or rules of thumb that are used to assist in decision-making. "A general law of least effort applies to cognitive as well as physical exertion. The law asserts that if there are several ways of achieving the same goal, people will eventually gravitate to the least demanding course of action. In the economy of action, effort is a cost, and the acquisition of skill is driven by the balance of benefits and costs. Laziness is built deep into our nature" [9].

Decision-making is mentally effortful, utilizing cognitive resources, which is classified as system 2 thinking, so the individual dips into thinking fast, the system 1 part of the brain which relies on impressions, feelings, a sense of cognitive ease and ignores the lack of evidence, ambiguity and even "suppresses doubt" [9]. Importantly, cognitive load or too much work for system 2 weakens self-control, is ego depleting, and reduces motivation. Think of system 2 as the electrical circuits in your home. When the demand for electrical current overloads the system, the breaker trips and all devices lose power simultaneously. System 2, on the other hand, selectively chooses which activity to focus on, leaving the other activities to the faster system 1. Kahneman calls this "the sophisticated allocation of attention".

The intelligence needed to steer a new business relies on focus for long periods of time and emotional or impulse control plus the ability to switch quickly from one task to another. All of these features are compromised when there is cognitive overload on system 2. Startups involve much adversarial collaboration and consensual disagreement—this can be mentally depleting but is vital in bringing awareness of the environment and of all the constituents involved in the process.

Asynchrony and Noise

There is one more aspect of connectedness that has had negative consequences. The decoupling of time and content or asynchrony made possible by new hardware and software creates a solitary consumption experience with concomitant loneliness. For example, text messaging, a favorite form of communication, has decoupled the time at which the message was sent and the time it was read. Linear television of the old days consisted of the large broadcasting networks deciding the timing and content of your viewing. On-demand television today eliminates this restriction by streaming content directly to your home from a massive library of movies.

Asynchrony has fostered a form of alienation. Communication via text messages, with asynchronous communication has allowed many in the entrepreneurial world to become completely alienated from ordinary people throughout the country—so there is little awareness of real needs and real problems. This arises because asynchrony allows more people to access information and be connected since there is no need to coordinate the timing of the interaction. With greater access, no curators or gatekeepers and more flexibility in content consumption, more content is imbibed, intensifying the content tsunami.

In addition to stretching the limits of comprehension, serial communication impedes coordination. Our species became the most powerful on the planet because language gave Homo Sapiens the unprecedented ability to cooperate in large numbers and coordinate their activities, according to Yuval Harare. [See the discussion from chapter 6]. With coordination foundering, the business rapidly disintegrates as the production side is out of sync from the marketing and sales side.

In contrast to the prevalence of asynchrony in content consumption, there is real-time connectivity in product and service consumption, as seen by the proliferation of platforms as-a-service and direct-to-consumer business models among startups. Software has replaced inventory. Platforms-as-a-service connect buyers with sellers, effectively creating a marketplace. The consumer is directly connected with the business. A wholesaler-retailer chain of intermediaries is not present, and buyers are confronted with a plethora of choices. In such a marketplace model, consumers can find it difficult to distinguish between products, becoming confused about the true nature of their preferences.

This development has led to choice-fatigue and preference reversals. In some cases, there is also intransitivity or inconsistency being displayed. As in Buridan's paradox, where a hungry and thirsty ass must choose between a bale of hay and a pail of water, decision paralysis results in death from both starvation and thirst. Subscription programs solve this decision problem by locking in consumers, building brand loyalty, as well as ensuring predictable cash flow. Brand loyalty eases the decision-making problem since the choice has already been made. Taco Bell released a subscription club, in January 2022, called the Taco Lover's pass which gets you a taco a day for a plan that costs $10 for a 30-day subscription. Cross country travel just became that much simpler since there is no longer a decision to be made at the end of a long road-trip—just head on over to the local Taco Bell.

Moreover, there is little slack ingrained into the direct-to-consumer framework of operation. Algorithms and data replace a warehouse filled with stuff, as businesses can evaluate the market demand directly from their mobile phone. However, some redundancy in the system is valuable as we have seen during the pandemic. Having multiple sources of supply, for example, may be inefficient, but guarantees the availability of inputs and services when needed. Super-efficient production processes are fragile to unknown variability in undiscovered areas. Not only is there variability in known outcomes, but there is also variability in the variability itself. Furthermore, the outcomes themselves are unknown, and have unknown variability.[4]

The unknown unknowns can lead to noise in judgment and decision-making. Noise is exacerbated when there is redundant information or extraneous information. Pandemic decision-making is replete with situations where individuals had to balance moral reasoning with risk evaluation. A cost–benefit calculation was constantly being made: when to wear a mask, when to stay home, how to interpret the data about hospitalizations and deaths. "People will take comfort when a coronavirus fatality

[4] Risk is uncertainty within a model such that there are known probabilities assigned to specified but outcomes. Ambiguity is uncertainty across models with unknown weights assigned to these alternative models. Misspecification is the uncertainty that results when you don't know the model nor the flaws about the approximations made in the model.

is attributed to 'underlying conditions—for instance, a patient's age or chronic maladies—that they do not share', surmising that they themselves are not at risk and perhaps need not wear masks. Cognitive scientists even have experiments to explain the 'declining marginal disutility' that people associate with others' deaths—the feeling that the difference between no deaths and one death is really bad, but the difference between 110,000 and 111,000 is negligible" [10].

An entrepreneur is constantly faced with vast amounts of information and an equally large number of decisions and choices. Kahneman et al. feel that "in real world decisions, the amount of noise is often scandalously high". Sometimes the same person can make opposing decisions on the same issue but on different occasions. This is occasion noise. In the early stages of a business, when a small number of founders and employees brainstorm ideas, they are subject to occasion noise from "seemingly irrelevant factors, such as who speaks first". Then the second person in the decision chain is likely to be influenced by the first person's judgment and may follow along, generating a cascade of "yes" decisions. In an attempt to stem the inadvertent impact of extraneous information, entrepreneurs and their financiers set strict guidelines, often in the form of simpler, numerical criteria such as revenue targets, product dimensions, etc. The problem with guidelines is that decisions become rigidly mechanical when the decision environment is incredibly complex and requires vigilant adaptation.

Worse, there is system noise, which arises from unwarranted confidence in one's decision-making capability. Confidence is established by the fluency and ease of similar decisions made in the past. The error arises in the subtle assumption that there is "a single interpretation of the world around us at any one time, and we normally invest little effort in generating plausible alternative to it... We do not go through life imagining alternative ways of seeing what we see". Hence, when comparable decisions arise for different individuals, their world-view influences the decision process, leading to system error [10].

Accelerators and the Support Architecture

In April 2001, an unarmed Black man was killed by police in Cincinnati, leading to massive riots. However, one well-meaning outcome was the creation of the Minority Business Accelerator (MBA), whose mission was to build scalable companies headed by minority entrepreneurs.

Twenty years later, the MBA has 40 African American and Hispanic firms, each earning $1million in annual revenue. Cincinnati has the highest percentage of minority businesses that make more than $500,000 annually and have been in operation for more than 6 years [11].

Cincinnati succeeds in part because it has matched minority-owned supply companies with its top science and research companies, from Johnson & Johnson and the Cincinnati Children's Hospital Medical Center to Procter & Gamble. From its perch within the city's chamber of commerce, the MBA often finds minority businesses making in the low millions annually and connecting them "with the buying power of that regional or national organization, building their revenue to $20, $30, $40 million or more", says MBA Executive Director Darrin Redus.

In 2014, the MORTAR startup accelerator was founded to help low-income, mostly African American entrepreneurs build or expand their businesses. Of the 180 graduates of the program, 172 are still actively pursuing their businesses as of last year. The Hillman Accelerator, created by Matthews Brackeen with former Cincinnati Bengals linebacker Dhani Jones in 2017, invests $100,000 and provides mentorship to female- and minority-owned Midwest startups. And in late June, Matthews Brackeen launched a $50 million fund to invest in companies led by racial, queer, and disabled minorities, the first to do so in the Midwest, and the largest fund launch to date by a Black woman. "It further feeds our pipeline of color", Redus says [11].

Ohio doesn't rank among the top states in startup activity, but the rapid establishment of accelerators, particularly for minority communities, is an encouraging policy. Accelerators have a competitive application process and provide equity capital and intense mentoring and training for several months, but typically less than a year. At the end of the program, founders pitch their idea or product to investors. Due to their highly selective nature, accelerators may not scale and are unique to each state or region.

The highest performing states, Massachusetts and California, have such institutions. The California Technology Council has a mission of advancing California's primacy in technology-led businesses through its diverse community. Based in Santa Clara, California, it initiated the California Business Incubation Alliance which is comprised of incubators and accelerators with a focus on education and networking. For example, in July of 2021, this group organized a meeting of biotech entrepreneurs on the question of matching biotech startups with incubators and addressing questions such as which lab space is best for a startup [12]. In Massachusetts, there is the Massachusetts Association of Business Incubators, a network of incubators and entrepreneur support organizations. The International Business Incubation Association, InBIA, a global non-profit with over 1200 members in 30 countries, has supported startups since the surge of connectivity triggered by the World Wide Web nearly 30 years ago.

However, a note of caution is voiced by Paul Graham, the founder of Y Combinator, the first and most recognized accelerator program. Graham writes, "[p]eople sometimes think they could improve the startup scene in their town by starting something like Y Combinator there, but in fact it will have near zero effect. I know because Y Combinator itself had near zero effect on Boston when we were based there... People came from all over... and afterward they went wherever they could get more funding—generally Silicon Valley" [13].

The weaker entrepreneurial landscape among mature firms could be the result of over-zealous intermediaries such as incubators, accelerators, and angel investors who play an active role in guiding startups even as they lend a financial hand. Hedge funds, corporate venture capital, and possibly mutual funds can be added to the list of intermediaries. Does venture backing select only winning opportunities, or do they play an active role in mentorship and networking?

Scaling, Again

Lerner and Nanda make the case that there is a sort of monopoly power held by this small band of intermediaries, "who hold and shape the direction of a substantial fraction of capital that is deployed into financing radical technological change" and that this may have "detrimental effects on the rate and direction of innovation in the broader economy". Using the initial public offering as a metric for success, these researchers find that 56% of firms that went public and traded on national stock exchanges between 1995 and 2018 were backed by venture financing in their early years. Since only 0.5% of startup firms receive venture financing this finding illustrates the concentrated power of venture backing in the U.S. economy. This concentration is incentivized by the fee structure where venture funds receive management fees as a function of the size of the portfolio. But management fees do not increase in lock-step with assets under management, there are economies of scale in management of these ventures. Moreover, more than two-thirds of the income for these funds come from these management fees which are a fixed cost to be paid out regardless of performance.

Not only is there a concentration of assets in few venture capitalists, but these investors are themselves geographically concentrated. According to the National Venture Capital Association Yearbook data, three areas account for over 66% of funding each year: the San Francisco Bay Area (or Silicon Valley), New York and Boston. This accords with the results in chapter 3 and 4 that rank California and Massachusetts high in startup activity. But what of New York, which remains relatively low in this ranking? [14].

Interestingly, there is also homophily or extensive similarities in background, and therefore behavioral preferences such as risk-taking, of decision-makers at the venture firms. Focusing on the 417 U.S.-based partners at the top 5 percent of venture capital firms, Lerner and Nanda write, "Eighty percent of partners are male... Three-quarters of the partner with at least one board seat attended either an Ivy League school, or one of Caltech, MIT or Stanford; moreover, nearly 30 percent of these individuals are graduates of just Harvard Business School or the Stanford Graduate School of Business". Does this influence the nature of products and services that are backed by these investors? Could it be that they lack the deeper feel of the larger economy and hence are grossly misinformed about which sectors to back?

Recall the discussion on scaling in the previous chapter and the role that finance plays in that process. Venture capitalists typically have a 10-year horizon and seek to exit from their investment in the form of the public offering or sale to a larger firm. This relatively short fund life is a relic of twentieth-century finance which focused on oil-and-gas exploration and real estate. Rapid commercialization of the idea is promoted since valuation for the sale of stock depends upon expected future cash flows that can be derived from the firm. Venture investors would thus be attracted to that class of high-risk investments that provide rapid exit. If the uncertainty lies on the demand side, the sooner the market provides positive feedback the quicker is the resolution of this investment uncertainty and hence exit. The longer-term innovative aspect and further spillovers are not the concern of these investors. For example, the recent decline in energy related early stage venture investments could have negative geopolitical, and social, implications. Data from CBInsights covering the first two quarters of 2022 show that the predominant sectors receiving seed and early stage funding in the U.S. were biotech, e-commerce, restaurants and Internet software and services, not energy [15].

Based on data from the National Venture Capital Association's yearbooks, Lerner and Nanda find that hardware software accounted for nearly 84% of venture investments during the late 1980s but has shifted, between 1985 and 2019, toward consumer and business products and services, biopharmaceutical and medical devices and software. Hardware, comprised of telecommunications, networking, materials and energy, accounted for less than 5% during the 1985–2019 period.

Bibliography

1 Matthew Haag. 2020. Facebook Bets Big on the Future of N.Y.C., and Offices, With New Lease. *New York Times*, 8/2/2020. https://www.nytimes.com/2020/08/03/nyregion/facebook-nyc-office-farley-building.html
2 Card, David, Jesse Rothstein, and Moises Yi. 2021. Location, Location, Location. *Center for Economic Studies. U.S Census Bureau,* CES 21–32. October 2021.
3 Glaeser, E. L., W. R. Kerr, and G. A. M. Ponzetto. 2010. Clusters of Entrepreneurship. *Journal of Urban Economics*. 67(1): 150–168.
4 Nanda, Ramana, and Jesper B. Sørensen. 2010. Workplace Peers and Entrepreneurship. *Management Science* 56 (7): 1116–1126.
5 Olav Sorenson. 2017. Regional Ecologies of Entrepreneurship. *Journal of Economic Geography* 17(5). https://doi.org/10.1093/jeg/lbx031
6 Zuora website. Accessed on 2/26/22 from https://www.zuora.com/our-customers/case-studies/gopro/
7 Kaur, Supreet and Mullainathan, Sendhil, Oh, Suanna and Schilbach, Frank, Do Financial Concerns Make Workers Less Productive? 2021. *University of Chicago, Becker Friedman Institute for Economics Working Paper No. 2021–07.* SSRN: https://ssrn.com/abstract=3770928 or https://doi.org/10.2139/ssrn.3770928
8 Mullainathan, Sendhil and Eldar Shafir. 2013. *Scarcity: Why Having Too Little Means So Much.* New York: Times Books, Henry Holt and Company.
9 Kahneman, Daniel. 2011. *Thinking, Fast and Slow.* New York: Farrar, Straus and Giroux.
10 Kahneman, Daniel. 2022. *Noise*. Farrar, Strauss and Giroux.

11 Fouriezos, Nick. 2020. Cincinnati's Secret Sauce to Help Minority Businesses Succeed. *Ozy.com.* https://www.ozy.com/the-new-and-the-next/cincinnatis-secret-sauce-to-help-minority-businesses-succeed/370356/
12 Fehder, D. C., & Y. V. Hochberg. 2019. Spillover Effects of Startup Accelerator Programs: Evidence from Venture-Backed Startup Activity.
13 Graham, Paul. 2009. Can You Buy a Silicon Valley? Maybe. http://paulgraham.com/maybe.html
14 Lerner, Josh and Ramana Nanda, 2020. Venture Capital's Role in Financing Innovation: What We Know and How Much We Still Need to Learn. *Journal of Economic Perspectives* 34(3).
15 https://www.cbinsights.com/reports/CB-Insights_Venture-Report-Q2-2022.pdf?utm_campaign=marketing_state-venture_2022-07&utm_medium=email&_hsmi=219299935&_hsenc=p2ANqtz--LgkjKQA8KqFGQ8cA52NHCMlRFYvi2RVpMeVgcIpI2lsQqIizgVBxSR1i3xQaI13ZJ6_SNcu2IRsEoaBApewaGvg7Msw&utm_content=219299935&utm_source=hs_automation.

CHAPTER 8

Experience, Age, Education, Gender, and Race

A question posed in many entrepreneurship classes is about the required knowledge and skills for a would-be startup. Internet foraging is not to be conflated with basic research and critical thinking. Rapid-fire enumeration of Google-charged, Wikipedia-fed data is not sufficient. There needs to be expertise, understanding and awareness, perhaps an intuition about the problems faced by people and their needs. In rare instances there a flight of the imagination that results in the creation of an iPhone, or iPad which at its inception had no obvious purpose but has since become a vital tool for all functions. This chapter posits that in the face of declining labor force participation among the prime age working population (ages 25–44) and the enormous slowdown in productivity growth, entrepreneurial ventures are the fruits of older, more seasoned adults, ages 45–54, as they ply their experience and age in reconfiguring this new phase of their lives.

The iPhone's success, its mass appeal, was not due to its technological superiority (though that was important), but the charismatic individual who introduced the product. The device was not Jobs' vision. There is rarely a single inventor, but rather a team who may be working in parallel or in sequence, standing on the shoulders of previous giants, that produces what the public sees as a brilliant idea. When Steve Jobs introduced the iPhone in 2007 at the Macworld conference, his message was about "1000 songs in your pocket" rather than 1 GB of memory. Jobs

S. Bhatt, *Entrepreneurship Today*,
https://doi.org/10.1007/978-3-031-11495-3_8

noticed that people wanted to listen to music as they moved about [1]. In the current context, is this awareness missing, and if so, can it be taught?

In addition to vision and awareness does an active work history play any role? Do years of experience in the workforce matter to invention or innovation? Do you recognize problems only if you are in the trenches? Steve Jobs had been immersed in the world of computing and is associated with the personal computer revolution of the 1980s, with the introduction of the MacIntosh in 1984. Later, it was the network of individuals in Jobs' team that was actively engaged with both the product and its users, promoting an understanding and a preparedness when the inevitable bug or glitch appeared. As Jobs' biographer, Merchant makes clear, "The story of the iPhone starts... not with Steve Jobs or a grand plan to revolutionize phones, but with a misfit crew of software designers and hardware hackers tinkering with the next evolutionary step in human–computer symbiosis" [1]. Hundreds of people, at Apple, Corning (maker of Gorilla glass, the surface of the iPhone) and Samsung, made key contributions to the success of the iPhone.

In this chapter we examine age, experience, education, gender, and race to either of these factors is correlated with what I refer to as "awareness" and a connection to the community.

Age, Experience, and the Undefined Factor

Both age and experience matter. The vision of a recent and youthful graduate starting a new business has not materialized. There are two paradoxes that emerge. First, there is declining labor force participation among the prime working age population (ages 18–64), which conflicts with the upsurge in startup activity during the years 2010–2019. Second, the economy-wide slowdown in labor productivity growth to 0.8% since 2010 combined with the declining labor force participation rate is hard to reconcile with the digital mobility revolution of these very same years. The resolution of these two paradoxes, of these opposing forces to creative business formation, comes from the active presence of older entrepreneurs and community involvement. Let me explain.

Paradox 1 - Who Are the Founders?

Active participation in the labor market is a measure of some kind of work experience, whether it is at an employer business or one's own business.

Absence from the labor force implies lack of experience. The first paradox is that the labor force participation rate, which defines the proportion of the civilian non-institutional population **actively in the labor force**, age 16 and older, has seen a secular deterioration since the mid-1990s, a time period we have labeled the digital revolution (Fig. 8.1). Actively working includes both those who are actually working as well as those who are looking for work in the past 4 weeks.

The participation rate includes the category for self-employment implying that low engagement in work is not restricted to employees in large firms but also encompasses non-employees who manage their own business. However, the process of disengagement started before the recession of 2009—there was sluggish performance since 1990.

Reflecting on the labor force participation curve in Fig. 8.1, the sharp upsurge in participation rates during 1980–mid 1990s reflects the entrance of the late boomer generation into the labor force. The boomer generation is defined as those born between 1946 and 1964, so the oldest boomer was around 40 in the mid-1980s and zestfully engaged in the labor force. The Pew Center defines the generations according to birth years, so, for example, those born between 1965 and 1980 are called Generation X, those born between 1981 and 1996 are the millenials and those born between 1997 and 2012 are gen Z [2].

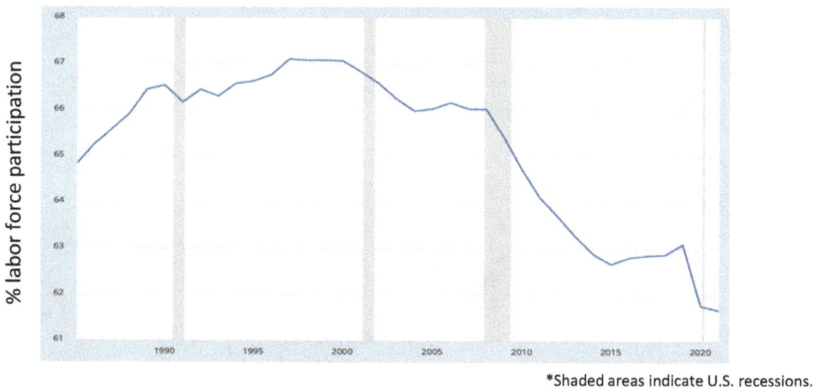

Fig. 8.1 Labor force participation rate (*Source* U.S. Bureau of Labor Statistics, compiled by FRED [fred.stlouisfed.org])

Now consider Fig. 8.2 which pictures the labor force participation rates of adults between the ages of 25 and 54. Matching this trend with the Pew Center generation definitions, it is possible to create a link between the economics of the labor market and its sociology. As we will see later, there is reason to start by focusing on the younger adults, those between the ages of 20 and 34. This is the group that is just entering the labor force, after having finished high school, and perhaps college. Call them the graduates.

There is an increase in the rate of actively engaged adults between 1995 and 2000, from 83.5% to 84%. Of this population, those who would have been between the ages of 20 and 34 were born during 1961 to 1975, the late boomers and early gen X (born between 1965 and 1980). Linking workforce dynamics with the startup revolution, there is a matching between early period I increase in startups during 1994–2000 and increasing labor force engagement during the same years. The late boomers and early gen X could have been the entrepreneurs during these years.

Subsequently, in 2005, the participation rate falls to 82.8% and then even further to 82.2% in 2010. The graduates in 2005 would have been born between 1971 and 1985, the late gen X and early millenials. In 2010, the graduates would have been born during 1976–1990, which also comprises late gen X and millenials.

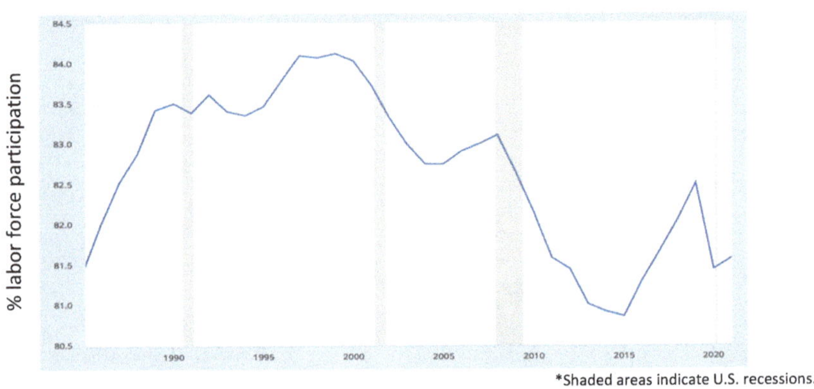

Fig. 8.2 Labor force participation rate: 25–54 years old (*Source* U.S. Bureau of Labor Statistics, compiled by FRED [fred.stlouisfed.org])

However, a paradox emerges during period II, the years between 2010 and 2020, the mobility revolution. The labor force participation rate falls dramatically from 2010 to 2015, when it is 80.9%. This low a rate has not been seen since 1984, about the time when the first desktop computers were created. The graduates in 2015 were comprised of those born between 1981 and 1995. This matches almost exactly with the definition of millenials. **Therefore, the downturn in participation arises precisely when the millenials were entering the labor force** [3].

The contradiction between increasing startups during the mobility revolution on the one hand and labor force participation rates of the prime working age group (those who might have been founders) lies at the heart of this paradox. Startups are rising and labor force participation is falling. Then who are the founders?

The founders must have been the older cohort, the patriarchs and matriarchs between the ages of 45 and 54. Label this group the *householders*. In ancient India, it was believed that one's life had multiple stages and the most venerable and dignified stage was that of the householder due to his/her sense of personal and communal responsibility, self-reliance and resourcefulness. The authors of the ***Dharmashastras***, the ancient Indian body of jurisprudence (1500–1200 BCE) that is the basis of family law in Hinduism, believed that the householder derived legitimacy from his fulfillment of obligations to others, and his contributions to the prosperity of family and community [4].

With this frame of reference, those born between 1956 and 1965, would be 45–54 in 2010, which is the definition of the late boomer generation. In 2015 and in 2019, the householders would be those born between 1961 and 1974, gen X. Figure 8.3 shows that, as of 2020, for every 100,000 adults in 2020 aged 45–54 there were 500 who started a new business, compared to 400 in the generation aged 35–44 and among millenials only 250 individuals started a new business. This trend is rather consistent in that entrepreneurial activity is increasing over the period 1996–2020 for all cohorts except those between 20 and 34. The proportion of this younger generation that have participated in new business creation has hovered around 0.25% since 1994.

In 2010, at the start of the mobility revolution, the graduates were the young millennials. They are the digital natives, having grown up with computers, smartphones, and the web. They had information at their fingertips. Yet the data suggest these individuals may *never have entered the labor force*, nor the startup world, during the decade of the mobility

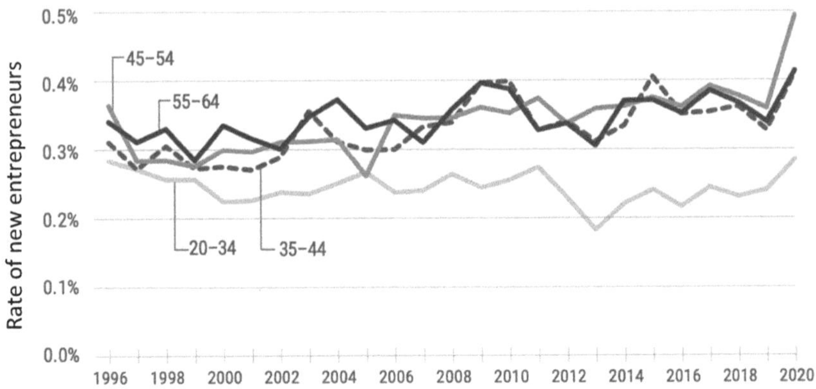

Fig. 8.3 Rate of new entrepreneurs by age group: 1996–2020 (*Source* Current Population Survey, compiled by Kauffman Indicators of Entrepreneurship)

revolution. Yes, age and experience matter in the sense that it is the older cohort, 45–54 that lies behind the startup movement, corroborating the data in Fig. 8.3.

Moreover, the householder generation is unlikely to exhibit declining labor force participation as they would have little incentive to exit from the labor force. They were rising up the career ladder and perhaps were at the peak of their careers. Remember that inclusion in the labor force means current employment or seeking employment. If you are unemployed for longer than 4 weeks, then you don't count in this statistic. The generation older than householders, 55–64 are close to retirement and would forfeit any benefits, both social and economic, if they exited the labor markets. Similarly, the generation younger than householders, 35–44, is more likely to switch jobs in their search for the best job and skill match, but they too are seeking a livelihood to support a family.

The trend for men has taken a deeper dive than that for women, falling consistently throughout two decades of the twenty-first century. The overall trend has fallen from a high of around 67% in 1994 to a low of 62% in 2020. The rate for women actually rose during the 1990s, which explains the mild rise in overall participation rates during that period. See Fig. 8.4. The decline in labor force participation for men accelerated after the Great Recession, the period after 2010. Male workers who lost their jobs during the economic slowdown were quite possibly scarred by the

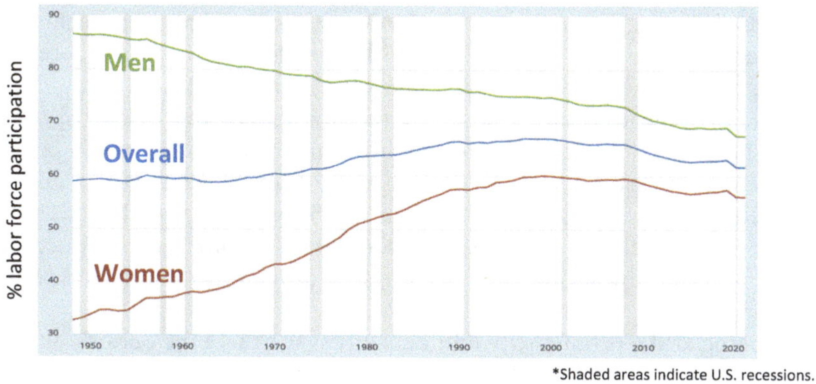

Fig. 8.4 Labor force participation rate by sex: 1950–2020 (*Source* U.S. Bureau of Labor Statistics, compiled by FRED [fred.stlouisfed.org])

experience: they became reluctant to return to their jobs or could not find replacement jobs.

Paradox 2: Productivity and Participation

At the same time, the pace of life has been increasing. Measuring the pace of life by the number of activities that can be crammed into a 24-hour day, the larger the number of activities, choices, modes of communication, the greater the pace, the speed, of life. It is perhaps paradoxical that with more being consumed, less effort is being placed in its very production. Psychologists define the pace of life as the speed with which actions are completed, or equivalently, the number of actions that can be accomplished in a given period of time. If more activities are executed within 24 hours, then they must be completed faster. Both the speed of actions and the number of actions translate into a perception that time itself has accelerated—the speed with which we perceive life passing by, the passage of time, has increased. This is the source of the second paradox. Despite an increasing pace of life, the growth in productivity has slowed down.

Increasing number of choices and activities, quite possibly the result of the mobility revolution, juxtaposed on declining labor force participation and productivity growth presents us with the second paradox. Overlaying productivity numbers with labor force participation numbers, we see that declining labor force participation has coincided with declining productivity during 2007–2019. Recall that we defined the mobility revolution, period II, as encompassing the years, 2010–2020. In Chapter 5 we discussed productivity growth in the context of the delay hypothesis, where technological change was not immediately apparent in labor productivity measures. Growth in real gross domestic output per capita declined from an average of 2.46% over the 50-years period, 1920–1970 to 0.35% during the 10-year period, 2006–2016, despite the introduction of digital communications technologies, such as the iPhone and streaming [3].

Looking at the productivity numbers across the two time periods under consideration in this book, the average annual percent change in productivity in the non-farm business sector was 2.6 during 2000–2007, the later years of the desktop revolution but has declined to 1.4% over the years 2007–2019, inclusive of the Great Recession. The post-pandemic increase to 2.1% during 2019–2021 has yet to be sustained in the coming decade.

However, the regions of the U.S. had variable rates of productivity growth. The West had a 1.6% rate of productivity growth during 2007–2018, while the South and Northeast both posted rates of 1% and the Midwest had a rate of 0.9%. In particular, North Dakota had the highest labor productivity growth followed by Washington and California, a result consistent with our results on young startups during the mobility revolution in Fig. 3.10. Note that the BLS productivity data stop short at 2018 and include the recessionary years.

The slowdown in productivity growth has three components: contribution of capital intensity, contribution of labor composition, and multifactor productivity growth. The latter is the largest contributor to the slowdown and also the most volatile. Importantly, MFP growth "cannot be measure or identified on its own but can only be ascertained as the ***leftover output growth*** that remains after all measurable inputs to production—in this case, labor and capital—have already been taken into account. With MFP growth, we are actually measuring something that is unidentifiable.. This is the reason that the question of what is driving MFP growth has puzzled so many economic observers in recent years and still remains incompletely explained following more than a decade of work on the issue" [5].

The U.S. economy slowed significantly following the adverse financial shock of 2008–2009, which put a damper on the supply side of the economy including research and development and technology adoption. Some researchers believe that this weakness started before the Great Recession, that there was slower long-term trend growth and that fiscal and monetary policy provided insufficient stimulus. Stock and Watson argue that demographics changes such as the "surge of women into the labor force in the 1970s–1990s, and more recently, the baby boomer beginning to retire" have been the cause of the declining long-term trend [5].

Institutions and their organization might play an active role in this diffuse measure of residual output growth. As in a large jig-saw puzzle, multiple agents need to be connected and perhaps federal and state governments, alone, are not sufficient for this task. Local institutions and community organizations can be vital in connecting people. The key policy goal in the U.S. going forward is to get the productivity growth rate back to its long-term historical trend of 2.1% measured over 1947–2018 (Fig. 8.5).

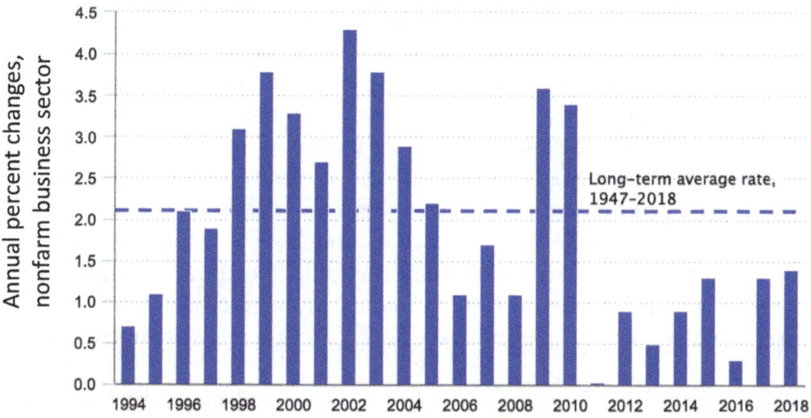

Fig. 8.5 Labor productivity growth: 1994–2018 (*Source* U.S. Bureau of Labor Statistics)

Labor Productivity Growth, Non-Farm Business Sector, Annual Percent Changes

Despite this paradox of productivity slowdown coinciding with declining labor force engagement, the number of new and young establishments grew rapidly, as an entrepreneurial force gripped states like Missouri, Idaho, Wisconsin, Massachusetts, and California. Perhaps community organizations or the "third pillar", to use Raghu Rajan's terminology, was instrumental [See chapter 1].

Gender

Labor force participation across men and women has a vastly different trajectory. There has been a secular downward trend in participation among men starting from 1950 to 2020, while women have increased participation until 2000 after which they too have reduced participation in the labor force. Recall that participation in the labor force includes both those who are working as well as those who have been actively looking for work in the past 4 weeks.

An entrepreneur is a person who desires to own their workspace and perhaps create similar workspaces for others. Yet, researchers have found there are less female than male entrepreneurs. Differences in risk appetite, identity, and gender norms might all be possible explanatory factors.

Gender norms could be playing a role where women do not identify with being entrepreneurs. However, network effects could kick in if a few women were to be upheld as role models. The gains from being a founder increase as more women join the ranks, both in changing gender norms as well as in providing mentorship, and therefore existing female entrepreneurs may be incentivized to encourage more women to consider this career path.

The Rate of New Entrepreneurs Index by Sex, calculated by researchers at the Kauffman Foundation, shows a wide disparity over the entire period 1996–2021. (Fig. 8.6). Moreover, female owners constitute less than half of the total entrepreneurs in the U.S. (more precisely 35%). Women owned approximately 20% of all employer businesses in the U.S. in 2018 and 25% of those were owned by minority women [6].

Even when women enter the entrepreneurial pool, they face financial constraints. They have a 10% higher probability of loan rejection, despite

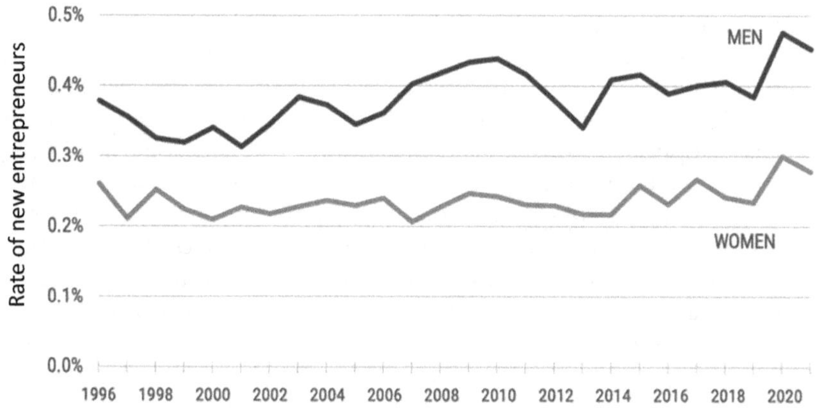

Fig. 8.6 Rate of new entrepreneurs by sex: 1996–2020 (*Source* Current Population Survey, compiled by Kauffman Indicators of Entrepreneurship)

the fact that "female-owned firms are neither riskier nor less profitable with respect to male-owned ones" [7].

Using data from the World Bank, recent research shows that less than 25% of businesses across 141 countries have female owners and that in women-owned businesses, the probability that the top manager is a woman is over 50%, as compared to 6.2% when the firm is owned by a male. This would suggest that encouraging female entrepreneurship might be a way to increase the participation of women in the labor market. With around half of the world's population being women, there is a significant loss of productivity and innovation due to this misallocation in the entrepreneurial labor market [8].

In some parts of the world, there is the belief "that a wife who works outside the home is a source of social stigma or shame for her husband, who is expected to earn enough to support his family". In a controlled setting in rural India, researchers found that directly depositing women's earning into an individual bank account, and giving them bank account management training, resulted in greater labor market engagement and private sector work. The group that was most impacted were the "socially constrained" women. These were women who had never worked outside the home. These women reported greater agency and mobility. Over the course of the experiment, gender norms became more liberal among the women who were directly paid, and they reported that their community was also more accepting of working women. On the other hand, while their husbands' own attitudes didn't change, they did feel that the community was more accepting and that the stigma was lessened. With an outside option, women's bargaining power had increased within the household, which not only gave them access to more household income, but also freed them from the constraints placed by the community norms. Their sense of self, their identity as good women and wives, was no longer threatened. The policy implication is enormous—provide incentives to change behavior and the norms will change of their own accord [9].

Consider the case of Norway. It has one of the highest female labor force participation rates at 48%. However, only 25% of the entrepreneurs are women, a fact not lessened by including educational differences or industry differences [10]. Following workers new to the labor market for 10 years after entry, occupational choices in Norway over 2002–2012 are strongly influenced by their older peers. Strong links with family, friends, classmates, neighbors, and importantly, same sex peers explains 50% of the gap in gender composition of founder.

The absence of women founders in individuals' social network as well as role models and mentors leaves a vacuum for women who are considering such a career path. The latter group do not possess the know-how and possibly are afraid to ask male peers for help, for fear of being downgraded, depreciated or not taken seriously. This might lessen their motivation and turn them off this particular career path.

Social influence is the impact of one's peers and this includes members of one's family, and friends and neighbors, groups that in many cases are quite distinct. Sociologists call this kind of persuasion membership closure. If a close friend has created a new venture then it is quite likely that there is plenty of opportunity, incentive, and trust for this choice of career to transmitted to the friend.

The opportunity to exert this influence is determined by, to a large extent, geographic overlap. One could argue that digital connectivity advances the influence but does not initiate it. Person-to-person contact is important where risk-taking activities are concerned. Body language—the straight talk, the unblinking visage, the squared shoulders—conveys confidence, however imperceptibly. The influence of neighbors thins out in sparsely populated areas since it would be effortful and costly to interact with the "founder crowd"—this might explain the low rates of women founders in Norway.

Migration might offset some of the geographical impediments to social influence and peer effects. Government policies, such as local taxes and subsidies, might motivate certain groups, formerly separated geographically, to arbitrage these differences by moving to favorable locations, and perhaps into closer proximity with entrepreneurial groups. In addition, the perception of what women as a group, are accomplishing or not accomplishing, could send a powerful signal that might be interpreted as general encouragement toward such a career path.

Education

One normally thinks of relevant education as high school graduation and college degrees. It would be useful to consider vocational skills, some measure pertaining to non-college-based skills. In order for inventiveness and ideas to thrive, there must be some requisite underlying skill set to support such a move. The Kaufmann Foundation data covering the entire U.S. show that since 2006, the largest cohort of new business creators has come from those with less than a high school education, outranking college graduate who count for a low of around 0.3% (Fig. 8.7).

There is considerable heterogeneity at the state level which can be seen in graduation rates by state. If we consider public schools in the U.S., state education agencies calculate the adjusted cohort graduation rate (ACGR)

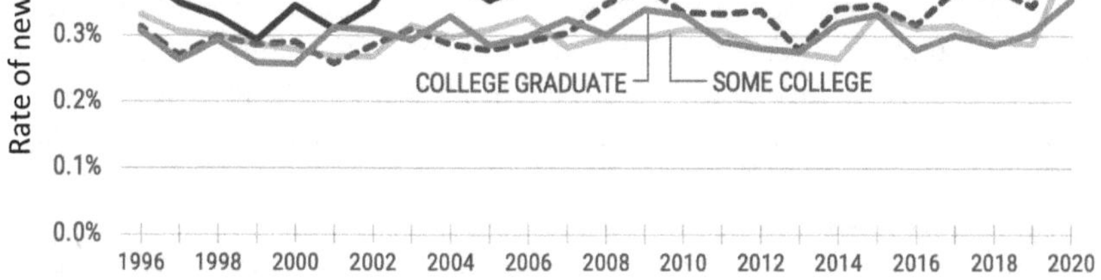

Fig. 8.7 Rate of new entrepreneurs by education: 1996–2020 (*Source* Current Population Survey, compiled by Kauffman Indicators of Entrepreneurship)

by identifying the cohort of first time 9th graders in a particular school year and then obtaining the percentage of students in this cohort who graduate within 4 years with a regular high school diploma. The ACGR is adjusted for students who immigrate from another country or transfer into the cohort after 9th grade and subtracting the transfers out of the school. The U.S average ACGR for public high schools increased from 79% in 2010–2011 to 86% in 2018–2019. Forty states reported ACGR's over 80%, with Alabama at the top with 92%, 69% in the District of Columbia, and 75% in New Mexico [11]. There appears to be little correlation between ACGR in states and their startup performance. Neither Alabama nor New Mexico stood out in the rankings for young startups.

These numbers suggest that high school graduation is neither a necessary nor a sufficient statistic for measuring the skills needed for entrepreneurship given its high rate across most states, regardless of whether or not the state ranked high in the uptake of business opportunities. Moreover, the ACGR only measures graduation of students who have already enrolled in a high school. It does not include those who never entered high school or who dropped out in junior high school. This might explain why Massachusetts has a relatively low rate of 88%, close to the national average, despite ranking high in the startup landscape.

Using the National Assessment of Educational Progress report card in 2019 across the top states might be more revealing. For example, on the math, reading and science scores for grade 8 students, 29%, 30%, and 24% of students respectively performed at or above the NAEP proficient level in California. The same numbers for Massachusetts were 47%, 45%, and 44%, while for Missouri they were 32%, 33%, and 40%, and for Idaho they were 37%, 37%, and 40% respectively. Clearly California doesn't rank high in this statistic. In fact, while many states west of the Mississippi ranked at or above proficient in grade 8 math scores in 2019 on the NAEP assessments, California, Texas, Nevada, New Mexico, Oklahoma, Arkansas, and Louisiana did not. On the other hand, Massachusetts and all the New England states, Pennsylvania and New Jersey were at the top of these rankings. Except New York, which was at average [12]. There appears to be little correspondence between test scores and entrepreneurial performance across states.

Admittedly test scores are not comprehensive in their assessment of adult competency and functionality. There is the danger of painting all students with a broad brush and assuming that a common curriculum meets a variety of different learning approaches and needs. The pandemic has made clear that the environment, via the social-emotional circuit, can impact a student's ability to learn. The energy and focus necessary to absorb knowledge when there are irregular school schedules are significantly diminished.

Learning depends on what students are being asked to comprehend and the attitudes that they are encouraged to have about that body of knowledge. Relevance to a students' interests, the topics that they care about, the kinds of work they see themselves performing, and the types of people they wish to become are factors that will determine the actual learning process and retention of information. Students learn more effectively, therefore, when the content is measured to their size.

Researchers in Milwaukee, Wisconsin conducted an experiment in 1987 where they created a 2-foot-by-2-foot replica of a baseball field in a classroom, complete with four inch wooden players. They asked 64 students to read a story about a hypothetical game stopped after half an inning and then use the model to replay the action. The students who did the best with transferring the abstract story into actual action on the miniature baseball field were not strong readers but rather students with an innate knowledge of baseball. Weak readers did as well as strong readers if they had similar levels of familiarity with baseball. The implication was that if these students were taking a learning and reading comprehension test based on a topic they knew little about, they would perform worse than if they were tested on their favorite activity. Prior knowledge is the key to superior performance in not only test taking but also success in college and life [13].

Entrepreneurship Skills

The skills required for founding a firm are less correlated with college degrees. Attributes such as collaboration, openness to new ideas, developing a sensitivity to the environment, and an awareness of people in your radius of interaction and their needs cannot be taught. They must be learnt through experience, usually at young ages, by grade 4 or grade 8.

There are five native skills that are acquired by experience rather than formal education: awareness, resourcefulness, practical intelligence, over-optimism, and personal initiative.

First is awareness. In a paper in the Harvard Business Review, Stern School of Business Professors Ashish Bhatia and Natalia Levina tell the story of how a Thai student's family rapidly converted the family's medical supply business to sanitizer production upon the onset of the pandemic in April 2020. They pivoted without a business plan or detailed analysis. "This approach to entrepreneurship is called 'effectuation' or leveraging what we know, who we know and who we are in order to take action. Business schools don't generally teach this approach, as they tend to focus more on lengthy risk and return calculations.... Moreover, developing a penchant for imagination, disruption and counterintuitive action required for effective entrepreneurship doesn't generally fit into a typical business school curriculum defined by abstract analytical models and precise calculations" [14].

Entrepreneurship can be thought of as the identification and exploitation of business opportunities and hence is "fundamentally personal" [15]. Awareness of one's surroundings enables individuals to notice business opportunities without searching for them. Business plans can be misleading as they are fixed and rigid structures, based on incomplete information about a future that is unknown and unknowable. It is hard to even conceptualize the many unknown unknowns.

Second is resourcefulness. Creativity is required when entrepreneurs need to take action to overcome financial constraints by using financial bootstrapping or acquiring resources without relying on bank debt or equity financing. It can take different forms such as owner financing (personal and family savings), speeding up invoicing or accounts receivable, delaying payments, obtaining subsidies from the public sector, minimizing inventory (to the extent possible). Capital constraints need not impact new venture creation when nascent entrepreneurs have innovativeness [16].

Third, another native skill which cannot be taught, is practical intelligence. Practical intelligence helps entrepreneurs make fast and accurate decisions because it encompasses general knowledge about ideas and processes that have proved to be successful [17]. This attitude of "gee-whizzery" fosters agility in taking action before others perceive the opportunity and a rapid reaction time to unforeseen events. Practical intelligence promotes repeated experimenting, testing, and revising of the business concept to continuously improve it.

Fourth, cognitive biases or overoptimism can actually promote risk taking by initiating the necessary activities to launch a venture and successfully introducing radically innovative products and services [18, 19]. Like the first penguin who plunges into the icy waters of the

Antarctic in search of food despite the danger of lurking sharks, the entrepreneur takes a leap into frosty waters to launch this particular business.

Fifth, personal initiative means that an entrepreneur's impetus for action is driven less by other people or immediate external demands but more from inner passion. Many commencement speeches are laden with the exhortation to pursue one's passion, but in this context, it translates into constant vigilance and anticipation of potential threats in the process of developing, launching, and managing a new venture, and being persistent in seeking solutions.

Despite the devastating effects of the bombing of the World Trade Center towers at the beginning of the twenty-first century, Americans became more determined after this disaster rather than letting a malaise creep into their life. But sheer resoluteness and dogged passion are not sufficient. Untiring persistence in the absence of awareness, resourcefulness, and practical intelligence is like scattering seeds into barren soil. These are the crucial three traits that are frequently lacking in the entrepreneurial ecosystem.

Grouping these traits into a category called acuity or the ability and willingness to incur information processing costs of decision-making ignores the critical aspect of information filtering in the first instance [20]. In the second instance, the sheer volume of information or the content tsunami creates an attention deficit which then leads to a cognitive apathy in decision-making and judgment. Entrepreneurs could be overwhelmed with information such that it clouds judgment and precludes the ability to be aware, resourceful, and street-smart (a more vivid interpretation of practical intelligence). Incorporating information about, and being aware, of one's surroundings and people can lead to cognitive overload—processing this content tsunami makes an enormous demand on mental acuity.

Race and Ethnicity

Centuries of socio-economic injustice tied together with persistence in present-day discrimination have left an iron mold of behavior across all parts of society. Like icebergs, formed by calving, or splitting, glaciers, segregation, sub-par education, and childhood poverty are simply the visible manifestation of the ice shelf. And the iceberg itself, the visible portion, is just the tip—approximately 90% of the iceberg is under water.

As with cooling temperatures in the early fourteenth century, the "Little Ice Age", deeply held beliefs about race and ethnicity developed like glaciers advancing in many parts of the world. By the mid-nineteenth century, the Ice Age had officially ended but the glaciers remained. The Gangotri Glacier, located in the Uttarkashi District of Garhwal Himalaya is one of the largest in the Himalayas. While it has been receding since 1780, studies show that its retreat has hastened after 1971. Over the past 25 years, the Gangotri glacier has retreated more than 850 m. Glaciers are sensitive to temperature fluctuations, and global warming has accelerated this melting. Has there been a similar warming of beliefs about racial differences? [21].

Average inequality and segregation in housing by income has risen in the U.S. between 1980 and 2010. Metropolitan areas are segregated by income and this segregation is correlated with the average measure of inequality across the nation. Skilled workers, with higher incomes, gravitate toward neighborhoods with benefits such as education, better public services, which in turn generate even more spillovers in terms of neighborhood effects. A reversal of causality is also observed when skilled workers with higher-paying jobs, pay more in local taxes, engage more with local public education and libraries and create a neighborhood effect or a culture of investing in higher education, exacerbating the existing inequality.

Research shows that such neighborhood choices are reflected in a greater concentration of income in precisely these locations, contributing to 28% of the increase in inequality between 1980 and 2010. Peer effects in new business formation are also segregated along these lines. Complementarities between highly skilled workers, higher incomes, higher local taxes paid, and increased provision of public services are the direct impact. There is also the indirect complementarity that arises due to the transmission of values and behavioral norms, the so-called social externalities or peer effects. The correlation between income and race would suggest that race-based segregation could be driving these results [22].

Deep-seated beliefs, the glaciers, that have given rise to the bergs of segregation, educational disparities, and childhood poverty, while still prevalent, are not reflected in recent data on entrepreneurship. What they do tell, however, is a more complex story. Figure 8.8 shows that the Latino population has dominated the rate of new entrepreneurs since the turn of the century, the year 2000. A stable fraction of new entrepreneurs is white, at roughly 0.3% while the percent of the Latino population that starts a new business has risen from 0.3% to over 0.5% between 1996 and 2020. The fraction of the Black population that have become entrepreneurs was at 0.2% in 1996, has risen to 0.38% in 2020, but dipped in 2021. The rate for immigrants was a much larger 0.59% relative to 0.35% for native-born Americans.

The groups that have demonstrated significant entrepreneurial ability in the past decade, or the mobility revolution years, 2010–2020, have been Latinos and immigrants. There are considerable complementarities or peer effects among both groups where members of the group provide information, mentorship, and social support to each other due to the strong links that exist due to a common heritage and beliefs. Newly arrived immigrants tend to gravitate toward metropolitan areas that hold substantial numbers of people with similar ethnic and racial histories. Transferring business information about markets and products is integrated with the social aspects of their interactions.

The labor force participation rate of the Latino population gives weight to this conclusion. Consider Fig. 8.9. It maps the rates of engagement across three demographic groups: White, Latino, and Black. The participation rates in 1994 for these groups were 67.1, 66.1, and 63.4 respectively. In 2021, these rates were 67.1, 65.5, and 60.9. The labor force participation rates had fallen the least for the Latino group. There are two penetrating questions that come to mind: Why has the downward

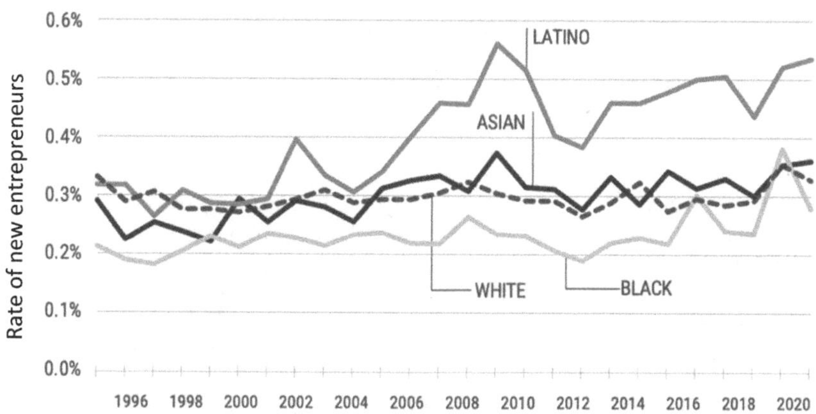

Fig. 8.8 Rate of new entrepreneurs by race and ethnicity: 1996–2020 (*Source* Current Population Survey, compiled by Kauffman Indicators of Entrepreneurship)

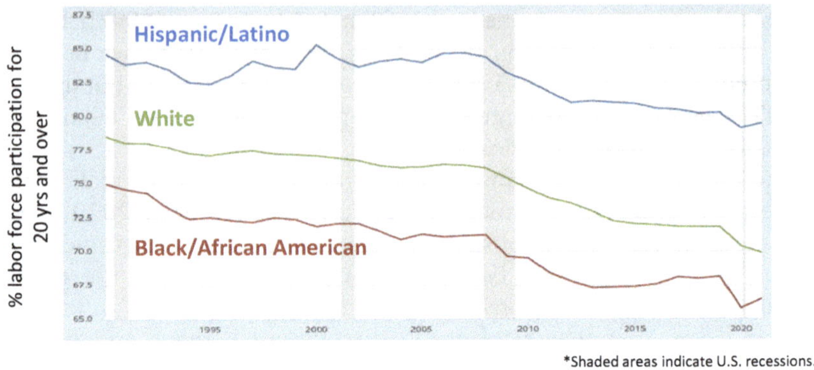

Fig. 8.9 Labor force participation rate by race and ethnicity: 1950–2020 (*Source* U.S. Bureau of Labor Statistics, compiled by FRED [fred.stlouisfed.org])

trajectory been so prominent for Whites? Why has this decline surfaced only since 2000 for Latinos and why has it been relatively slower for Blacks?

Bibliography

1 Merchant, Brian. 2017. The One Device: The Secret History of the iPhone, Little, Brown and Company.

2 Dimock, Michael. 2019. Defining Generations: Where Millennials End and Generation Z Begins. Pew Research Center. https://www.pewresearch.org/fact-tank/2019/01/17/where-millennials-end-and-generation-z-begins/

3 Bureau of Labor Statistics. 2022. Labor Productivity and Costs, 1947–2021. https://www.bls.gov/lpc/prodybar.htm

4 Olivelle, Patrick. 2019. *Grhastha: The Householder in Ancient Indian Religious Culture*. Oxford Scholarship Online. https://oxford.universitypressscholarship.com/view/10.1093/oso/9780190696153.001.0001/oso-9780190696153

5 Monthly Labor Review, Bureau of Labor Statistics. 2021. The U.S. Productivity Slowdown: An Economy-Wide and Industry-Level Analysis. https://www.bls.gov/opub/mlr/2021/article/the-us-productivity-slowdown-the-economy-wide-and-industry-level-analysis.htm

6 Number of Women Owned Employer Firms Increases. U.S. Census Press Release, 2018. https://www.census.gov/newsroom/press-releases/2018/employer-firms.html

7 Morazzoni, Marta and Andrea Sy. 2021. Female Entrepreneurship, Financial Frictions and Capital Misallocation in the U.S. https://www.cmu.edu/tepper/faculty-and-research/seminars-and-conferences/assets/docs/morazzonisy.pdf
8 Chiplunkar, Gaurav and Penny Goldberg. 2021. Aggregate Implications of Barriers to Female Entrepreneurship. *NBER 28486*. https://www.bls.gov/opub/mlr/2021/article/the-us-productivity-slowdown-the-economy-wide-and-industry-level-analysis.htm#_edn8
9 Field, Erica, Rohini Pande et al. 2019. On Her Own Account: How Strengthening Financial Control Impacts Labor Supply and Gender Norms", *Working Paper, Economic Growth Center, Yale University*. https://papers.ssrn.com/sol3/papers.cfm?abstract_id=3456234
10 Simen Markussen and Knut Røed. 2017. The Gender Gap in Entrepreneurship – The Role of Peer Effects. *Journal of Economic Behavior & Organization* 134. https://www.sciencedirect.com/science/article/pii/S0167268116302955
11 Public High School Graduation Rates, National Center for Education Statistics. 2021. https://nces.ed.gov/programs/coe/indicator/coi
12 State Performance Compared to the Nation. 2019. *The Nation's Report Card.* https://www.nationsreportcard.gov/profiles/stateprofile?chort=2&sub=MAT&sj=AL&sfj=NP&st=AP&year=2019R3
13 Recht, Donna and Lauren Leslie. 1988. Effect of Prior Knowledge on Good and Poor Readers' Memory of Text. *Journal of Educational Psychology* 80(1).
14 Bhatia, Ashish and Natalia Levina. 2020. Can entrepreneurship be Taught in a Classroom? *Harvard Business Review, August 7, 2020.* https://hbr.org/2020/08/can-entrepreneurship-be-taught-in-a-classroom
15 Baum, J. R., M. Frese, R. A. Baron and J. A. Katz. 2007. Entrepreneurship as an Area of Psychology Study: An Introduction. In J. R. Baum, M. Frese, and R. A. Baron (Eds.), *The Psychology of Entrepreneurship* (pp. 1–18). Lawrence Erlbaum Associates Publishers.
16 Shane S. 2000. Prior Knowledge and the Discovery of Entrepreneurial Opportunities. Organization Science 11(4): 448–469.
17 Baum, J. R., B. J. Bird, and S. Singh. 2011. The Practical Intelligence of Entrepreneurs: Antecedents and a Link with New Venture Growth. *Personnel Psychology* 64(2): 397–425.
18 Baum J. R., M. Frese, R. A. Baron. eds. 2007. *The Psychology of Entrepreneurship*. Mahwah, NJ: Erlbaum.
19 Simon M., and R. C. Shrader. 2012. Entrepreneurial Actions and Optimistic Overconfidence: The Role of Motivated Reasoning in New Product Introductions. *Journal of Business Venturing* 27(3): 291–309.

20 Heiss, Florian and Daniel McFadden. 2021. Inattention and Switching Costs as Sources of Inertia in Medicare Part D. *American Economic Review, September* 111(9).
21 National Snow and Ice Data Center. 2022. https://nsidc.org/cryosphere/glaciers/quickfacts.html
22 Fogli, Allessandra and Veronica Guerrieri. 2019. The End of the American Dream? Inequality and Segregation in U.S. Cities. *NBER Working Paper 26143*. DOI: https://doi.org/10.3386/w26143

CHAPTER 9

The Big Quit: Reimagining Lifestyles

The pandemic made us realize that other than work there is nothing else going on in our lives. There are few hobbies or interests—so why not quit and try something diametrically opposite to current work like starting a new business. It is quite possible that a connection exists between the recent uptick in new business formation, shown in Fig. 1.1, and the big quit. The delay hypothesis, discussed in Chapter 5, may in fact be quite pertinent in this context. Are the inventions we saw in Chapter 7 now coming to fruition? Perhaps not precisely, but in a circuitous manner. The exciting opportunities that had only been imagined before can now be implemented if there was a boldness in action. That would mean quitting. However, the quit rates are highest for the 25–34 year old cohort, followed by the 35–44 cohort, the very same cohorts with the lowest labor force participation, as inferred from the data in Chapter 8. Is quitting just another facet of declining activity in the labor market or are these individuals at the vanguard of a startup revolution?

Approximately 4.35million workers quit their jobs in February 2022, compared to 3.44million in February 2021. That is an increase from 2.4% to 2.9% of the employed labor force. Of the total, the largest number, 991,000 workers, have departed from the trade, transportation, and utilities sector, while 863,000 have quit from the leisure and hospitality sector. [1] Many have made the leap from blue-collar jobs and hourly work to

S. Bhatt, *Entrepreneurship Today*,
https://doi.org/10.1007/978-3-031-11495-3_9

jobs that required more tech skills, such as software and IT more generally. There appears to be a talent migration as job switchers follow where there are job postings. Does the switch occur before the job posting or do workers quit after locating another job? If the switch occurred after the job posting for skilled work that required software and other information technology skills, then it would be more likely that the worker already has these skills and would like to deploy them more broadly in another enterprise. For low-wage, unskilled workers it is more likely that they quit, learnt the skills, and then applied for the job.

For example, Zack Williams took a landscaping construction job after losing his bartending job in March 2020. In August 2020, he enrolled in a coding boot camp for nine months at a cost of $15,000, earning a software engineering certificate. He started at a new job in January 2022 as a software engineer at media company Gannett Co. [2]

These are the "New Collars" or blue-collar workers who acquired new, tech-based skills to search for better jobs. They are entering the world of software, information technology, data processing, and electronics manufacturing, and leading a revolution of sorts: their departure from the blue-collar labor market is creating a shortage of workers in that segment. "More optimistic, **community oriented**, resilient, and risk-taking than the general population, they reinvented themselves. They learnt new skills to get the compensation and flexibility they crave and deserve" [2]. [Emphasis mine]

These workers are primarily between the ages of 25 and 34 and urban millennial males, born between the years 1980 and 1996. Most of them desired more flexibility rather than simply higher compensation. They are eschewing standard education programs, as 59% attended a free course while 42% used social media, such as YouTube; 38% enrolled in a paid online course, while only 2% went to school. Certificates and licenses were the most sought after credential, rather than college diplomas. This age group, 25–34, the millennials, are also digital natives, who "desire control and connection,.. are non-conformists, with a shared sense of having suffered a trauma together" but have "an overall sense of disconnection". Flexibility and free food are perks that are highly valued, and key to hiring, as 69% said they would take a pay-cut for more flexible work. [3] Incredibly, as we saw in Chapter 8, this very cohort was the least entrepreneurial as well as the least engaged in the labor force.

This chapter probes three major arguments as an explanation for the recent surge in quits. Apart from the anecdotal evidence above, we proceed by scrutinizing the data and then assess the impact of the pandemic and the role of government support.

Quits

A dramatic trend toward reimagining lifestyles and starting one's own business appears to have taken off in the past two years.[1] Was there some feature of the labor market that prompted such bold shifts?

Perhaps low wage growth prompted many workers to move to self-employment. Figure 9.1 shows that wage growth in period I, 1994–2007, is observationally different from that during period II, 2010–2020. The former time period saw declining wage growth overall, from a peak of 4.5% in March 1997 to 4.3% in October 2007, just before the great recession. On the other hand, wage growth post-Great Recession went from 1.6% in January 2010 to a high of 5.1% in January 2022. But that is not a complete story. If you look carefully, wage growth was relatively stagnant during the 2010–2019 period, and lower than the average rate of growth between 1994 and 2007. The sharp uptick in 2020 and 2021 was a **result** of workers quitting or simply not returning to work after the forced closure of many establishments during the stay-at-home norms prevailing during the height of the pandemic years.

What are the demographics and trends of quit rates? Fig. 9.2 shows quit rates have been steadily rising since the pandemic, from 2million workers in April of 2020 to over 4million in January 2022. Have many of those who have been asked to remain away from the office during the early months of the pandemic never came back to their old jobs? Many might have been rehired elsewhere or become self-employed.

The Demographics

Consider the age profile of those who quit over the past 26 years. Figure 9.3 depicts separation levels by age. Not surprisingly, individuals over the age of 55 show little change in quit rates over the entire

[1] Two data sets are explored: one from the U.S. Census, housed in the Department of Commerce, and the other from the BLS, housed in the U.S. Department of Labor. The Commerce Department also houses the Bureau of Economic Analysis, which produces some of the most influential indicators of the economy: GDP and trade balance, among others.

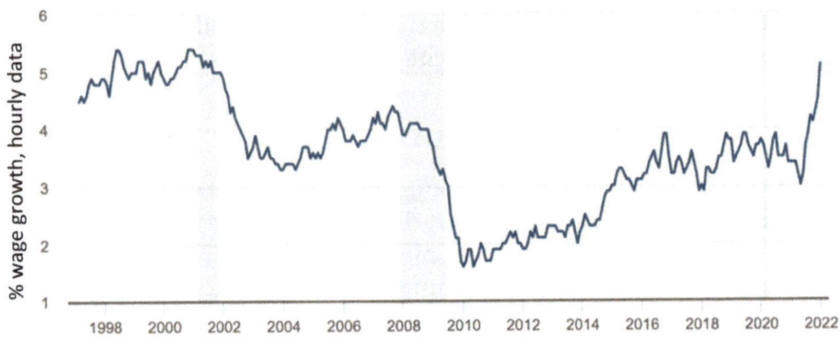

Fig. 9.1 Wage growth: 1998–2022 (*Source* Current Population Survey, compiled by Federal Reserve Bank of Atlanta)

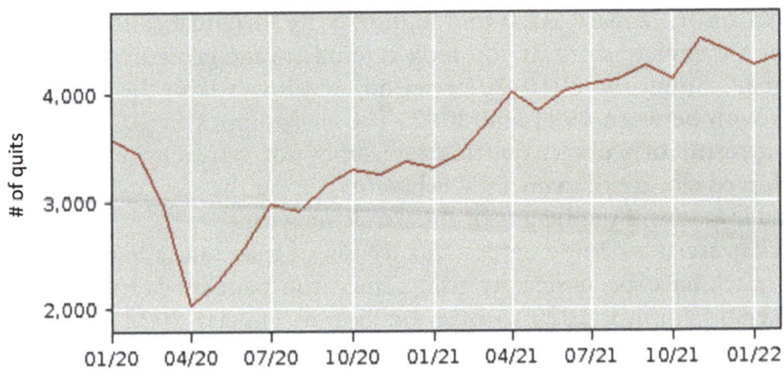

Fig. 9.2 Quit rates: 2020–2022 (*Source* Bureau of Labor Statistics, JOLTS dataset)

time period. Employees close to retirement age have probably become accustomed to the work, which might even have become routine, and, additionally, are likely to forfeit any benefits that may accrue due to longer job tenure.

Ranking third in average quit rates over the entire 26-year period, individuals in the 45–54 year group also show a relatively flat separation trend. These are employees at the peak of their careers and are looking to climb the job ladder at their current establishment. Consequently, they might be unwilling to risk the next promotion in search of a better alternative.

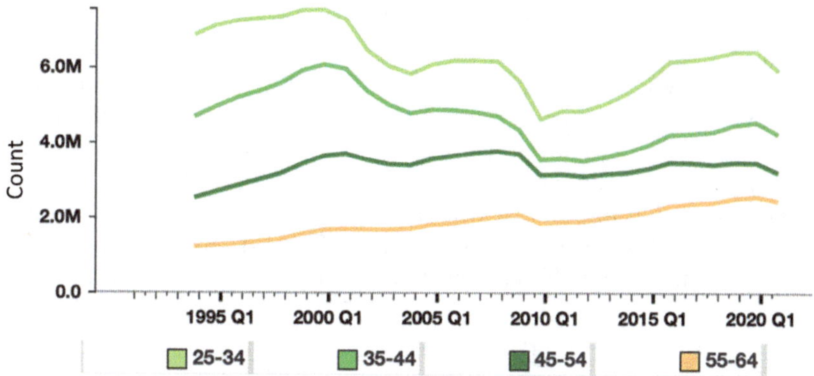

Fig. 9.3 U.S. separation counts: 1994–2020 (*Source* U.S. Census Bureau)

Similarly, individuals between the ages of 19 and 24, with the lowest average quit rate over the two decades, show a milder decline in separations. Having just entered the labor force, the 19–24-year-old group not only rank at the lower end of average quit rates over the 1994–2020 timeframe but have shown a relatively mild drop in separations.

The most meaningful pattern is shown by the 25–44-year-old demographic. With the highest average quit rate over the 26-year period, this group first exhibits a dramatic drop in separations between 2000 and 2010 and then turns sharply upward around 2010.

Within this group, the 25–34 age cohort ranks highest in separation count over the entire 26-year period. During the early aughts, this cohort's quit rate dropped precipitously after 2000 to a low point in 2010, before rising during the decade of the teens. During the desktop revolution years, 1994–2007, these workers were wedded to their jobs with little job churning.

While their average quit rates were lower than the younger cohort, the older group between the ages of 35 and 44, had a similar trajectory. They showed reluctance to leave their current job in period I, the desktop revolution years, and then began quitting around 2010 until the present, the mobility revolution years. Were these quitters the founders of startups or joining a startup as one of their early employees?

The 45–54 year cohort had the lowest separation count and remained steady over the period 1995–2020. Recall the discussion in Chapter 8 about the 45–54 year-old demographic being the source of startups because the precipitous declines in the labor force participation rates among the younger cohorts eliminated them (i.e. 24–35 year old) from the startup world. See Fig. 8.2. [The U.S. Census includes the self-employed in calculations of employment and unemployment data. The incorporated self-employed are classified as wage and salary workers because, they are paid employees of their own corporation.]

The intriguing question is whether higher separation rates among the 25–34 year-old cohort is another facet of the decline in labor force participation. Perhaps this cohort simply is not interested in work.

The State Trends

As with entrepreneurial activity, so also with separations—there are differences across states. See Fig. 9.4. Most relevant would be the correspondence between separation and startup activity by state during the years of the mobility revolution, 2010–2020. Examining the data on state level quit rates or separations, five observations stand out, particularly among the states with superior entrepreneurial activity.

First, most states that are at the center of startup activity have a similar pattern to that of the entire U.S. The levels are highest for the age group 25–34 followed by 35–44 and then the 45–54 group. Workers in the younger cohort could be in the job switching mode and very well start their own business. One can postulate that rising separation levels might be correlated with increased entrepreneurial activity in that state.

Second, the separation levels have a general pattern of rising during the late 1990s, then precipitously falling starting around 2000 and reaching a floor in 2010. A sharp upturn around 2010 occurs, most predominantly in the 25–34 age group. Third, the sharp hike in separations coincides with the startup trends during the years 2010–2020, the years defined as the mobility revolution, suggesting that workers might have swapped jobs and entered the startup world.

Fourth, the separations rise faster for the 25–34-year-olds after 2010, widening the difference in quit levels between that group and all other groups. These are the millennials, born between 1981 and 1996. This league of younger workers, who have recently entered the labor force, are quitting their initial jobs and venturing into new territory at a faster rate. As mentioned earlier, and worth repeating for emphasis, this is also the group with the lowest labor force participation rates.

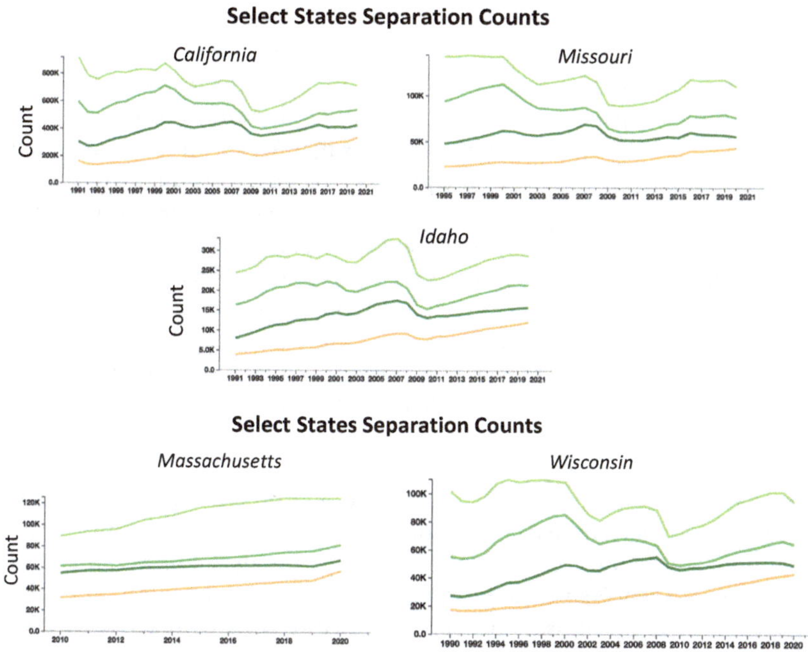

Fig. 9.4 Select states separation count: 1994–2020 (*Source* U.S. Census Bureau)

Fifth, Massachusetts stands apart—it exhibits a steady rise in separation counts throughout the mobility revolution or 2010–2020 time period, with slowdown in the years following the Great Recession. [The BLS doesn't have data for Massachusetts prior to 2010]. There is a significant upward trend in separation among the younger cohort, 25–34, widening the gap between this cohort and all the older cohorts who had more subdued upward trajectories. People in Massachusetts were quitting even before the term became part of the popular lexicon. Were they quitting to start new businesses? The evidence on high startup activity in Massachusetts among the younger startups during the years 2010–2020 is consistent with higher quits over the same period.

In general, the slowdown in separations across all states during the years 2000–2010 had economists lamenting that this lack of churning in the labor market might be the result of declining business dynamism during the early years of this century. Business dynamics is the lifecycle of new business creation, growth, decline, and finally exit. An outcome of this dynamism is job reallocation as workers gravitate toward innovative firms with higher productivity. If there is little innovation or idiosyncratic productivity shocks there is no incentive for new, or existing, businesses to create or destroy jobs. Even in the presence of these productivity shocks, frictions to job reallocation from older, less productive firms to newer, more productive firms would slow labor market churn.

There is, indeed, evidence of both establishment-level and firm-level dispersion in labor productivity. The output per worker differs across firms and across establishments even in a given firm. Workers are not identical, and the organization and culture of a particular establishment incorporates the attitudes of workers in that place of work. It would be specious to assume that all organizations, whether startups or established businesses, have similar worker output performance; they may not even face the same distribution of labor productivity, which can be geographically determined, in addition to organization and culture. [4]

Consequently, the recent trend toward separations is a form of reallocation, ensuring renewed dynamism. These workers are quitting and being rehired in other businesses and perhaps starting their own business. New businesses move the technological frontier upwards and workers "reallocate from old, obsolescing incumbents to new, more productive entrants" [5] "Although this process takes time due to labor market frictions, it does not necessitate workers spending time in unemployment. Instead, a large share of this reallocation takes the form of direct job-to-job moves".

Perhaps the conjecture that "ideas are getting harder to find", according to a Bloom et al. [6] is the source of labor productivity dispersion.

The Pandemic

By April 2020, as the coronavirus continued to spread uncontrollably across the U.S., most cities and states issued stay-at-home orders, which limit the circumstances under which people can leave their homes. Under such an order, all non-essential workers were required to stay at home. People could leave their homes only for essential needs like groceries and medical supplies, or for outdoor exercise. That meant that restaurants had to close or only offer take-out and delivery, salons and barber shops must close, schools and businesses that could function remotely must do so.

These stay-at-home orders and social distancing guidelines had a basic aim: flatten the curve or reduce the spread of the virus and prevent the disease from overwhelming the health care system, which was being stretched beyond its normal limits. The lockdown was not a simple quarantine, which would involve isolating infected individuals. It was a mass quarantine.

There was fairly high compliance with these orders. Researchers from the University of Pennsylvania and the Federal Reserve Bank of Chicago found that these orders were successful—county level measures of mobility decreased by 7% within the first two days of the order. [7]

The pandemic had given pause to normal work life and allowed people to imagine, become aware of, and connected to their environment. Time spent away from the constrictions of a daily commute and routine job may have provided the right impetus for soaring on a dream of owning one's own livelihood, of following a passion conceived in earlier days. The forced break created by the pandemic was an unimagined savior.

Many Americans have been taught skills that are no longer in demand. Having the wrong skills means an unfulfilling job so the incentive to quit is higher—people don't want to work just to earn a livelihood, they want to own their livelihood. As a nation grows richer and people have enough to eat and a shelter over their heads, they seek to flourish in life and will accommodate their lifestyle to achieve this goal. If they have been trained for the industrial age, they are mismatched for the digital age. It follows that they feel unfulfilled, not just redundant.

Goods are undelivered for want of truckers. Code is unwritten for want of coders. Hotel beds are unmade for want of bed makers. Hilton Worldwide Holdings and Marriott International Inc have dispensed with automatic daily housekeeping at their non-luxury properties.

The obvious reason is the coronavirus pandemic, supercharged by multiple follow-up strains of the original virus. Yet this phenomenon highlights problems that were already in place or at least on the radar screen. Already visible is the demographic squeeze that was the inevitable consequence of retiring baby boomers and declining fertility rates or birthrates. Labor supply depends upon the fraction of the population that is able bodied and working. That is, the fraction of the total population that is between the ages of 25 and 54. "America has thrived in the long term because of a generous supply of both people and skills, delivered by a combination of high fertility and immigration". [8]

The low fertility future is captured by the population growth of 0.1% in 2021, the slowest rate since the eighteenth century. In addition, the civilian labor force participation rate, the fraction of potential working age people actually working, declined from 67% in 2000 to 62% in December 2021 (Source: U.S. Census). It is even lower for prime-age men as 10% of men ages 25–54 are neither employed nor looking for work. In addition, as discussed above and in Chapter 8, the group between the ages of 25 and 34 has been quitting the labor force for a decade, measured by the decline in labor force participation rates.

Nor is the rest of the world an important source of talent. "A growing proportion of foreign-born Ph.D.'s now return to their native countries either to teach or, more frequently, to start their own companies. From 1978 to 2007, only 25% of the 1.2 million Chinese who went abroad to study returned; from 2007 to 2017, that proportion had risen to 80%". [8]

In a study that examines the employment outcomes of college graduates between the years of the Great Recession and those encompassing the COVID-19 economic distress, a period that corresponds to the mobility revolution, Jesse Rothstein (2021) finds that "employment rates fell precipitously for recent cohorts of labor market entrants. The cohort that entered the labor market in 2010 had an employment rate, averaged over its experience to date, that is two percentage points lower than what would have been expected based on prior cohorts' age profiles and the state of the economy". There are long lasting effects of unemployment, called scarring. Long periods of unemployment can leave scars on individuals' resumes and these scarring effects on employment paths can be permanent. "Cohorts that face high unemployment when they enter the labor market have statistically and substantively lower employment rates throughout their careers, not just at the beginning". "Something seems to have changed in the labor market with notable negative effects on new generations' employment rates, and the long, steady recovery of the 2010s did not fix it". [9]

Lower employment rates are a reflection of lower labor force participation rates, a trend we have seen in Fig. 8.1. Attributing this outcome to "scarring" places all the causality to labor market phenomena. Could there be deeper social and psychological forces that have made workers, particularly young workers, drift away from conventional work? Newer generations could be learning archaic skills or being taught in a manner that is disconnected from their world and therefore harder to internalize.

Recall the discussion in Chapter 8 about students in Wisconsin being taught reading comprehension using a model of a baseball field.

To address the weak supply chain of workers, particularly from the perspective of new business creation several structural changes must be made. Skill-based, vocational education instead of an expensive, debt-fostered college education might train workers in competencies where they already have a comparative advantage. In recent years, America has been perseverating over the merits of a college education over any other form of post-school learning. Any platform of learning that is disconnected from the constraints of the individual's life is meaningless—it is quickly obliterated. The value of years spent in college emanates from interaction with peers, from socialization and creating lasting networks during the college years. [8]

The Government

Support from the federal government played a role as well. The Paycheck Protection Program (PPP), enacted in March 2020, involved allocating more than $800b dollars over three years with an aim to help small businesses (under 500 employees) meet their payroll.

According to the Small Business Administration, the vast majority of loans approved in 2021 went to firms with fewer than 10 employees, as firms in the accommodation and food services sector accounted for the largest share of the program at 15% of the total, while health care and professional, scientific and technical services obtained 10% each.

The last mile in this pipeline of funding was undertaken by the community banks. The relationships they created with new and existing customers reinforced the community bank business model of relationship banking, with implications for community building and startup creation. Historically, a smaller fraction of small business loans have been initiated by community banks compared with their larger competitors, but this recent activity might provide a life-line to community banks. This financial assistance provided a cushion against the fallout from the pandemic, which could have placed a damper on all small businesses, young and old.[10] [11]

Bibliography

1 Bureau of Labor Statistics. 2022. https://stats.bls.gov/news.release/jolts.t04.htm

2 Fuhrmans, Vanessa, 2022. Blue-Collar Workers Make the Leap to Tech Jobs, No College Degree Necessary. *Wall Street Journal*, April 8, 2022. https://www.wsj.com/articles/tech-jobs-no-college-degree-necessary-11649371535
3 Oliver Wyman Forum, 2022. The New People Shaping Our Future. https://www.oliverwymanforum.com/global-consumer-sentiment/the-new-people-shaping-our-future/the-new-collars.html
4 Decker, Ryan, John Haltiwanger, Ron Jarmin and Javier Miranda. 2018. "Changing Business Dynamism and Productivity: Shocks vs Responsiveness", *NBER Working Paper* 24236. January 2018. https://www.nber.org/papers/w24236
5 Bilal, Adrian, Niklas Engbom, Simon Mongey and Giovanni Violante. 2021. Labor Market Dynamics When Ideas Are Harder to Find. *NBER Working Paper* 29479. http://www.nber.org/papers/w29479
6 Bloom, N., C. Jones, J. Van Reenen, and M. Webb. 2020. Are Ideas Getting Harder to Find? *American Economic Review*, 110(4), 1104–1144.
7 Diane Alexander, Ezra Karger. 2021. Do Stay-at-Home Orders Cause People to Stay at Home? Effects of Stay-at-Home Orders on Consumer Behavior. *The Review of Economics and Statistics*. https://doi.org/10.1162/rest_a_01108
8 Wooldridge, Adrian. 2022. America is Facing a Talent Recession. *Bloomberg Opinion*. https://www.bloomberg.com/opinion/articles/2022-02-04/2022-worker-shortage-u-s-needs-to-boost-top-talent-to-stack-up-to-china
9 Rothstein, Jesse. 2021. The Lost Generation? Labor Market Outcomes for Post Great Recession Entrants. Forthcoming, *Journal of Human Resources*. https://doi.org/10.3368/jhr.58.5.0920-11206R1
10 White, Carl, 2020. Small Business Lending Gives a Boost to Banks. On the Economy Blog, *Federal Reserve Bank of St. Louis*. https://www.stlouisfed.org/on-the-economy/2020/september/small-business-lending-gives-boost-banks
11 White, Carl, 2021. A Post-Mortem of the Paycheck Protection Program. On the Economy Blog, *Federal Reserve Bank of St Louis*, June 29, 2021. https://www.stlouisfed.org/on-the-economy/2021/june/post-mortem-of-paycheck-protection-program

CHAPTER 10

Conclusion Culture, Society, and Government

Digital connectivity, a deep desire to engage in the community and a mistrust in formal institutions has been driving entrepreneurship over the past two decades. Connectivity and shared experiences create communities which provide a sense of belonging and identity through the narratives portrayed and the shared values established. By providing meaning and context, both online and in-person communities build deep relationships and understanding. A risk-taking culture, based on mutual trust and shared values, an ethos that the rules of the game are accepted by all, that the process must be inclusive of all constituents, is born in such an environment. The marvel of this nation is its optimism, its forward-looking attitude and a belief in advancing rather than mulling over both the great and the shameful past. This business wisdom implies an entrepreneurial resurgence.

The past 26 years have been punctuated by the events of September 11, 2001, the Great Recession of December 2007 through 2009 and the pandemic emerging in March 2020. These historic episodes created a powerful force binding communities. In these recent years, we had the shared experience of sheltered isolation during the pandemic. Having faced a once-in-a lifetime crisis of epic proportions, people may be more tolerant of risk. Attitudes toward risk change when individuals face such unimagined shocks. They become emboldened by having passed through

S. Bhatt, *Entrepreneurship Today*,
https://doi.org/10.1007/978-3-031-11495-3_10

the crisis and survived. That it was possible to live a reasonable life under such formidable circumstances can be empowering.

Correspondingly, America has been in the rising tide of a startup revolution, since before the pandemic. The creative applications of technology, ideas, and imaginative concepts that make it beyond the drawing board, are all new ventures and individuals behind these ideas form the kernel of an entrepreneurial resurgence. At the heart of this resurgence is a risk-taking culture that spreads imperceptibly like a contagion through communities and leads to bold action along new pathways. Attitudes of trust, personal responsibility, awareness of others, resourcefulness and restraint diffuse through the community, cementing bonds that are vital for commerce of any kind. The economic network, which is a trading network, rests on such interactions between individuals where each transaction is undertaken in the belief that it will be fully accomplished within the bounds of available information.

This trust network is fragile and could have been shattered by the events of September 2001, the Great Recession and more recently, the pandemic. The subsequent pullback of financial resources could have stymied any forward movement of entrepreneurial activity. However, the recovery was swift as Americans drew upon flexibility of mind and a sense of historical perspective to move forward. Failure acted as an engine of renewal.

Money was pouring into the venture capital space, especially the seed and angel stage where funding for early-stage businesses is the goal. At the funding level there was a belief that *glamour* takes precedence over *user-friendly*. The practical fulfilment of this "shooting-for-the-stars" objective left much unexplored new venture terrain on earth, such as businesses that address real-life problems or that are affiliated with marginal communities. Funding practical businesses was unappealing. An app that matches a local handyman with homeowners in the neighborhood would provide local efficiencies: if the individual is working on house X on a street, it would be efficient to match that person with houses Y and Z that need work and are located on the same street. The low survival rate of young startups could be traced to the lack of community support, poor mentoring and insufficient funding at critical moments in their growth trajectory. While the venture capital space is bulging with funds for late-stage ventures, these funds tend to be allocated toward glamorous technologies with quick payback rather than the more grass-roots technologies that have a slower time scale of growth and expansion.

Since the invention of the transistor in 1947, many magnificent technologies in the digital communication and information universe have made their appearance, but their application for the business startup appears to be some distance away. Research laboratories are in the race for generating inventions, with a goal of shooting for the stars, most of which remain far removed from actual implementation.

Speed is the other demon, after glamor, as new businesses seek to rapidly expand their customer base. Startups are typically online businesses, either in existing markets or in an entirely new market. The emphasis on quickly scaling-up is often fueled by investors who want a quick exit and a high return. This helps them establish larger market shares, inspiring more funding with higher valuations. Improvement of the product or service after early feedback is typically short-circuited, or rapidly accomplished, in the service of an ultimate goal: going public.

The mission of a startup may not be directed toward scaling up rapidly and expeditiously exiting via an initial public offering, an IPO. That is the investor's perspective. The founder, on the other hand, cares about the company, the early employees and the market—the people who buy the product or service. The growth-at-all-costs mentality has led to the demise of too many startups. Time sensitivity, manifested as impatience and immediacy, is frequently expressed as the convenience factor in individual decision-making. Much like maximizing one's well-being, minimizing the time required for activities has become a powerful driving force.

The skills required for founding a firm are less correlated with notions of efficiency and college degrees. Attributes such as collaboration, openness to new ideas and an awareness of people in your radius of interaction and their needs cannot be taught. They must be learnt through experience, usually at younger ages.

Broadly speaking, there are five native skills, acquired by experience rather than formal education: awareness, resourcefulness, practical intelligence, over-optimism, and personal initiative. In recent years, America has been perseverating over the merits of a college education over any other form of post-school learning. Any platform of learning that is disconnected from the realities of the individual's life is meaningless—it is quickly obliterated. A skill-based, vocational education instead of an expensive, debt-fostered college education might train workers in competencies where they already have a comparative advantage. In reality, the value of years spent in college emanates from interaction with peers, from socialization and creating lasting networks, the community aspect.

I started writing this book to investigate the disconnect between economists' doomsday picture of declining economic dynamism, a startup deficit and dismal job creation against market intelligence discovered amidst the weeds of data that suggested a slow but steady rise in new businesses. I discovered that both sides were right, they were looking at the same picture from different perspectives and this led to conflicting policy recommendations on the one hand and a rather dispiriting sense of unease about the U.S. economy among would be founders. Of course, it becomes a self-fulfilling prophecy when potential startups remain dormant on the basis of this forbidding picture. My goal is to dispel this negative outlook with evidence that portrays a set of vibrant and creative individuals laden with good ideas but lacking the direction and the motivation.

Let me recount the evidence behind this enthusiastic outlook. First there has been growth of startups since the beginning of the period under examination, 1994–2020. Second, this upward trajectory is reinforced after 2010 by a powerful blast of creative energy with increasing numbers of startups till the present day. Third, while the ideas germinated, they did not flower since startup survival was weak during the overall period, and particularly during the recent decade. Rapid scaling may be the bane of startups, in addition to an inadequate foundation and structural rootedness in the community and local economy. Fourth, startup activity is present across all states in the nation, but predominantly in states west of the Mississippi River, and Massachusetts and Wisconsin from the east. Georgia and South Carolina are the rising stars with Georgia first making an appearance among the leading states during the early years and subsequently joined by South Carolina in the past decade. The key point is that, in states that exhibited strong early venture creation, such as Massachusetts, Missouri, Idaho, California, and Wisconsin, survival remained strong and persistent.

Fifth, these startups are in the professional and business sector, which comprises technical services as well as research and development. Sixth, population growth rates, rather than population density, are correlated with startup activity. The late boomers and gen X, bracketed by the ages of 45–54, are in the entrepreneurial vanguard. Latinos are in the advance guard after 2000, while women, Blacks and the younger demographic are weakly represented among the entrepreneurs. Individuals, especially white males, between the ages of 25 and 44 are absent from the venture ecosystem and, in fact, are increasingly absent from the labor force, more so after the onset of the pandemic.

The takeaway is that the recent decade of 2010–2020 has been bubbling with startup ventures and entrepreneurial enthusiasm, but these new businesses have been short-lived and unevenly observed across various socio-economic categories.

New ventures start small and are entrepreneurial even if they do not employ large numbers of workers. They may, in fact, generate employment in complementary or ancillary markets within their respective regions. Most small business owners care for work flexibility rather than income, and at least a third of business founders "wanted to create a new product or had a very good business idea". Innovation means a new way of solving an old problem, so new ideas and products may not suggest invention, but they do flag innovation. The point is that growth incentives, job creation incentives, are not the first order reasons for startup creation—creating a culture of risk-taking is of the first order. Perhaps it is time to think outside the box and develop the community supports and business climate first in order to encourage an entrepreneurial risk-taking culture.

A Broader Perspective—communities

What does this imply as we move into the third decade of the twenty-first century? It means that taking a narrow perspective is imprudent. Over the course of my research, I discovered that the entrepreneurial world encompasses multiple frames of reference, besides economics. These include engineering, psychology, sociology, politics, and law.

Having studied the data, it is time to reflect on what resurgence and application of technology implies for our social and economic systems and our individual world views. Technology has conferred more control and agency to individuals, and therefore to society. The growing number of startups with a small number of employees suggests an increasing degree of control at the individual level. Will individuals cooperate when they have more control? Will there be consensus in the governance of common pool resources such as the Internet? Will communities in rural and impoverished regions have access to the Internet for charting new ventures?

Chapter 8 showed that female business activity lagged that of males, as measured by the Rate of New Entrepreneurs Kauffman Index. This index measures the fraction of a given population that is forging new businesses. When race was factored into the analysis, this index was highest for Latinos since 2000, when they overtook Whites. Blacks show increasing activity since 2013. There is some structural factor, something in the environment, that has changed since 2000 for Latinos, and since 2013 for Blacks.

It is not education, as we also saw that the rate of entrepreneurs was highest for those with less than a high school diploma, while those with a college degree lagged in this measure. It cannot be technology alone, as access to broadband and computers, was at least as high among Whites as among other racial and ethnic groups.

Social norms that favor community building and embeddedness in local networks are that crucial structural factor. Embeddedness is best described by the overlap in relationships between individuals; where, for example, persons A and B share a common circle of friends and acquaintances. Variation in entrepreneurial activity across nations and cultures is best predicted by social norms, according to a recent study. There is little evidence for other explanations of such differences: national funding of research and development, government assistance, science-based education, availability of venture capital, and spillover effects from clusters of incumbent businesses.[1] The strongest cultural factors associated with entrepreneurial norms were a "humane orientation and institutional collectivism". The former refers to communities where fairness and generosity were valued, and the latter refers to institutions that foster collective action and a just distribution of resources. Note that both these traits correspond with the previously mentioned traits of community embeddedness and trust.

Societies based on this culture developed norms that include granting agency to the founders and gender equality. "[G]ender-egalitarian societies and societies that value and reward performance and endorse status privileges had on average higher rates of organizational founding, net of differences in national national income and economic growth". [1]

[1] Valentina Assenova examines a large longitudinal sample comprising 192 countries over 2001–2018. [1]

The growth of startups is associated with agency or control coupled with rewards equitably conferred across gender, race, and ethnicity, establishing legitimacy. These are the social norms that convey underlying cultural values such as trust, personal responsibility, awareness of others, resourcefulness, and restraint for a thriving business community. Shared experiences are a strong vehicle for building these communities since all share in the profound dislocation of major external events, albeit unequally. For instance, the time period we examined was marked by three such shared crises: the national-security crisis of September 2001, the financial crisis of 2008, and the pandemic of 2020. Nevertheless, entrepreneurial activity has thrived.

Will we continue to have shared experiences as we fragment into hybrid work and education spaces? A remote lifestyle preserves connections and provides more control over the extent of engagement with the community but curtails shared experiences. Serendipitous sharing around the water cooler and other common public spaces is absent. Despite the collective awakening created by the shared pandemic experience there might be a retreat into divided, non-communal spaces. From the perspective of new business formation, this development might provide opportunities serving segmented groups much like the motion picture industry where there is a movie for every kind of taste. The result is likely to be a flood of consumption choices targeted toward distinct groups. While people may not connect over a common food, such as pepperoni pizza or onigiri or idli they are quite likely to enlarge the very concept of shared experiences via the online emoji, those that go viral.

The past year has shown us how technology can be our partner, not our enemy. Access to information is the key to unlocking ideas, but the ensuing content tsunami and endless choices that inundate would-be entrepreneurs leaves them in decision paralysis, like Buridan's ass. In the conception of free will, the paradox is satirized in the form of a hungry and thirsty ass who is incapable of choosing between a bale of hay and a pail of water and dies of both hunger and thirst while pondering the decision. [2] Buridan's ass paradox is the cause of system glitches. The idea of metastability in electronics is the persistence of instability in a digital electronics system due to the inability to choose between a zero or one within the time required for proper circuit operation. This situation can result in system failure. The fault lies not with the technologies, but with the way they are used. Like a sharp knife in the hands of a cook, the outcome of its deployment depends upon the knowledge and skills of the cook, not the knife. The solution to the choice problem may be to proceed with caution, taking measured steps in an ongoing exchange with customers, suppliers, and the other constituencies in the world of the founder.

To recapitulate, new ventures have steadily grown across the nation from 1994–2020, particularly after 2010 in states west of the Mississippi. The new founder is more likely to come from the 45–54-year-old demographic and may not have a college education, but is likely to possess native skills, which comprise an awareness of the environment, its people and their problems. Like birds sensing the barometric pressure and then soaring into the sky after a storm, these founders are quick to perceive opportunities. The startups' jugular, its underbelly, is survival beyond the first year. There is a cry for help with sustaining the new venture. The new enterprise depends upon suppliers, customers, employees, community, financial, and legal institutions.

Policy and Entrepreneurship

In addition to financial incentives such as taxes and subsidies, how can the public sector be enlisted as a partner in establishing these social norms, this national ethos? What are the social norms of underperforming regions in the U.S. like the rust belt or coal country that work against entrepreneurship? States have been labelled as hostile against business like the blue states of California, Massachusetts or Washington seem to do better with sustaining new businesses. Despite high tax rates and onerous regulation, entrepreneurs continue to flock to these states. However, sectors that are innovative are weakly regulated, precisely because they are novel, and the law generally follows technological developments.

It is often stated that California's "at will" employment rules are a boon to innovation as ideas can spread quickly throughout a sector. California's Labor Code contains a presumption that the employee–employer contract is written at will, which means that either can terminate employment at any time without prior notice or cause.[2] Flexibility in the labor

[2] Labor Code Sect. 2922 establishes the presumption that an employer may terminate its employees at will, for any or no reason. A fortiori, the employer may act peremptorily, arbitrarily, or inconsistently, without providing specific protections such as prior warning, fair procedures, objective evaluation, or preferential reassignment. Because the employment relationship is "fundamentally contractual" (Foley, supra, 47 Cal.3d 654, 696), limitations on these employer prerogatives are a matter of the parties' specific agreement, express or implied in fact. The mere existence of an employment relationship affords no expectation,

market allows both employers and employees to continue the matching process as conditions change. A superior match creates a culture that continues to innovate.

The taxi industry is heavily regulated but that didn't stop Uber from starting up in California. The auto industry is heavily regulated but that didn't stop Tesla from being first manufactured in California. Aerospace is also heavily red-taped, but that didn't stop Jeff Bezos or Elon Musk from starting up Blue Origin or Space X on the West Coast. The term "at-will employment" is a legal term used in the US. It means that an employer can terminate an employee for any reason without warning, except if the reason for firing is illegal, such as firings due to race, gender, or religion.

Market observers were debating during the summer of 2020 whether economic growth would snap back to its previous trends in a V-shaped pattern or whether there would be a slower "whoosh" recovery as in the letter W. In fact, the former has materialized. A crises mindset is a strong driver of resourcefulness. In 2020 most companies were forced to try remote work, and many will continue this format in the future. This opened up a talent pool and allowed companies to draw from around the globe, creating opportunities for people as well as granting startups access to talent.

Unmet consumption needs in areas such as education, fitness, and friends led to new products and services. "The Zoom boom is a clear example of how changing consumer habits have prioritized new tech solutions. Activity on the platform increased from 10 million daily participants in December 2019 to about 300 million daily participants in April 2020", an increase of just under 3000% in 5 months. [4] Communication platforms, such as Zoom video conferencing, became the standard for connecting with others face-to-face in work and social settings.

The pandemic upended two major institutions shaping young people's lives and early pathways—education and the job market—with potentially disastrous effects. Without targeted policy responses, young people might have suffered long-term consequences, especially those whose connections to school and work were already tenuous. Social exclusion and

protectible by law, that employment will continue, or will end only on certain conditions, unless the parties have actually adopted such terms. Thus, if the employer's termination decisions, however arbitrary, do not breach such a substantive contract provision, they are not precluded by the covenant. [3]

inequality at such a scale could seriously threaten social cohesion and community well-being.

The $1.9 trillion American Rescue Plan (ARP) has entered—and quickly exited—national consciousness six months after its inception, but its effects have lingered at the state and local level. The rescue plan allotted $330 billion to support state and local fiscal recovery, with the first outlay released in May 2021 and the second by May 2022. State and local leaders were working in real time to deploy this funding to stabilize their budgets and respond to economic disruptions. [5]

ARP dollars were flexible and investments in educational and career opportunities for young adults would have been the appropriate move. They offered the chance to disrupt long-established patterns of who succeeds in education and the labor market, and who doesn't. An improved learning environment that includes skill-based education and knowledge related to individuals' actual lives fosters truly applicable learning.

The path from high school through postsecondary education to a good job has long been more like an obstacle course. Before the pandemic, millions of young adults cycled through postsecondary education, unemployment, and low-wage jobs without being gainfully engaged. The low labor force participation rate could be due to lack of direction and mentorship. These individuals might have been startup entrepreneurs. This problem doesn't solve itself over time. More young people are isolated, being neither employed nor at school. This cohort, from age 16 to 26, has been increasingly disconnected as they age from the early years to 26, when 34% drop out of the labor force and are not seeking employment. [6][7]

This group of individuals exhibits tremendous variation. A 19-year-old who is on the cusp of graduation is different from one who dropped out in 10th grade. A 26-year-old with a high school diploma and a low-wage job is yet another category. Some young adults are parents themselves; others lack stable housing. Some were once enrolled in college but left for financial or other reasons and may have student debt. State and regional data can identify the key points where young people disengage from education and the relative size of different subgroups.

A rethinking of the educational environment is the most important policy issue at the national as well as the local level. It is a task that will require coordination across state and local governments as well community organizations.

My Take

My take on entrepreneurship is that supportive relationships within the community provide dignity and foster the sentiments of awareness of others, resourcefulness, practical intelligence, optimism and initiative—the culture of risk-taking. Culture is a mental model of decision-making based on underlying values and beliefs. The values and beliefs that foster a risk-taking, entrepreneurial culture are marked by connectivity and embeddedness in a strong community. Trust-based relationships provide networking in an uncertain labor market. For millions of young people there is a path from high school to entrepreneurship, with support from the community in which they learn and mature, as well as local organizations.

Bibliography

1 Assenova, Valentina. 2019. Why are Some Societies more Entrepreneurial than Others? Evidence from 192 Countries over 2001–2018. SSRN: https://ssrn.com/abstract=3449762 or https://doi.org/10.2139/ssrn.3449762
2 Buridan's Ass. 2022. Wikipedia. https://en.wikipedia.org/wiki/Buridan%27s_ass
3 This paradox is not to be confused with Buridan's Bridge sophism, which is Plato's decision problem when he is guarding a bridge and says to Socrates that he will be allowed to cross the bridge if he speaks the truth but will be thrown into the water if he speaks falsely. To which Socrates replies that he be thrown into the water.
4 See Guz v. Bechtel National, Inc., 24 Cal. 4th 317, 8 P.3d 1089, 100 Cal. Rptr. 2d 352 (2000).
5 Tai, Jack. 2021. Startup Surge: Pandemic Causes New Businesses to Double. *Forbes,* January 20, 2021. https://www.forbes.com/sites/theyec/2021/01/20/startup-surge-pandemic-causes-new-businesses-to-double/
6 Ross, Martha, Lilli Allen, Annelies Goger and Avni Nahar. 2021. American Rescue Plan Can Jump-Start Stalled Opportunities for Youth. *Brookings Papers on Economic Activity*, 2021. https://www.brookings.edu/blog/the-avenue/2021/10/27/american-rescue-plan-funds-can-jump-start-stalled-opportunities-for-youth/
7 Lewis, Kristen. 2021. A Decade Undone: 2021 Update. New York: *Measure of America, Social Science Research Council*, 2021. https://ssrc-static.s3.amazonaws.com/moa/ADecadeUndone2021Update.pdf
8 Millet, Catherine and Marisol Kevelson. 2018. *Doesn't Get Better With Age: Predicting Millennials' Disconnection.* ETS Policy Information Report and ETS Research Report Series No. RR-18–42, Princeton, NJ.

Appendix

Data Sources

All data in this book are accessed from the following websites.

1. https://www.bls.gov/bdm/
2. https://www.bls.gov/bdm/bdmann.htm
3. https://www.bls.gov/bdm/business-employment-dynamics-data-by-age-and-size.htm
4. https://www.bls.gov/news.release/cewbd.tn.htm]
5. https://www.bls.gov/bdm/entrepreneurship/bdm_chart1.htm
6. Business Formation Statistics can be found at: https://www.census.gov/econ/bfs/index.html
7. Kaufman Index. www.kauffman.org/indicators
8. Business and economy. https://www.census.gov/topics/business-economy.html
9. Business formation statistics, https://www.census.gov/econ/bfs/index.html
10. Business Employment Dynamics for job gains and losses by firm size, https://www.bls.gov/bdm/business-employment-dynamics-data-by-age-and-size.htm
11. https://data.bls.gov/cgi-bin/surveymost?bd
12. Current employment statistics (CES) https://www.bls.gov/data/#employment

S. Bhatt, *Entrepreneurship Today*,
https://doi.org/10.1007/978-3-031-11495-3

13. Job Openings and Labor Turnover Survey (JOLTS) https://data.bls.gov/cgi-bin/surveymost?jt

Business Employment Dynamics—Chapter 2

Business Employment Dynamics consist of a quarterly series of statistics on gross job gains and gross job losses. These statistics "*reveal some aspects of business dynamics, including establishment openings and closings, and establishment expansions and contractions*".

The Bureau of Labor Statistics describes the data in detail. The following description is excerpted from their website.[1]

The Business Employment Dynamics (BED) data are a product of a federal-state cooperative program known as Quarterly Census of Employment and Wages (QCEW). The BED data are compiled by the U.S. Bureau of Labor Statistics (BLS) from existing QCEW records.

Most employers in the U.S. are required to file quarterly reports on the employment and wages of workers covered by unemployment insurance (UI) laws and to pay quarterly UI taxes. The QCEW is based largely on quarterly UI reports which are sent by businesses to the State Workforce Agencies (SWAs). These UI reports are supplemented by two additional BLS data collections to render administrative data into economic statistics. Together these data comprise the QCEW and form the basis of the Bureau's establishment universe sampling frame.

These reports are used to produce the quarterly QCEW data on total employment and wages and the longitudinal BED data on gross job gains and losses. The QCEW is also the employment benchmark for the Current Employment Statistics (CES), Occupational Employment Statistics (OES), and Job Openings and Labor Turnover Survey (JOLTS) programs and is a major input to the Bureau of Economic Analysis's Personal Income Accounts.

Establishments are used in the tabulation of the BED statistics by industry, and firms are used in the tabulation of the BED size class statistics. An establishment is defined as an economic unit that produces goods or

[1] Details are available from the Bureau of Labor statistics website at https://www.bls.gov/news.release/cewbd.tn.htm.

services, usually at a single physical location, and engages in one or predominantly one activity. A firm is a legal business, either corporate or otherwise, and may consist of several establishments.

> Establishment **openings** are *either establishments with positive third month employment for the first time in the current quarter, with no links to the prior quarter, or with positive third month employment in the current quarter following zero employment in the previous quarter.* ***Closings*** *are either units with positive third month employment in the previous quarter, with no employment or zero employment reported in the current quarter.*
> ***Births****. These are units with positive third month employment for the first time in the current quarter with no links to the prior quarter, or units with positive third month employment in the current quarter and zero employment in the third month of the previous four quarters. Births are a subset of openings not including re-openings of seasonal businesses.*
> ***Deaths****. These are units with no employment or zero employment reported in the third month of four consecutive quarters following the last quarter with positive employment. Deaths are a subset of closings not including temporary shutdowns of seasonal businesses. A unit that closes during the quarter may be a death, but we wait three quarters to determine whether it is a permanent closing or a temporary shutdown. Therefore, there is always a lag of three quarters for the publication of death statistics.*

We interpret this statement to mean openings signify businesses that have non-zero employees for the first time this quarter or non-zero employees following a zero-employment quarter. For establishments less than 1 year old, this definition is transparent—a business with non-zero employees indicates a new business.

For establishments between 1 and 4 years old, an establishment opening can mean a business that was around for over a year, had temporarily "shut down" or slowed down, and was now "starting up" again. We count this in the category of startups. According to the BED website "openings include seasonal and other re-openings and closings include temporary shutdowns" [23]. This data set is particularly relevant for our purposes, since we are interested in the number of startups or establishment openings.

Firm or Employer = EIN, employer identification number at the national level;
Establishment = A physical place of work within the firm; a single EIN firm can have multiple establishments;
Employee = identified by social security number but coded to Protected Identification Key (PIK); Earnings for each PIK are reported on a quarterly basis—Q1 is Jan–March, Q2 is April–June.

Age of establishment is the "*difference between the reference period and the first time an establishment reported positive employment*" [20].

- The age of a firm is classified using the age of the oldest establishment within a firm and can be in one of five bins: less than 1 year old; 1–4 years old; 5–9 years old; 10 years and older; all ages.

Size of an establishment is based on its reported employment and can be in one of 8 bins:

- 1 to 4 employees; 5 to 9 employees; 10 to 19 employees; 20 to 49 employees; 50 to 99 employees; 100 to 499 employees; 500 or more employees; All sizes

The research data series are classified in 40 age-by-size bins: gross job gains and losses; gross job gains and losses as a percent of employment; the number of establishments by direction of employment changes and as a percent of total establishment. **We focus on the third bin—the number of establishments by direction of employment change and by age and average size of establishment (Table 3-A-E in [22]). In particular, we focus on the number of establishments with net positive employment change, which is the difference between opening establishments and closing establishments.**

Statistical Details—Chapter 3

First Order Autoregression Model

Using data from the BLS, chart 3-A-E, we obtained the number of new establishments each year, defined as establishments less than 1 year in existence, with under 100 employees and denoted by S_t with t indicating the year.

More formally, S_t is the number of new establishments in any given year, growing at rate θ in a single time period.

$$S_t = a + \theta S_{t-1} \tag{1}$$

When indexed by S_{2007}

$$\text{we have } \hat{S}_t = \frac{S_t}{S_{2007}} = \hat{a} + \hat{\theta}\frac{S_{t-1}}{S_{2007}} \tag{2}$$

The **slope** of this regression is theta hat, $\hat{\theta}$.

The subscript i denotes the states. All the states are ranked by $\widehat{\theta_i}$ within the following bins

$$(i)\widehat{\theta_i} > 0(ii)\widehat{\theta_i} < 0(iii)\widehat{\theta_i} = 0$$

Regression: Time Trends

The trend over period I, 1994–2007, was labeled, $\hat{\theta}^I$, and the trend over period II, 2010–2020, was labeled $\hat{\theta}^{II}$. Both of these trends, $\hat{\theta}^I$ and $\hat{\theta}^{II}$, reflect startup activity indexed by 2007.

Across the entire period, $\theta = 0.6\%$. During period I, $\hat{\theta}^I = 1.12\%$, and during period II, $\hat{\theta}^{II} = 3.31\%$. It is clear that $\hat{\theta}^{II} > \hat{\theta}^I$ and, in fact, the trend in period II is **significantly** larger than that in period I.

a. Number of new establishments regressed on time; 1994–2020

Regression	*Statistics*
Multiple R	0.58840617
R^2	0.34622182
Adjusted R^2	0.3200707

(continued)

(continued)

Regression	*Statistics*
Standard error	0.06930642
Observations	27

ANOVA

	df	*SS*	*MS*	F	*Significance* F
Regression	1	0.06359325	0.06359325	13.2392696	0.00124533
Residual	25	0.12008451	0.00480338		
Total	**26**	0.18367776			

Coefficients		*Standard error*	t *stat*	P-*value*	*Lower 95%*	*Upper 95%*
Intercept	−11.562049	3.43690229	−3.3640902	0.00247861	−18.640482	−4.4836167
X variable 1	**0.006231**	0.00171244	3.63858071	0.00124533	0.00270402	0.00975771

b. Number of new establishments regressed on time; 1994–2007

Regression	*Statistics*
Multiple *R*	0.90758383
R^2	0.82370842
Adjusted R^2	0.80901745
Standard error	0.02439612
Observations	14

ANOVA

	df	*SS*	*MS*	F	*Significance* F
Regression	1	0.03337065	0.03337065	56.0690463	7.3516E-06
Residual	12	0.00714205	0.00059517		
Total	13	0.0405127			

Coefficients		*Standard error*	t *stat*	P-*value*	*Lower 95%*	*Upper 95%*	*Lower 95.0%*	*Upper 95.0%*
Intercept	– 23.302518	3.23570934	– 7.2016721	1.0842E-05	– 30.352523	– 16.252513	– 30.352523	– 16.252513
X variable 1	**0.012111**	0.00161745	7.4879267	7.3516E-06	0.00858721	0.01563544	0.00858721	0.01563544

c. Number of new establishments regressed on time; 2010–2020

Regression	*Statistics*
Multiple R	0.98597943
R^2	0.97215543
Adjusted R^2	0.96906159
Standard error	0.01962656
Observations	11

ANOVA

	df	*SS*	*MS*	F	*Significance* F
Regression	1	0.12103922	0.12103922	314.222795	2.6429E-08
Residual	9	0.0346682	0.0003852		
Total	10	0.12450603			

Coefficients		*Standard error*	t *stat*	P-*value*	*Lower 95%*	*Upper 95%*	*Lower 95.0%*	*Upper 95.0%*
Intercept	–65.870464	3.77071275	–17.468969	2.9841E-08	–74.400409	–57.340519	–74.400409	–57.340519
X variable 1	**0.033172**	0.00187132	17.7263306	2.6249E-08	0.0289384	0.03740484	0.0289384	0.03740484

Averaging Across the Trends for Each State and Comparing Trend in Period I with Trend in Period II Using T Test

	theta I	*theta II*
Mean	0.0057407	0.02979911
Variance	0.00014905	0.00041579
Observations	53	53
Hypothesized	0	
df	85	
t Stat	−7.3695474	
P(T < = t) one-ta	5.1642E-11	
t Critical one-	1.6629785	
P(T < = t) two-ta	1.0328E-10	
t Critical two-	1.98826791	

Conclusion: Theta I < theta II

Index

S. Bhatt, *Entrepreneurship Today*,
https://doi.org/10.1007/978-3-031-11495-3

SPRINGER NATURE

GPSR Compliance

The European Union's (EU) General Product Safety Regulation (GPSR) is a set of rules that requires consumer products to be safe and our obligations to ensure this.

If you have any concerns about our products, you can contact us on ProductSafety@springernature.com

In case Publisher is established outside the EU, the EU authorized representative is:

Springer Nature Customer Service Center GmbH
Europaplatz 3
69115 Heidelberg, Germany

Kolibri 360 GmbH
Ferdinand-Jühlke-Straße 7
99095 Erfurt, Deutschland
produktsicherheit@kolibri360.de